Happy Birthday

Norman Nichols

12/28/74

Natalie & Dink

NEW HAMPSHIRE'S UNIVERSITY

The Story of a New England Land Grant College

1974

NEW HAMPSHIRE'S UNIVERSITY

Everett B. Sackett

New Hampshire Publishing Company, Somersworth

University of New Hampshire, Durham

Library of Congress Catalog Card Number: 74-82893
Standard Book Number: 0-912274-44-1

New Hampshire Publishing Company, Somersworth 03878

© 1974 by the University of New Hampshire

Designed by George Lenox

To Martha,
who has shared more than three good decades
in the University community and who on a
series of Saturday nights in 1962-63 served
brick-oven baked beans to all members of the
Liberal Arts faculty and their spouses.

Contents

Preface

This is the story of the University of New Hampshire, formerly known as the New Hampshire College of Agriculture and the Mechanic Arts. The institution completed its first century in 1966. Not until 1973, however, did it mark the fiftieth anniversary of its charter as the University of New Hampshire. It was a sobering experience, for those of us concerned with the development of the university, to realize that New Hampshire College was still the senior establishment.

In the century-plus of its existence, this institution has witnessed new charters, buildings, benefactors, administrators, trustees, faculty, students, and curricula. Such elements are basic to its history. Nevertheless, the official record presents only the skeleton of the living institution. It has been my earnest goal to put flesh upon the skeleton. I have tried to go beyond the record, to the people of the university community and the society of which they were a part. I have eliminated detail with a light heart. To do otherwise would have been to compile a fat volume—or two or three—ideally suited to gather dust upon library shelves. The excess material has been left on the cards on which it was recorded; these cards have been deposited in the University Library for the benefit of future historians.

Among those who have been slighted in this process are the scores of public-spirited citizens who served without pay as trustees of the college and the university. In the early days, they at least had the satisfaction of being directly involved in governing the institution. More recently, with the advent of professional administrators and an active faculty-student senate, their initiative has been eroded. The trustees continued to be hard-working, committee members on occasion having several meetings a month. At times they have the thankless task of explaining to poorly informed or prejudiced acquaintances and others activities at the university criticized by the press or state officials.

Slighted also are the contributions of many able and devoted faculty members. Among them was a gentleman who had a very large role in compiling this history: Philip M. Marston. Phil graduated from the university in 1924 and joined its faculty a year later. He was appointed assistant professor of history in 1928, chairman of the department in 1949, and University Historian in 1962. He died on November 11, 1966, mourned by everyone who knew him.

At the time of his death, Phil had completed a draft of the university's history through the Engelhardt administration. I was asked to finish the work he had begun. I might have taken this assignment literally, but the result would have been two conflicting styles within the same book: Phil was a historian, whereas I was trained as a journalist and have never completely recovered from the experience. Furthermore, a shorter volume was desired than the one Phil had been in the process of creating.

A copy of the Marston draft has been bound and deposited in the University Library. With it is an annotated copy of my own first draft, cross-referenced to Phil's, to show the numerous instances where I have relied upon his research or even his prose. Crediting Phil as co-author was considered, but if he were here he might not have approved. His aim was a volume completely documented from authoritative sources. I have endeavored to be factual, but at the same time to give a sense of the university as a living institution—even if this meant eliminating material that a historian would have deemed significant, or including material that a historian would have regarded as trivia.

In addition to Phil Marston's fundamental contribution, several others have helped in the preparation of this book. Among them are Edward Y. Blewett, former dean, whose exceptional memory and long association with the university have made him an authority on its history; John W. McConnell, former president, who read the entire manuscript and made valuable suggestions for reorganizing parts of it; Philip A. Wilcox, former curator of the University Museum, who checked the manuscript for its factual content and supplied many interesting sidelights in the process; Adrian O. Morse, executive secretary during the Hetzel administration, who shared his intimate knowledge of that period and the interregnum that followed; Donald C. Babcock, professor emeritus, who recounted his experiences as a faculty member beginning in World War I; Arthur S. Adams and Eldon L. Johnson, former presidents, who checked the chapters dealing with their administration; and Doris Beane, former university recorder, who located information on the World War II military training programs and the enrollment of veterans thereafter. It is impossible to list all who were helpful in gathering data. Acknowledgment is given in the text to those whose unpublished materials were of particular assistance.

Emily Ketterson Smith, director of university publications, did preliminary editing of the first draft and in the years since has remained a steadfast supporter and effective negotiator. Daniel F. Ford '54—alumnus, journalist, editor, and novelist—as the publisher's editor by judicious pruning and some modification of organization made the volume more forthright without altering its flavor. A word must be said about the photographs. They were gathered by Sally Paine Ford from a number of sources, and in many cases it has not been possible to identify the photographer. Accordingly, photo credit has not been given anywhere in the book. Most of the recent photographs are the work of John P. Adams, the present university photographer, or Richard D. Merritt, who filled that post for many years.

Having duly acknowledged those who contributed to this volume, I must now make the customary admission that anything that is not right should be blamed on me. I make one exception to this assumption of blame; that is in reporting enrollment statistics. I was not always there to count, and those who were evidently used varying criteria in arriving at their totals. But though there are discrepancies in detail, the enrollment trends are accurately reflected.

EVERETT B. SACKETT

Lee, New Hampshire
December 1973

PART ONE

For Farmers' Sons

(1866-1912)

*The Concord Turnpike in the winter of 1893, with
Ben Thompson's barn in the foreground. Thompson
Hall is at left and the original College
barn is just visible at right of photograph.*

1. Dartmouth Becomes the Host

New Hampshire's interest in higher education goes back at least to 1815. In that year, in Hanover, the trustees of Dartmouth College became embroiled in an intramural dispute which pitted President John Wheelock against the other trustees. State politics soon became involved. As a result, the New Hampshire state legislature passed an act on June 26, 1816, changing the name of Dartmouth College to Dartmouth University and enlarging the board of trustees so that a majority would be political appointees—in effect making the college a state university. Confusion and litigation followed. For a time two separate institutions, the college and the university, operated on the Hanover campus. The matter finally went to the United States Supreme Court where an eloquent espousal by Daniel Webster, a Dartmouth alumnus, resulted in a precedent-setting decision in favor of the college trustees, February 1, 1819.

This attempt by a state government to take over a private college was not unique to New Hampshire. It was part of a national movement to extend to higher education the separation of church and state that had come with the American Revolution. The colonial colleges had been church institutions, characterized in 1754 by President Clap of Yale as "Societies of ministers for training up persons for the work of the ministry." Of the nine colonial colleges, only Brown, Princeton, and Rutgers escaped state interference before the precedent of the Dartmouth case ended the trend.

As an aftermath of the Dartmouth controversy, a Literary Fund was set up by the New Hampshire legislature in 1824. Supported by a tax on bank stock, this fund was to be used solely for the purpose of supporting a state college or university. It accumulated $55,000 by 1828, with no

steps being taken to start the institution it was to nourish. So much idle money in the state treasury was too much for the legislators to leave unmolested. In 1828, in spite of the strict limitation which had been put on the use of the money when the law was passed, it was voted to distribute the sum to the towns for the support of the common schools. Commenting on this diversion nine years later, Governor Isaac Hill declared: "That Literary Fund was pledged by a law of the State to a particular purpose; it was raised from a tax which was paid into the treasury for that purpose and no other. Yet a law of the Legislature, violating the pledged faith of the State, diverted it from the original purpose and distributed it among the towns for another and a different purpose."

Following diversion of the Literary Fund, the interest of the New Hampshire legislature in public higher education lay dormant until passage by the U.S. Congress of the Morrill Act, July 2, 1862. This act, passed after years of agitation by agricultural interests, provided for the distribution of public land to each state. The land was to be sold and the proceeds used "for the endowment, support and maintenance of at least one college where the leading object shall be without excluding other scientific and classical studies, and including military tactics, to teach such branches of learning as are related to agriculture and the mechanic arts . . . in order to promote the liberal and practical education of the industrial classes in the several pursuits and professions in life."

The New Hampshire legislature in 1863 accepted the terms of this act. It instructed Governor Joseph A. Gilmore "to appoint a committee consisting of ten persons, one from each county, who from their professions and pursuits, may in their judgment be best qualified for the duty, who shall, after the fullest inquiry and consultation, prepare a scheme for the establishment of a college for education in agriculture and the mechanic arts, and make a printed report thereon to the Legislature at the next June session."

The committee reported at the appointed time, but it was less than forthright in espousing a "scheme." True to its political nature, it decided not on one location but suggested three: Hanover, Lyme, and Manchester. Favoring the Hanover location was an offer by Dartmouth College, at that time the only institution of higher education in the state, to add instruction in agriculture to its curriculum. For Lyme was the offer of General David Culver (a member of the committee of ten) of his 400-acre farm plus an additional $30,000 gift if the college were located in his home town. The suggested Manchester location was on the farm connected with what later became the state Industrial School. It was not an accident that all three proposals involved free land or housing. None of the federal money could be used for physical facilities, with the result that in many states the location of the "land grant" institution was determined by the willingness of local communities to furnish these essentials.

In seeking the land grant funds, Dartmouth was following a national pattern. Typically the private colleges were under church control and had rigid, classical curricula, stressing mental discipline rather than acquisition of knowledge. They were interested not in teaching agriculture but in the money available through the land grants. Between 1862 and 1879, in six states the grants were awarded to private colleges; in nineteen, to state universities or colleges; and in twelve, to newly founded agricultural and mechanical colleges. Elsewhere in New England, Connecticut's land grant funds went to Yale's Sheffield Scientific School, Rhode Island's to Brown, Vermont's to the University of Vermont, Maine's to a new college of agriculture and the mechanic arts, and Massachusetts's in part to the Massachusetts Institute of Technology and in part to a new college of agriculture.

As the New Hampshire study committee had been reluctant to make a decision, so was the legislature. No action was taken in the 1864 or 1865 sessions. Before the convening of the 1866 session, General Culver died, leaving his farm and $30,000 to the state provided the college was located in Lyme, otherwise to Dartmouth for agricultural education.

A new committee of ten was appointed. Under General Culver's will, the committee was able to combine the benefits of Dartmouth's willingness and Culver's generosity. This it did. Its recommendation, which was accepted by the legislature, was that a new college be established in Hanover in connection with Dartmouth.

The new institution, however, was to have its own identity. The act of establishment provided for a board of nine trustees, five to be appointed by the governor and council and four by the trustees of Dartmouth College. The terms of office would be for three years, with a third of the board appointed annually. They were to appoint a secretary, a treasurer, and "a faculty of instruction, prescribe their duties, and invest them with such powers, for the immediate government and management of the institution, as they may deem most conducive to its best interests." Governor Frederick Smyth signed this act on July 7, 1866.

In establishing the New Hampshire College of Agriculture and the Mechanic Arts in Hanover "in connection with Dartmouth College," the trustees were to make all necessary contracts between the two institutions. After fourteen years the contracts could be terminated by either party on a year's notice. Dartmouth was required to provide for "the free use of an experimental farm, of all requisite buildings, of the libraries, laboratories, apparatus, and museums of said Dartmouth College, and for supplying such instruction, in addition to that furnished by its professors and teachers, as the best interests of its students may require; and also as to any legacy said Dartmouth

College may receive from the estate of the late David Culver." In addition the trustees were to provide "as far as may be practicable, free tuition to indigent students" and "to make provision for the delivery of free lectures in different parts of the State upon subjects pertaining to agriculture and the mechanic arts." The act stipulated that all funds from the sale of the land scrip issued to New Hampshire be invested in bonds of the state or of the United States; the income was to be paid, not to the treasurer of Dartmouth, but to the treasurer of New Hampshire College.

Trustees appointed by the governor and council were John B. Clark, Chester C. Hutchins, John D. Lyman, Joseph B. Walker, and William P. Wheeler. The Dartmouth appointees were Asa D. Smith (the college president), Ira A. Eastman (who declined to serve), Anthony Colby, and Governor Frederick Smyth. The governor convened the first meeting of the board in the council chamber in the State House, September 28, 1866. They elected Asa D. Smith president, Joseph B. Walker secretary, and Frederick Smyth treasurer.

A state was entitled to 30,000 acres of land grant scrip for each senator and representative in Congress. As New Hampshire then had three representatives, it was entitled to 150,000 acres. Sale of the script at fifty-five cents an acre, the going rate, was authorized by the trustees. The net amount received was $80,000. This amount went to the state, which agreed to pay to the college annual interest at six percent.

A committee of Lyman, Walker, and Wheeler was appointed to work out the necessary contract with Dartmouth, which was done by June 1867. The contract would have linked the new college closely with the Chandler Scientific Department, which enjoyed a certain degree of autonomy within Dartmouth. The Board of Visitors of the department had the right of veto over decisions of the Dartmouth board relating to the department. Unfortunately for the plans of the trustees, but perhaps fortunately for the eventual develop-

ment of the new college, the Chandler Board of Visitors exercised its right of veto and refused to accept the contract. Accordingly, a new contract was drawn and signed April 7, 1868. Instead of tying the new college to the Chandler Department, it was treated as a separate department of Dartmouth College. Dartmouth agreed to furnish the necessary classrooms and the use of its library, laboratories, and museums, with appropriate payment to be made for such use. Dartmouth faculty members were to teach in the new college when that could be arranged, and the faculty of the new college were likewise to teach in Dartmouth. As in the first contract, an experimental farm was to be secured and the proceeds of the Culver bequest were to be used for agricultural instruction.

With the new contract in effect, the trustees of New Hampshire College proceeded with plans to start instruction in September, 1868. Although no faculty was on hand, the trustees outlined a curriculum to make "intelligent men in the broadest sense, worthy citizens of a state in which the people ultimately rule, and of whose dearest interests knowledge and virtue are the only safeguards." The means to this end were carefully prescribed:

Mathematics and Engineering—Algebra; Trigonometry; Surveying and Mensuration; Engineering, with its application to agriculture; Book-keeping, with special reference to farm accounts.

Natural Philosophy—Including Meteorology and Astronomy, with practical application of the Mechanical Forces, as in various Machinery.

Chemistry, Geology, and Mineralogy—Inorganic and Organic Chemistry, vegetable and animal; Analytical Chemistry; Agricultural Chemistry, including Soils, Elements of Plants, Manures, and Agricultural Products, with Analyses.

Botany—Structural and Systematic Botany, with special reference to Plants pertaining to Agriculture; Natural History, varieties, description, and culture of Grasses, Grains, Fruits, and Woods, with special attention to Arboriculture and Horticulture; Obnoxious Plants, Weeds, etc.

Zoology—Elementary Zoology; Comparative Anatomy and Physiology; Natural History, Breeding, Feeding, and Economic Products of Domestic Animals;

Veterinary Surgery; Wild Animals, Insects, etc., beneficial or injurious to the farmer.

Physical Geography—With particular reference to the geographical distribution of plants and animals.

Agricultural Mechanics, Aesthetics, and Economics—Rural Architecture; Farm Implements; Mechanism of Tillage; Drainage; Fencings; Landscape Gardening; Rural Economy; Aesthetics of the Farm.

Literature—French; Rhetoric; English Literature; History.

Intellectual, Moral, and Political Philosophy—Including in the latter, the Science of Government, with special attention to the Constitution of the United States.

Military Tactics—As required by the Act of Congress, and the Statute of New-Hampshire.

The trustees concluded their course outline by saying: "Some of the subjects may be most advantageously treated in lectures. As to a considerable number of them, it will at once occur to all who are familiar with the processes of education, that, in the time that can be assigned to them, they can be mastered only in their principles and outlines. Yet even that will be of great advantage; and it is believed that, with the object we have in view, more or less attention should be given to all the topics named." The program was to be three years in duration. The terms were to correspond to those of the Dartmouth calendar, except that the summer term was to be omitted. Of the calendar, the trustees said: "This plan of limiting the time of study to the cool months of the year, and having a recess in the summer, is a novel feature, so far as similar institutions in this country are concerned, though there is one precedent for it, we are informed, in Europe." It also enabled the students to work on their farms during the summer.

To a college faculty of today it would seem presumptuous for a lay board to fashion a college curriculum. But at that time few were trained for college teaching in any field except the classics. Agricultural education was so embryonic that all was speculation and experimentation. The first attempts to interest American farmers in better practices had taken the form of fairs—one of the first being that at Rye, New Hampshire, about 1726. The 1754 prospectus for King's College (now Columbia University) mentioned husbandry and commerce, but there is no record of instruction in husbandry until 1792 when state funds for a time supported Dr. Samuel L. Mitchill as professor of natural history, chemistry, and agriculture. What became Rensselear Polytechnic Institute was founded in 1824 for teaching engineering and agriculture, but by 1850 it had become a school of engineering. The first college of agriculture to persist and flourish was that of Michigan, founded in Lansing in 1855.

Agricultural education had fared better in the more developed society of Europe. A proposal for an agricultural school had been made in England as early as 1651, and by the early nineteenth century such schools were to be found not only in England but on the Continent. A college of agriculture started at the University of Leipzig about 1812. As the sciences basic to agriculture—chemistry, botany, geology, zoology—were developing rapidly in Europe, it was there that Americans went for graduate study.

It was apparent that the New Hampshire College trustees recognized the tentative nature of their proposed course of study. That was fortunate, as French was not offered for two decades and military science not until the college had moved to Durham.

In addition to the three-year program, the 1868 trustees' report indicated that at some future time consideration would be given to a short course for those unable to follow the basic program. Agricultural extension also was previsioned: the trustees observed that, during the summer and fall vacations, the faculty would have "an opportunity to visit in different parts of the state, making desirable observations and investigations, and delivering occasionally popular lectures."

Having decided what was to be taught, the trustees addressed themselves to the problem of finding someone to teach it. They had, of course, given prior consideration to this matter. Dr. Boulton, a Concord preacher, had suggested one of his former parishioners, Ezekiel Dimond. Dimond was spending the year in Europe, but before his departure one of the trustees had interviewed him, and there had been correspondence between him and the board. The trustees now elected him Professor of General and Agricultural Chemistry at an annual salary of $1,500. (That its first faculty member should have been a chemist probably influenced the development of this science at the institution. Throughout its first century the chemistry department was the strongest on the campus, owing to the leadership of such notables—following Dimond—as Charles L. Parsons, Charles James, and Harold Iddles.)

Ezekiel Dimond was born August 7, 1836, in Warner, New Hampshire. His farmer father died in 1842, his mother two years later, and the orphaned boy went in 1846 to live with Daniel Knowlton on his farm in Concord. Dimond had inherited $300 from his father, and in nine years he had saved an additional $200 from wages paid him by Mr. Knowlton. With this capital, he decided to seek an education above that of the common schools. After attending New London Academy and Kimball Union Academy—with periodic returns to the Knowlton farm—he entered Middlebury College in 1861. Self-supporting, Dimond was fortunate to get a job as laboratory assistant to chemistry professor Henry M. Seely. Graduating with honors in 1865, Dimond spent the next year studying at Harvard under the famous Louis Agassiz. In the fall of 1866 he was teaching chemistry at the Oread Institute in Worcester, Massachusetts. In addition to his teaching duties, he was commissioned by a boiler inventor to investigate the chemistry of combustion. This project resulted in a 162-page treatise, *The Chemistry of Combustion Applied to the Economy of Fuel, with Special Reference to Construction of Fire Chambers for Steam Boilers*, published by Edward R. Fiske of Worcester in 1867.

Tired by a year of sixteen-hour days, Dimond decided to combine relaxation and education in a trip to Europe. He sailed in July, 1867. During the fall, in addition to sightseeing, he visited some of the pioneering agricultural schools of Europe. That winter in Dresden he attended scientific lectures. It was there that he was notified of his election as a professor of the New Hampshire College of Agriculture and the Mechanic Arts. Since little scientific equipment was made in the United States at that time, he was authorized to spend about two thousand dollars on material to bring back with him.

Ezekiel Dimond was just under six feet tall and a bit inclined to stoutness. His ruddy complexion, auburn hair, and full beard contrasted with his gray-blue eyes. His struggle to get an education had accustomed him to hard work. This habit stood him in good stead when he arrived in Hanover, August 1, 1868.

2. Professor Dimond Takes Charge

New Hampshire College was scheduled to open on September 4, 1868. When Ezekiel Dimond arrived in Hanover, he discovered that because of the illness of Asa D. Smith (president of both Dartmouth and New Hampshire College) little had been done to prepare for the opening. The college had no building of its own. Worse yet, it had no students.

Dimond prepared a circular of which two thousand copies were distributed. All the newspaper editors of the state received copies with a request for publication. Many complied, and a number also wrote editorials favoring the new institution. State senators, the now-recovered President Smith, and some Dartmouth faculty aided the recruitment drive, with the result that "a respectable number of young men presented themselves for admission." Attendance figures, like prices, were lower in those days. The "respectable number" was ten.

Tuition had been set at fifteen dollars for each of the two terms. Twelve scholarships, one for each senatorial district, had been established. As a result of the abundance of scholarships, the treasurer's report for the year showed a fifteen dollar income from tuition, paid by the lone out-of-state student.

During the first year Dimond was the only full-time college faculty member. Thomas R. Crosby, M.D., a Civil War surgeon who had taught at Norwich University, was added on a part-time basis; his contribution to the development of the college was cut short by his death in 1872. The Dartmouth faculty completed the instructional staff. President Smith taught rhetoric; Edwin D. Sanborn, history; Charles A. Young, natural philosophy and astronomy; and Charles A. Emerson, mathematics. John E. Sinclair of the Chandler faculty taught free hand drawing the second term. For this teaching in the "Agricultural Department" the Dartmouth men were paid two dollars an hour. Dimond (who taught all of the chemistry offered by Dartmouth except for that in the medical school) and Dr. Crosby were paid a like sum for the courses they taught for Dartmouth.

What of the students? Requirements for admission were modest. The candidate had to be at least sixteen years old, of good moral character, and able to pass examinations in English grammar, geography, and arithmetic based on preparation offered in the common schools. With few academies in the state and no system of public high schools, an institution dedicated to the higher education of the "industrial classes" could ask for no more in terms of academic preparation. Similar admission standards, if they can be called such, were typical of the land grant colleges across the United States during the first decades of their existence.

The work of the college evidently was not attractive to the students, for only two of the first-year students returned for the second. These two were joined by a third man, and they constituted the first graduating class in 1871. William Ballard of Concord took the agricultural course; Lewis Perkins of Hampton and Charles Sanders of Fisherville took the mechanic arts course. (All three were able to attend their fiftieth reunion in 1921.) One of the students who dropped out was an Indian, Albert Carney, a Confederate soldier who had come to Dartmouth on funds provided for the education of Indians. He was transferred to the "Agricultural Department" but soon left for preparatory school to acquire a background of Greek and Latin. The records show him in 1887 to be a hotel keeper in Choctaw Nation, Indian Territory.

If the curriculum designed by the trustees did not suit most of the original students, neither did it satisfy Professor Dimond. Toward the end of his first year in Hanover he prepared a lengthy statement for the 1869 report of the trustees. Dimond deplored the views of those who "have either innocently misapprehended or willfully misrepresented" provisions of the Morrill Act. To him the term Agricultural College was "an improper title—a name misapplied—because it fails to comprehend what is embraced and explicitly set forth in the statute which gave these institutions birth." After reviewing the colleges which had been established, Dimond went on to conclude that "whatever name may have become attached to these institutions, and whether they have been established as independent institutions or in connection with older colleges, the liberal education of the industrial classes is as much of an object as their practical training, and the mechanic arts are placed upon the same footing as agriculture, and so is mining or any other branch of productive industry. Indeed, we are led to infer that any branch of human knowledge may be taught in these colleges, provided that those sciences relating to agriculture and the mechanic arts, and the liberal and practical education of the industrial classes, are kept prominently in view."

Emphasizing the importance of thorough training in writing and speaking the English language, Dimond pointed out that lack of such ability had been a handicap to our "practical men" who were obliged "to call upon the educated lawyer or minister" to write or speak for them. Such a "subservient position of the industrial classes" was "entirely needless" for all that they had to do was "to avail themselves of, and give to their children, that *liberal education*" which Congress . . . proposed to furnish them."

Although Dimond's concept of the mission of the land grant colleges was limitless, the resources of his institution were not. The program of studies for the beginning year remained much as the trustees had proposed, except that the offerings were narrowed by the dropping of history and geometry. The work of the second and third years became more specialized. Students interested in agriculture pursued one program; those interested in mechanic arts followed another. The emphasis on English composition and declamation was retained by keeping them in the program for all three years. The same was true of the weekly biblical exercise. It would be decades before the rich educational offering foreseen by Dimond would become a reality.

President Smith had been disappointed when the legislature set up the Agricultural Department as a separate college instead of a true department of Dartmouth. Once the arrangement was set, however, he supported the new college. Dimond and others commended him for his tact and patience in working out the problems the arrangement created. A good deal of his patience was expended in adjusting to Ezekiel Dimond. In addition to being the major part of the teaching faculty of the college, Dimond also was its administration. His ideas often differed from Asa Smith's, and he was slow to give ground.

More pressing than reform of the curriculum was the need for physical facilities. It was true that the legislation setting up the new college had specified that Dartmouth was to provide the necessary classrooms, laboratories, museums, and so on; but Dartmouth had no excess space and certainly no entire building which could be designated as the headquarters of New Hampshire College. The trustees and Dimond alike lamented that the institution lacked a building for its "own local habitation and use." Furthermore, Dimond had definite ideas about the facilities his proposed building should contain. He wanted more than classrooms. There was to be a chemistry laboratory where the student could learn by doing and, very important, space for what he termed the "New Hampshire Museum of General and Applied Science." He believed that museums are "the only means of efficiently teaching those branches of knowledge which relate to agriculture and the mechanic arts." The proposed museum was to "contain geological and mineralogical specimens arranged and classified for instruction; samples of soils, marls, and peat; botanical specimens, especially those illustrative of the botany of our own state; native wools, textile fabrics in all stages of utilization; collections of grains and straws; vegetable products; skeletons of domestic animals; specimens of the birds, fish, and reptiles of our state; insects injurious to vegetation; agricultural implements; samples of everything manufactured in the state; models to illustrate the art of mining, glass-blowing, calico printing; and machinery sufficient to illustrate the principles of practical mechanics." Included in the museum would be the specimens then being collected by Charles H. Hitchcock, state geologist and professor in the Chandler Scientific Department. Hitchcock supported Dimond's request for the building.

Dimond's list of needs did not end there. He asked for the experimental farm mentioned in the act establishing the college. By working on the farm, a student would see the application of scientific knowledge; the manual labor would also serve to promote his health. Dimond also asked for an experimental machine shop.

The trustees, meeting April 27, 1869, voted that a building for use of the college was an immediate necessity. They authorized Dimond to secure "such plans and drawings as may be necessary." (This authorization was not to require much additional work or time on Dimond's part, for he already had plans for all four floors together with a seven-page description of the facilities to be provided.) The trustees then adjourned until May 4 in Concord, where the Dartmouth trustees were also meeting. In Concord the New Hampshire College trustees unanimously adopted a resolution and conveyed it to the Dartmouth trustees:

They [the Dartmouth trustees] will cooperate in the erection of a large building for such purposes as are indicated in the resolutions of the Trustees of the Col-

lege of Agriculture and the Mechanic Arts, the said building to cost not more than $40,000.

For this purpose, they will appropriate of the moneys that shall come to them from the estate of the late David Culver, the sum of $15,000 and they will add to this the sum of $10,000 to be received from the estate of the widow of the said David Culver . . . . The further sum of $15,000 shall in some way be furnished by the Trustees of the College of Agriculture and the Mechanic Arts, making a total of $40,000 . . . .

Said building shall contain appropriate recitation and lecture rooms, and also suitable rooms for the collections of the New Hampshire Museum of General and Applied Science, and shall, in honor of the chief donor, be designated as CULVER HALL.

One floor of said building shall contain a well appointed chemical laboratory, which shall be for the joint use of Dartmouth College and the New Hampshire College of Agriculture and the Mechanic Arts . . . .

In case the Trustees of Dartmouth College shall deem it advisable to place in said building any collections they may have . . . they reserve the right to do so, and if it is found desirable to place collections belonging to both colleges in the same room or case, each specimen shall be distinctly marked with the name of the college to which it belongs, and any Professor in either college shall have, under proper regulations, the free use of the same for purposes of instruction.

Dartmouth College shall have free use of the lecture, recitation, and other rooms, for all required instruction in any department of mineralogy, geology, or natural history . . . .

The expense of warming, lighting, and keeping in repair said building shall be paid by each college in proportion to the use made of it . . . .

Should any appropriation towards said building be made by the Legislature of New Hampshire, the [Dartmouth] Trustees bind themselves, in case the connection between Dartmouth College and the College of Agriculture and the Mechanic Arts shall hereafter be dissolved, to refund the State, if requested by the Legislature, the amount appropriated, without interest.

The Dartmouth trustees endorsed the resolution. The trustees of New Hampshire College then petitioned the state legislature for an appropriation of $15,000 for the proposed Culver Hall. At its June 1869 session the legislature voted this amount. In a later report to the trustees on the start of construction, Dimond noted that the state appropriation of $15,000 "was the *first* substantial recognition of the claims of scientific education which the Legislature of New Hampshire had ever made. And this, too, made when the people were groaning under the burden of excessive taxation, and when the best paying stock in the political market was supposed to be retrenchment and economy . . . ."

Edward Dow of Concord designed the building, making it twenty feet longer than had been proposed. Work was started promptly, but a flood in the fall of 1869 damaged the brickyards where the brick was to be made and washed away the firewood which had been collected for the kilns. Enough progress was made, however, so that in the winter of 1870-71 Professor Charles H. Hitchcock of the Chandler Scientific Department was able to occupy an office in the building. Hitchcock's office was connected by a direct telegraph wire to a scientific expedition housed that winter on the top of Mt. Washington. It was the only room in Culver Hall fitted for occupation, reached by struggling through piles of lumber, and by crossing a single plank over perilous depths.

Culver Hall was ready for dedication in the spring of 1871. For the ceremony on June 23, Governor James A. Weston and members of his council and the state legislature were present. The ceremony was a major public relations effort: $496 of the college's total budget of $7,138 for the year was spent on it.

While Culver Hall was still under construction, twenty-five acres of land opposite the site were purchased from S. M. Cobb for an experimental farm. The price was $150 an acre. The tract was too small for the college's purposes, but the institution had no money with which to purchase more. Not dismayed by his duties as business agent, supervisor of construction, curriculum planner, student recruiter, extension lecturer, lobbyist, and teacher of four or five classes a day, Dimond undertook to be a one-man holding company. He

personally committed $7,000 for a farm of 135 acres adjoining the Cobb land, for eventual sale to the college. While holding the farm he also had to manage it, assured by the trustees that he would be repaid for any loss when the college acquired title.

John Conant relieved the trustees of making good on this promise. Conant was eighty when in the fall of 1870 he made a three-day visit to New Hampshire College. He had been born in Stow, Massachusetts, one of sixteen children of a prosperous father. When he was eighteen his father gave him a $1,500 mortgage on a well-timbered farm. He soon possessed the farm, cut the timber, and hauled it to Boston where he sold it for a good price. He then sold the place, having doubled his capital, and bought property in Jaffrey, New Hampshire. It was 1816, the "year of no summer," and crops were short. Conant, however, sold his hay for nearly enough to get back his purchase price. He built a large house and became a leading citizen of Jaffrey, serving at various times as selectman, delegate to the state legislature, and town moderator. He spent little and invested shrewdly. In 1851 he became president of the Monadnock Bank. Though active in financial matters he remained for years a successful farmer with an interest in improved methods. In later years he became a remarkably generous philanthropist. His gifts made possible the founding of Conant High School in Jaffrey; he contributed $6,000 toward the founding of the State Insane Asylum, forerunner of the State Hospital; he gave $3,000 to churches and a like sum for indigent families, as well as $12,000 to New London Academy. Because of these gifts and those to New Hampshire College, at his death there remained in his estate only $9,412 of a fortune estimated to have been $200,000 at one time.

When Conant paid a visit to New Hampshire College, he was so impressed by its potential that he bought the farm from Dimond and gave it to the college. In appreciation the trustees named it the Conant Farm. Dimond was made acting manager and was authorized to spend $1,000 for livestock and farming tools.

The completion of Culver Hall made possible the realization of Dimond's third request, a machine shop. This was established in a room previously used to house the museum collections. The shop was not so large or well equipped as desired, but it was a shop.

While in Hanover, John Conant had noted that the living accommodations for the New Hampshire College students were unsatisfactory. Dartmouth had purchased for $3,500 a hotel at South and Main streets and had spent nearly $2,000 on renovations. Students in other departments lived in it, but it was known as the "Ag" dormitory; it was unpopular with the residents and they left as soon as they could find other quarters. To improve the situation, Conant offered $5,000 towards a dormitory to be built on the newly acquired farm. At a special meeting on March 1, 1871, the offer was considered by the trustees. They thought the proposed building would be too small, so they voted to ask the legislature for $15,000 to add to Conant's offer. Instead, the legislature came up with $5,000 in the June 1871 session.

While plans were being made for the dormitory, word came that Conant would like to see representatives of the trustees. A visit by President Smith and William P. Wheeler of Keene resulted in an agreement being drawn whereby Conant turned over to the college securities and other property to the value of $48,000, with the provision that he be paid the income on this for the next year. Not over $5,000 could be spent for the purchase of land or for improving the land already owned by New Hampshire College. Another $5,000 could be used for a dormitory in which students not able to pay would have free room rent. The balance of the gift was to be a perpetual fund for scholarships, the income on each $1,000 to go to a student studying agriculture. Residents of the town of Jaffrey were to have two of these scholarships, with one each

reserved for the other towns in Cheshire County. Any of the income not distributed as scholarships could be added to the principal or, in case of "pressing need," be used for the general purposes of the college, especially for agriculture. Fortunately Conant was foresighted enough to agree that the trustees should have authority to increase the amount of the individual scholarships: they amounted to $40 each in 1872. (At present the Conant scholarships are adjusted to the individual student's needs and sometimes go as high as full tuition.)

With a total of $10,000 now available from Conant for student housing, plus $5,000 appropriated by the legislature in 1871, the trustees successfully sought an additional $7,000 from the 1872 legislature. Five acres across from Culver Hall were purchased, and in 1873 construction started on the dormitory to be called Conant Hall. It was completed in 1874 at a cost of $22,358. The first floor was used for a dining room where 135 students, most of them from other departments of Dartmouth College, ate for $3.25 a week. Dimond had figured that by use of produce from the farm the cost could be kept to about $2.75 a week, but even at the higher figure the dining hall never broke even. For several years it was let out to a Mrs. Durgin who ran it with rigid economy. The upper floors were a dormitory where the rent for a double room ranged from fifteen to twenty-five dollars a year.

The new institution was doing better in building its physical plant than its student body. The enrollment of ten the first year dropped to seven the second, but it went up to eleven in the third year. The new Conant scholarships evidently stimulated recruitment: the entering class in the fall of 1872 numbered eighteen, more than three times the number who had entered the previous year. (There also were two "middle class" men and three seniors.) This was the largest entering class for some time, and eleven of them stayed to graduate in 1875. The year 1872-73 saw an enrollment of thirty-three—a peak which was not equaled again for a decade. A low point was reached in 1877-78 when there were only ten students, including a lone freshman, Charles H. Hood, who stayed on to be the entire graduating class of 1880. (A son of the founder of the H.P. Hood Dairy Company and later its president, he prospered with that concern and became a major benefactor to the university through the building and endowment of Hood House, the present infirmary.)

The dearth of students could hardly have been due to high costs. Tuition remained at fifteen dollars a term, and most students had scholarships. Board and room charges were low. With a tuition scholarship, work on the experimental farm during the academic year, and earnings during the four-month summer vacation, it was believed that a young man of "prudent and industrious habits" could nearly support himself while getting his education.

In addition to their farm work—which was not compulsory at New Hampshire College, as it was at some of the new land grant institutions—the students had other employment opportunities. They did maintenance work on the college buildings and even provided much of the labor for a new barn. Built with $5,000 appropriated by the legislature in 1874, the barn measured 50′ x 100′ and was considered a model for its time. The trustees reported that New Hampshire College paid out $828 for student labor in 1873-74 and $1,298 the following year. Some of this money, earned at the rate of twelve or fifteen cents an hour, went to Dartmouth students who had joined the college work force.

There was no problem of an out-of-state quota in the early years. Except for the Indian from the West the first year, the only out-of-stater during the first six years was a boy from Vermont in 1870-71.

Agricultural interests, which had been important in the establishment of the college, were disappointed by the small enrollment. They were even more disappointed when they learned how few of the graduates made agriculture their life work. Only one of the graduating members of the first class became a farmer. Two of those graduating in the class of 1873 were in agriculture, but in the next two classes there was but a single farmer. These figures so disturbed John Conant that he changed the provisions of his scholarships to restrict them to those making agriculture their "life pursuit" and "none others." To allay such concerns, the trustees in 1874 declared:

It has often been urged, in objection to institutions like this, that few of the graduates devote themselves to agricultural pursuits. This objection is based, in part, on a too prevalent misapprehension. From the use, for brevity, of the term "Agricultural College"—a use so infelicitous as it is misleading—it is concluded that they were established solely to fit men for a farmer's life. This was, indeed, one of the objects, and one of great importance, but . . . it was by no means the only one . . . . It is no strange thing, and often not unwise, for a young man to change his life purpose. This happens sometimes even with students of theology, and will doubtless happen in the case of some who enter this institution with an industrial pursuit in view. We may turn out, now and then, a doctor, a lawyer, or even a clergyman—possibly a gentleman of affluence and of leisure. But the discipline and knowledge gained here will not be lost: they may even save the leisure from perversion, and give wise direction to the affluence.

New Hampshire agriculturalists were not alone in being dissatisfied with the land grant colleges because of their lack of concentration on training farmers. The Connecticut Grange complained that virtually no farm boy could pass the Yale entrance examinations, and that in twenty-four years during which Yale had been receiving the land grant funds it had graduated only seven farmers, at an average cost to the state of $25,700 each. In Rhode Island the farmers were upset because most of the free scholarships provided by Brown University with the land grant money were going to city boys, and what little agricultural instruction Brown was offering was entirely theoretical. Vermont had set up a separate land grant college attached to the University of Vermont, but the funds were given to the trustees of the university, and the new college existed principally in name. An agricultural course was announced, but it had no takers. Even in Maine, where a new state land grant college had been set up on a farm, with no ties with any other college, the agricultural interests were unhappy. The Massachusetts College of Agriculture concentrated more on farming than did any of the other New England colleges: it claimed that over half of its graduates during the first twenty years were in fields related to agriculture.

Beginning in the first year that instruction had been offered by New Hampshire College, oral examinations were conducted, usually but not always, at the end of each term. The trustees' report of 1875 is the first to mention theses submitted by seniors to an examining committee. Topics that year were Drainage and Its Advantages, Drawing, Steam and Its Utility, Rural Architecture, Forest Trees, Education, Water-Wheels: Their History and Comparative Utility, Should Government Support Industrial Colleges?, Topography: Its History and Mechanical Improvements, Iron, and Advantages of a Scientific Education to the Industrial Classes.

The degree awarded to the class of 1871 was the Bachelor of Philosophy. However, the following year it was decided that the degree to be awarded by the college would be the Bachelor of Science, and this was made retroactive for the first class.

In the spring of 1876, Professor Dimond became so ill he was forced to stop all work. His illness was, according to the trustees' report, "undoubtedly the result of overwork, he having performed, in superintending the erection of our buildings, in his various courses of instruction, in the management of the farm, and in the general care of the affairs of the institution, twice the amount of work that should have been required of any one man." In spite of his accomplishments, Dimond had not escaped criticism. John Conant wrote the trustees in 1875 saying that he

had heard that Dimond suffered from epilepsy and suggested that the professor was not qualified for his position. Conant quoted a student who charged that Dimond's management of the farm was rather shiftless, among other things accusing him of having allowed two acres of potatoes and twenty bushels of beets to freeze in the ground. The trustees, closer to the operation than Conant, wrote in their 1876 report that Dimond's care of the farm had been excellent, "despite certain false rumors."

With Dimond incapacitated, Benjamin Blanpied (who had been hired as an instructor in chemistry in 1871-72 and promoted to associate professor with a salary of $1,500 in 1873) was asked to take over Dimond's responsibilities. The ill man hoped to recover his health by taking a trip to Philadelphia where he viewed the Centennial Exposition, but he did not improve and died in Hanover on July 6, 1876, in sight of Culver Hall to which he had made such a vital contribution. An autopsy showed death due to a disease of the brain. In a memorial sketch, one of the original trustees listed Dimond's attributes as a "wonderful power of producing important results from slender means . . . not vivid imagination but strong common sense . . . keen and ready wit." And the trustees said of him: "With a persistency and courage alike honorable to his head and heart, he surmounted many obstacles in his way, and with the aid of a few noble souls, and a legislature that sympathized with him in the good work in which he was engaged, he was enabled to open the doors of a college for the education of the sons of farmers and mechanics . . . . In the midst of his usefulness, with brilliant prospects for the future as a man of science, and deeply wedded to the cause of popular education, he died when less than forty years of age, yet he had accomplished, in his brief day, more than a giant's work." At the funeral President Asa D. Smith declared: "He has accomplished in a little more than seven years the work of an ordinary lifetime."

The college's midwife was gone. The trustees looked about for others to nourish its infancy —but first there were financial accounts to settle.

Dimond's widow was given free use of rooms in Conant Hall until the spring of 1877. Meanwhile a committee of the trustees was chosen to settle the account between the college and Dimond's estate. They found that, not only had Dimond neglected to pay himself all of his last year's salary, he even had advanced money to pay some of the college bills. Total indebtedness of the institution to his estate was $4,075—a sum the college treasurer did not have available. The committee turned to John Conant for help. He gave the college an advance on his legacy, on which sum he was to be paid interest at four percent as long as he lived. This brought his total benefactions up to $70,000, or not much less than the amount realized from the federal land grant under the Morrill Act.

With the Conant money, Dimond's notes at the banks were paid and Mrs. Dimond received a partial payment in cash and a college note for the balance. These transactions left just thirty-eight cents in the treasury when Frederick Smyth, the treasurer, filed his annual report on April 1, 1877. It was not a generous working capital for the new management.

A TECHNICAL SCHOOL of high grade with WORK SHOP instruction.
Specialties: AGRICULTURAL SCIENCE, CHEMISTRY, and MECHANICAL ENGINEERING.
Scientific instruction by graduates of the best Technical Schools.
For catalogue or information apply to Prof. C. H. PETTEE, Hanover, N. H.

An early recruiting poster showing all the buildings of New Hampshire College at Hanover.

3. Growing Up in Hanover

More than one man was required to perform the duties that had been undertaken by Ezekiel Dimond. The trustees held a special meeting on August 10, 1876, to consider the problem. They authorized Benjamin Blanpied to take charge of all the details of managing the college, "as did the late Professor Dimond," except for the farm. (On his own initiative, Blanpied also took on Dimond's family responsibilities by marrying his widow. Although given the charge that had been Dimond's, Blanpied did not possess the energy and dedication that had characterized his predecessor. He left the college in 1889.) To manage the college farm, the trustees unanimously elected Jeremiah W. Sanborn of Gilmanton, New Hampshire. The new manager was to begin his duties on September 1.

Sanborn's formal education had gone no further than attendance at the Pittsfield and Gilmanton academies. He was superintendent of schools in Gilmanton in 1868 and 1869, meanwhile serving in the state legislature as chairman of the committee on New Hampshire College. When the trustees hired him in 1876, he was a member of the New Hampshire Board of Agriculture.

Sanborn was an impressive administrator. He began publication of monthly bulletins about research done on the experimental farm; they may have been the first regular publications of this kind in the country. In 1881 the trustees voted him an honorary Bachelor of Science degree—the first honorary degree given by the college. He resigned in 1882 to be dean of agriculture at the University of Missouri, and in 1889 he became president of the Agricultural College of Utah. He returned in 1894 to his native state, where he developed his 2,000 acres in Gilmanton into a model farm. He gave further service to New Hampshire College as a trustee from 1896 to

1899; as a trustee he was a severe critic of the experiment station.

Within a year of Dimond's death, Asa D. Smith resigned as president of Dartmouth and of New Hampshire College. Pending appointment of a new Dartmouth executive, George W. Nesmith of Franklin in 1877 became president of New Hampshire College. Nesmith was a trustee. Rev. Samuel C. Bartlett, upon being named president of Dartmouth, took Asa Smith's place on the New Hampshire College board of trustees, but Nesmith did not step aside for the new man. Instead, Bartlett was given the title of "President of the Faculty." Nesmith has traditionally been credited with being the second president of New Hampshire College, but the point might be debated. In any event, the trustees never did elect Bartlett president of the college.

Bartlett did initiate the practice of starting the trustee meetings with prayer—a custom which continued through President Murkland's administration—but he was not as actively involved in the affairs of the college as Asa Smith had been. An Old Testament scholar, he was not interested in agriculture and the mechanic arts. His mind was swift, his decisions firm, his patience short. He was soon at odds not only with the New Hampshire College of Agriculture and the Mechanic Arts but also with the Medical School and the Chandler Scientific Department of Dartmouth. An investigation of Bartlett's administration was requested by a group of Dartmouth alumni in 1881. Shortly thereafter a memorial asking Bartlett's resignation, and signed by members of the different faculties of Dartmouth including all of those in New Hampshire College and the Chandler Scientific Department, was presented to the Dartmouth trustees. A public hearing was held. It was charged that Bartlett was "habitually insolent, discourteous, and dictatorial," had destroyed freedom of discussion by the faculty, had humiliated students, and had lost the confidence of the faculty. The charges dealt more with the general air of dissension than with specific acts. Bartlett's defense was brilliant. The result was that the trustees asked for no resignations but urged everyone to get on with less friction. This proved easier for the trustees to advise than for those involved to practice.

Bartlett's attitude did nothing to lessen the dissatisfaction of the agricultural interests in the state. As the leading farm organization, the Grange was an important instrument for voicing criticism. Among other things it was felt that the location of the college on the Dartmouth campus was unfortunate because it resulted in making agriculture a minor part of the total institutional picture. Some believed that the Dartmouth students and faculty looked down upon the students in the "agricultural college." To counter this, the trustees had invited Dudley T. Chase, master of the state Grange, to visit the college. In a report dated February 18, 1879, he stated that as a result of his examination he could "not too highly commend the college to the farmers of New Hampshire . . . . The social position of the students is unobjectionable, and they are regarded and respected by their comrades, by their fellow-students in other departments, by their instructors, and by the faculty of Dartmouth College, for their merits and good conduct. No parent and no young man need fear that the agricultural student will be degraded by his connection with the college."

Even this favorable report did not still the complaints about the location of New Hampshire College in Hanover. The 1885 report of the college trustees reviewed the matter of the title to Culver Hall: the title remained with Dartmouth even though the building had been financed by the Culver bequest for agricultural education, plus a state appropriation. The New Hampshire College trustees contended that Dartmouth College should deed the building to the state institution.

Probably influenced by this trustee report, the legislature in 1885 created a commission to study removal of New Hampshire College from Hanover. The commission held public hearings, and the Grange also conducted a separate investigation. The only result of this activity was a revision by the legislature in 1887 of the board of trustees of New Hampshire College. The governor was to be on the board, ex officio, and there would be seven state-appointed trustees, including at least two practical farmers. To the enlarged board Dartmouth was to appoint five trustees. Dartmouth protested dilution of its representation, but did not cancel its contract with the state college.

To take the college to the people, the faculty in the winter of 1885-86 held a series of meetings at Colebrook, Lancaster, Whitefield, North Haverhill, Cornish, Acworth, Belmont, Canterbury, Wilmot Flat, and Short Falls. The next winter, meetings were held at fifteen other locations in the state. There usually were both afternoon and evening sessions. Charles H. Pettee spoke on the "Work of the Agricultural College" and sometimes lectured on "Weather Predictions." Clarence W. Scott was heard on "The History and Work of the College," on "Agricultural Education," or on "Industrial Education." George H. Whitcher offered advice on fertilizers and dairying, while Benjamin Blanpied's topic was the chemistry of fertilizers. On occasion a senior went along to talk on the education of farmers. Dr. Robert F. Burleigh, a graduate of the class of 1882, spoke on the treatment of the diseases of domestic animals.

With Bartlett more a critic than a leader, the college administration fell mainly on the shoulders of George Nesmith and Benjamin Blanpied. Although Blanpied had been expected to do the things which Dimond had done, except to manage the farm, Nesmith carried a good share of the load. It was he who received the funds from treasurer Frederick Smyth with which to pay the college bills. In 1888 Nesmith sought to resign his responsibilities. He agreed to remain as presiding officer of the board when, on February 20, 1888, Charles H. Pettee was appointed dean of the faculty. As chief executive officer of the faculty, Pettee was charged with supervision of instruction and of student behavior. He was also the financial agent of the college, under orders to see that expenditures did not exceed appropriations. He continued to teach, of course, and for all this his salary was set at $2,000.

Before he died, Ezekiel Dimond had asked Pettee—a young instructor in the Thayer School of Engineering at Dartmouth—to teach a course in meteorology to the agricultural students. Pettee confessed complete ignorance of the subject. Dimond replied: "That's all right. You can keep ahead of the boys." Once having gotten into meteorology, Pettee must have liked it: beginning in 1876 he taught it for fifty-two years.

Pettee's appointment as dean was not his first venture into administration. Upon the resignation of Jeremiah Sanborn in 1882 he had been appointed farm superintendent "for the time being." He continued to run the farm until George H. Whitcher, a graduate of the college in 1881, took over on April 1, 1884, at a salary of $600. Pettee at this time was made treasurer and auditor of farm accounts, for which he received use of a garden and the new farm house, except for certain rooms assigned to Whitcher.

Clarence W. Scott began a long association with the college about the same time. A teacher and the librarian of Dartmouth, he was for three years a part-time lecturer in rhetoric and algebra, and in 1881 he was elected Professor of English Language and Literature at an annual salary of $1,000.

When Benjamin Blanpied resigned in 1889, Fred W. Morse, who had been appointed an assistant chemist in the Experiment Station the year before, was named Professor of General and Agricultural Chemistry. At the same time Charles L. Parsons, an assistant chemist in the Experiment Station, was made an instructor in chemistry, to be promoted the following year to associate professor.

The first teacher in mechanical engineering was Lieutenant Thomas W. Kinkaid, USN, a graduate of Annapolis loaned to the college by the Navy from 1886 to 1889. When Kinkaid was recalled to active duty, Albert Kingsbury was chosen professor of mechanical engineering.

The salaries paid—$2,000 to Pettee as dean, $1,000 to Scott, $600 to Whitcher—sound niggardly today. But at the time the average salaries of professors in twenty-four of the larger institutions in the country averaged only $1,750. Cornell, a relatively wealthy college, paid its professors $1,375 to $2,250.

The trustees called attention to the fact that state appropriations for buildings had come to about $40,000 as of April 1, 1878. Contrasted with this were the gifts of $70,000 from Conant and $25,000 from the Culver estate. The only major source of continuing income was $4,800 coming each year from the state as interest on the funds realized from sale of the Morrill Act land grant. Against this income, the annual operating budget was nearly $10,000, not including necessary repairs to buildings. The only unused source of money was the income from the Conant gift, beyond what was expended annually for scholarships. Legal opinion held that the only uses to which the excess Conant funds could be put were gifts to needy students or payment for student labor.

The financial troubles of New Hampshire College were duplicated in its sister institutions around the country. The Massachusetts College of Agriculture had a $32,000 debt in 1878 and was kept in operation only because a trustee, William Knowlton, personally endorsed the college notes. The *Boston Post* referred to the college as a "hungry buzzard" and a "water-logged and beggarly institution." The Maine State College did better than most, but in 1879 the legislature sought to transfer some of the costs from the taxpayers to the students by ordering that tuition be charged. This resulted in applications for the next class dropping from fifty to seventeen. The University of Vermont also was having financial problems.

With enrollment down to ten, in the fall of 1877, special meetings of the New Hampshire College trustees were held to consider the plight of the institution. Samuel Bartlett proposed that part of Culver Hall be used by the Thayer School of Civil Engineering, with Dartmouth assuming a larger share of the cost of upkeep. Professors Blanpied and Pettee submitted a plan whereby some of the students in New Hampshire College and in the Chandler Scientific Department could attend the same classes, thus eliminating duplication of courses and instructors. The proposals were referred to a committee. How much the special meetings profited the college is problematic, as they ended with the trustees voting themselves ten cents a mile one way and three dollars a day for all other expenses when attending meetings.

The state at this point started to contribute to the operation of the college. In 1877 the legislature voted $3,000 a year for the next six years. When the six years were up, the legislature voted $2,000 a year for 1884 and 1885 for operating expenses. In 1886 a "perpetual" appropriation of $3,000 a year was voted. The parsimony of the state government nearly starved the college to death, but it did from the outset establish the college's fiscal independence. Having to do most of the worrying about where the money was coming from, the trustees were left free to decide how to spend what they could get. And the state appropriations did help. During 1877-78 about three thousand dollars was paid on the old debts, and the farm buildings were repaired and enlarged. The secretary was authorized to advertise the college in newspapers, which apparently had results: sixteen freshmen entered in the fall of 1878 compared with one in 1877. By 1881 the trustees were "happy to be able to an-

nounce . . . that for the last two years we have enjoyed increased prosperity. We have paid off all our indebtedness."

More students did not mean a substantial increase in student payments, since nearly all of them were on full-tuition scholarships. But it did release more of the income from the Conant fund, because out of the scholarships paid from it, tuition was deducted by the college.

As the founding of New Hampshire College had been due to federal financial help, so also was the largest expansion of its activities during the Hanover era. Congress passed the Hatch Act, providing funds for agricultural experiment stations in the various states. On August 4, 1887, the state of New Hampshire accepted the provisions of the act, under which $15,000 a year would be provided the state. Of the original payment, up to one-fifth could go for construction. Thereafter the construction allowance would be cut to five percent of the annual grant. The trustees named George Whitcher director of the proposed experiment station at a salary of $2,000. They then voted to spend $3,000 in Hatch Act funds and up to $4,000 in college funds for construction of the new facility, which would have the use of the Conant Farm. Two new professors were authorized, as was the hiring of necessary assistants for the station. These assistants were to be "superior college graduates" with the understanding that they would have an opportunity to pursue graduate work. Thus began today's extensive program of encouragement of graduate study through financial support of graduate students.

For the laying of the cornerstone of the Experiment Station on June 26, 1888, a special train starting at Nashua brought hundreds of farmers to Hanover. Governor Charles H. Sawyer spoke. State agricultural organizations, including the Grange, took a leading part in the ceremonies.

Upon completion of the station building in 1889, a number of additions were made to the faculty, several of whom had joint appointments in the Experiment Station. Fred W. Morse replaced Benjamin Blanpied as professor of chemistry. Albert H. Wood was engaged as associate professor of agriculture and George L. Teeple as instructor in mechanical engineering and physics. The staff of the station numbered eight. The college faculty was nine, plus three part-time members.

Congress soon gave further encouragement to the land grant colleges by passing the second Morrill Act, giving each state $15,000 a year, to be increased by $1,000 a year until the annual payments reached $25,000. This new money was "to be applied only to instruction in agriculture, the mechanic arts, the English language, and the various branches of mathematical, physical, natural, and economic science, with special reference to their applications in the industries of life, and to the facilities for such instruction . . . ." This money so improved the financial situation of the college that at the end of fiscal year 1891 Treasurer Smyth reported an unexpended balance.

In 1878, two basic changes had been made in the curriculum of the college. To raise the standards, the length of the college year was changed from twenty-eight to thirty-eight weeks. The option of substituting mechanical courses for agriculture courses was removed, but surveying, mechanics, geology, workshop applications, mechanical drawing, and construction of roads and bridges were included. The adoption of the new curriculum, which forced every graduate of the college to be trained for farming, was a response to criticism by agriculturalists. It necessarily reduced the opportunity for courses of a cultural nature. In adopting the curriculum, the trustees noted that no ancient or modern language was required but observed that in some cases a knowledge of French, German, or Latin was "important and desirable."

The new curriculum did not meet with universal favor. In April 1881, the trustees "authorized and requested" the faculty "to arrange a complete four-year course of study leading to the Bachelor of Science degree, provided that students completing the first three years of the course shall receive the Bachelor of Agricultural Science degree." This proposal brought quick reaction from the students. Thirty-five of them petitioned the trustees to rescind the four-year curriculum. The students also requested that the Bachelor of Science degree be restored. The trustees held a special meeting on June 28, 1881, and acceded to both demands. However, they decided to provide an optional fourth year for anyone who desired it. Robert F. Burleigh '82 took the extra year and was listed as a resident graduate student in 1882-83. He was doubtless the first graduate student in the college.

Although the trustees backed down on that occasion, they adopted a four-year curriculum in 1883. The first year was of two terms, ending in April; the sophomore, junior, and senior years were of three terms, ending in June. For admission to the first year, students were required to pass examinations only in arithmetic, algebra through simple equations, English grammar, geography, and United States history. Those who were able to pass examinations in algebra through quadratics, plane geometry, English language and composition, ancient history, physiology, and bookeeping were allowed to begin with the second year of the curriculum. (Students who had attended high schools or academies were excused from the entrance examinations in subjects in which they were certified by the school.) The students were allowed some choice of subjects, but most subjects were required, including French in the junior year. The French requirement was later reconsidered. At their annual meeting in 1886, the trustees voted: "*Resolved*, that the Trustees do not approve of the introduction of Foreign Languages into the Curriculum."

Since the founding of the college there had been debate—which was to last for a decade after the move to Durham—on the legitimacy of offering languages and other cultural subjects in a land grant college. On the other hand offering military science was clearly prescribed in the Morrill Act. Inquiry in 1890 revealed that the Secretary of War was willing to detail an officer to give instruction, but there were too few students to make it worthwhile.

Although a committee of three trustees had been appointed in April 1882 to consider whether it would be legal and advisable to admit women students, nothing more was heard of the matter until the trustee meeting of December 31, 1890. Dean Pettee reported that a woman had applied for admission. Six months later, the trustees voted to admit women. The programs prior to this time all had been directed toward preparation for vocations which women in that day did not enter. Perhaps in anticipation of the advent of coeds, the catalog of the college for 1890 listed a "general course" which was "arranged with a series of electives which can be taken by women in place of shop work and surveying."

The spread of high schools and the existence of established academies made it possible in 1891 to increase the requirements for admission to the freshman year. In his 1891 report, Dean Pettee wrote: "We desire that the advantages of the excellent academies and high schools, scattered over our State, may be enjoyed and utilized by those who propose to study here, in order that their progress after entering may be more rapid and satisfactory."

In its first quarter-century, the New Hampshire College faculty had grown from one to nine, with an additional eight on the staff of the Experiment Station. Whereas admissions had once been open to those with a reasonable knowledge of the subjects taught in the common schools, the entrance examinations now were based on secondary-school subjects. The original three-year curriculum, with an option for specialization in agriculture or mechanic arts, had expanded into a four-year program with seven options. The college year had increased from twenty-eight to thirty-eight weeks.

The first College baseball team, 1890.

Tuition was unchanged at thirty dollars a year, but a library and reading room tax of six dollars had been added, in effect making a twenty percent increase. The rate of pay for student labor had kept pace with this advance, rising from a low of twelve cents an hour to fifteen cents. Room rent for the year had gone from $12-$15 up to $18-$30. Board remained available in a range from $2.50 to $3.50 a week. In 1884 college officials estimated the total cost of a year's attendance at from $146 to $177, on the assumption the student would have a scholarship covering his tuition.

The trustees in 1890 adopted new regulations covering scholarships and other financial aids. Thirty Conant scholarships for students of agriculture, each paying seventy dollars, were approved. Each town in Cheshire County was to have one, except Jaffrey which had two. Those not used in Cheshire County could be awarded to other in-state residents. Since the number of senatorial districts had been doubled in 1877, there now were twenty-four senatorial scholarships; they now paid fifty dollars a year. If a senatorial district did not have an eligible student in the college, the scholarship for that district could be awarded elsewhere. Any New Hampshire student not holding a scholarship could get free tuition. Further financial aid for needy agricultural students was available from the Conant fund at Dean Pettee's discretion, provided the student pledged not to use tobacco or intoxicating liquor. The claim that any energetic and frugal student could work his way through the institution seemed well founded, especially if he had the foresight to enroll in agriculture.

Cash prizes for outstanding academic work also offered the student a chance to supplement his income. Beginning in 1879, Professor Henry G. Jessup started giving twenty dollars a year to the students preparing the best herbariums. Two years later Frederick Smyth established prizes for the best work in public speaking, public reading, and writing. The awards totaled one hundred dollars a year. In 1883 the Alumni Association offered prizes of fifteen dollars and ten dollars for the best essays on political economy. The Bailey Prize for proficiency in chemistry, given first in 1888 was ten dollars contributed by Dr. Charles H. Bailey '79 and Edward A. Bailey '85. The Erskine Mason Memorial Prize for the student making the greatest overall improvement was given by Mrs. Catherine M. Mason of Stamford, Connecticut, in memory of her son, a member of the class of 1893 who had died before graduation.

In view of the modest admissions and financial requirements, it might have been expected that the enrollment would rise steadily. But this was the nineteenth century, when a graduate of an academy or high school was rated a well-educated person. The procurement of dollars to support the institution was a major problem; the procurement of students was equally formidable. Dean Pettee spent much of his summer driving about with horse and buggy to persuade farm boys to enter the college. He found it more fruitful to talk with the mothers than with the fathers, who typically were of the opinion that if they passed on their knowledge of farming to the boy, he would know all he needed to practice agriculture successfully. On occasion, when an expected freshman did not show up for registration, the good dean would hitch up and go after him. The allocation of scholarships to senatorial districts appears to have been more to encourage each senator to recruit a student from his district than to give him a political plum to dispense.

Although most of the out-of-state students were from Vermont, one or more came from Connecticut, Maine, Massachusetts, New Jersey, New York, and Virginia. There were two American Indians, Albert Carney and Rollins K. Adair. The only Canadian was Angus O. Patton of Montreal, who attended in 1880-82. The only European was Belezar Stoinanoff Rouevsky, a Bulgarian, who stayed for four years and graduated with the class of 1886.

With a small enrollment, the paucity of student organizations is understandable. The Culver Literary Society started in 1872, the Christian Fraternity in 1881, and the Q.T.V. Fraternity (which became a chapter of Kappa Sigma) sometime in the 1870s. The only attempt at a student publication was the *Culver Literary Journal* put out by the Culver Literary Society from about 1871 to 1876. Containing essays, poems, jokes, and some news, it was copied in longhand and circulated among the students. Religious activity was more a part of the curriculum than an outside activity: Sunday morning, students were expected to attend church, which was followed by a "Biblical exercise" in the afternoon. The college contributed to the salary of the local pastor. In 1890 Dean Pettee purchased a pew for one hundred dollars in order that the seniors might be as properly seated as the Dartmouth students.

One other college organization should be mentioned: the Alumni Association. It was established in 1880, a healthy sign of the institution's growth from infancy to adolescence.

4. A Philanthropist in Durham

On February 12, 1856, Benjamin Thompson signed his will in Durham, New Hampshire. In it, Thompson left nearly his entire fortune to his native state "to promote the cause of agriculture" by the establishment of a school for that purpose on his land in Durham, "wherein shall be thoroughly taught, both in the schoolroom and in the field, the theory and practice of that most useful and honorable calling." The content of the will was a closely guarded secret until his death in 1890.

Ben Thompson was a descendant of William Thompson, a Scottish soldier captured by Cromwell's forces at the Battle of Dunbar, sold into servitude in the colonies, and sent to Boston. After serving out his time, William moved to Dover, New Hampshire. His oldest son settled in Durham—then part of Dover—and from him Ben Thompson descended. Ben was born April 22, 1806, in the Thompson farmhouse at the corner of Main Street and Madbury Road, where the Durham Post Office is now located. At that time Durham was a thriving community with twelve stores, two clothing mills, and four taverns. It was the starting point of the first New Hampshire turnpike, incorporated in 1796, leading generally along what is now U.S. Route 4 to Concord. During the early years of the nineteenth century, the development of competing towns drained off much of Durham's trade and industry, so that by 1840 it had become an agricultural rather than a commercial center.

Ben was educated in the common schools and at Durham Academy (long since passed out of existence). He worked on his father's farm and in his store, where he learned bookkeeping. At the age of nineteen he taught in the district school and also joined the militia. On December 8, 1828, his father conveyed to him the Warner farm and some other tracts of land in Durham. For seventy-one years, from April 4, 1828, to January 8, 1889, he kept detailed accounts of his extensive farming and other operations—including a sawmill, a cider mill, and a hay press. His crops, principally hay and apples, were sold in the Boston market. During his later years, he frequently gave these crops for some worthy cause, such as the Durham Library Association or the local church. Although not a church member, he purchased a pew when the present Community Church was built in 1848-49 and was a regular attendant thereafter. In 1850 he became engaged to a Portsmouth widow, but the marriage never took place. The story (undocumented, but true in spirit if not in fact) is that Ben gave her a thousand dollars with which to buy new furniture for his house. The first pieces to arrive were too fancy and fragile for Ben's taste, so he put them in the barn. Faced with the choice of living in the barn with her furniture or in the house with Ben, the widow called the whole thing off.

To the end he managed his investments, which made up the bulk of his estate at his death. What caused Ben Thompson to leave his fortune for the support of agricultural education? The idea was not uncommon: John Conant had offered his farm for a school of agriculture before 1850, and in 1863 General Culver offered his farm plus cash if the proposed New Hampshire College of Agriculture and the Mechanic Arts would be established on it. In 1885 Charles E. Tilton offered his farm and perhaps $40,000 in cash if the institution were moved to the town of Tilton. Interest in seeing their acres utilized for agricultural instruction was not confined to New Hampshire citizens. The institution that has become the University of Connecticut was founded on a farm given by Augustus Storrs, a site eight miles from the nearest town and two and a half miles from a railroad station, so remote that it was not joined to the outside world by an all-weather motor road until 1916.

Ben Thompson died January 30, 1890. In 1874 a codicil had been added to his original will, permitting his bequest to be used for an institution teaching the mechanic arts as well as agriculture, but providing that there should "be taught only such other arts or sciences" as were necessary to allow the state to take full advantage of the Morrill Act. Other codicils added later merely reduced the rate of interest to be paid on the trust funds from five percent to four, exempted his Durham real estate from inclusion in the trust funds, and named executors.

In its final form, the will provided that the state of New Hampshire was to hold the Thompson estate for twenty years and to guarantee on its appraised value a net annual compound interest of four percent. The fund thus established was to be known as the Benjamin Thompson Trust Fund. Ben shrewdly stipulated that the state was to establish another fund for furnishing the necessary buildings, stocking the farm, providing the necessary apparatus, and starting a library. This was to be known as the Benjamin Thompson State Trust Fund. It was to be secured by a state appropriation of $3,000 a year for twenty years, on which the state was to pay compound interest of four percent.

New Hampshire was given two years in which to accept the terms of the will. If New Hampshire failed to act, Massachusetts was to have second choice and Michigan the final option. The state accepting the bequest would be permitted to set up the college before the prescribed twenty-year period, if it wished. To do so, it would have to set aside money equivalent to the future value of the trust funds—in effect, prepaying the interest and the state appropriations.

Thompson's estate was appraised at $408,392, including "farming utensils and mechanic tools" valued at $132 and "miscellaneous articles" worth

Benjamin Thompson of Durham,
from a contemporary photograph.

$40. Nearly three-quarters of the estate was in the form of stock in railroad, bank, and industrial corporations. After deducting the value of the Durham real estate, the expenses of administration, legacies, funeral expenses, executors' commissions, and other expenses of settling the estate, the principal of the Benjamin Thompson Trust Fund was $363,823.

The provisions of the will and the value of the estate were known to the public when the trustees of New Hampshire College held their annual meeting in Hanover, April 22, 1890. Lyman D. Stevens, Warren Brown, and Charles W. Stone were appointed to represent the interest of the college in the will. Shortly after this President Nesmith died, and Lyman Stevens was elected to succeed him. At a meeting on the last day of 1890, President Stevens was authorized to act for the board of trustees on any matter coming before the 1891 legislature regarding the Thompson will.

Public reaction to the terms of the will found expression in the newspapers. To quote the Manchester *Mirror and Farmer:*

Our State has one agricultural college, which is all that kind of educational luxury she can afford. She needs another, such as Mr. Thompson provides for, about as much as she needs a million dollar pest house, and the offer of such a one, coupled with a condition that she shall forever support it, is about the last act of mistaken generosity she should be thankful for. If we were millionaires and wanted to bankrupt New Hampshire we would give it about four agricultural colleges, and three normal schools, and if we desired to put our money where it would do nobody any good, where it would remain a lasting monument to our misconception of the needs of the time, we would found an academy . . . . We have many more of this kind of educational institutions than we have or ever shall have students for, and it is mortal strange that natives of the State with sense enough to accumulate fortunes should continue to throw them away by making such wills as the one referred to.

The Dover *Enquirer,* on the other hand, supported acceptance of the bequest: "The Manchester *Mirror* proposed to have the State of New Hampshire reject a gift which at the end of twenty years will probably be worth a million and a half of dollars. We say give the farmers a chance to educate their boys; the more chances the better." The *Enquirer*'s was a lonely voice. Its competitor in Dover, *Foster's Daily Democrat,* referred to Thompson's will as "the last epistle of St. Benjamin to whom it may concern, showing his intent to establish a turnip yard over in Durham if the State will agree to fence it and keep it fenced." And the *Portsmouth Journal* expressed a sincere hope that the will would be broken: "we think it good *prima facie* evidence of an unsound mind, when a man will deliberately try to foist another incubus in the shape of a state agricultural college upon New Hampshire." Opposition to the will continued up to the meeting of the 1891 legislature. On January 3, 1891, the *Daily Press* of Manchester said:

We confess that the $400,000 of Benjamin Thompson of Durham does not dazzle our eyes nor does the object which he desired . . . seem to us worth the price . . . . The state has had some experience with agricultural colleges . . . . It does not produce agriculturalists, not at all, and if it does anything it turns away the thoughts of the few farmers' sons that enter its portals from the highly honorable profession it is supposed to foster and makes three of them into lawyers, doctors, ministers or business men where it returns one to be a farmer even though of the "gentleman" variety . . . .
The agricultural interest of the state is a declining one, incapable of competing in most respects with the broader fields and more wholesale methods possible in the west, and it is also a fact that mere book knowledge will never make a farmer . . . . The theory that farmers or the farming industry are to be bettered by sending farmers' sons to college is pretty well played out. All the agricultural colleges between here and the setting sun will not convert the rocky hills of New Hampshire into Gardens of Eden.

The attacks of the press did not sway the farming interests, however. Five days after the above article appeared, the state Board of Agriculture voted unanimously in favor of accepting the will.

This was also the sentiment of the majority of the members of the Grange.

The 1891 legislature appointed a committee on the matter. After a hearing at which many appeared in favor of acceptance and none opposed, a bill entitled "An Act to Accept the Provisions of the Thompson Will, and to Provide for the Present Disposition of the Funds" was passed and signed by Governor Hiram A. Tuttle on March 5, 1891. The two trust funds were set up as specified. The Benjamin Thompson Trust Fund was credited with a principal of $363,823 as of January 30, 1890; to the Benjamin Thompson State Trust Fund $3,000 was credited as of the same date, with a like sum to be added each year. On each fund interest at four percent was to be paid until the maturity date, January 30, 1910. The real estate in Durham was put in custody of the state Board of Agriculture. In case the state decided to establish the new campus at an earlier date, it could do so by appropriating the amount which the two funds would equal in 1910. So doing would relieve the state of making further contributions to the Benjamin Thompson State Trust Fund and also of guaranteeing the interest on the Benjamin Thompson Trust Fund.

The state of New Hampshire was ready to accept Ben Thompson's money, but some of his heirs were reluctant to see it go. A cousin, James F. Joy, approving the provisions of the will, had been named by Ben Thompson as one of the executors of the estate. Other western relatives, however, sought to have the will set aside. Their counsel held that the matter at issue was not the "capacity" of Benjamin Thompson to make the will but "the power of the State to accept and administer such a trust as that imposed by the will." It was on this ground that appeal was taken from the probate court, but as papers were not filed in the stipulated time, the appeal was dismissed. Under date of May 8, 1891, Joshua G. Hall of Dover, an attorney for the executors of the estate, notified Dean Pettee that the Thompson will was finally and definitely settled.

5. The New Beginning

With the knowledge that by 1910 New Hampshire College would move to Durham, unhappiness with the Hanover location reached a new intensity. Dean Pettee, Director Whitcher, and the ten-year-old Alumni Association lobbied in favor of making the move immediately.

A special committee of the state legislature was appointed to consider the matter. The result was "An Act providing for the removal of the New Hampshire College of Agriculture and the Mechanic Arts from Hanover to Durham, and for other purposes." Becoming law on April 10, 1891, it authorized the trustees of the college to give Dartmouth the stipulated one-year notice that the contract between the two institutions would be terminated. All lands and buildings owned by the college in Hanover were to be sold. Dartmouth was to get full title to Culver Hall upon paying to the state the $15,000 which the legislature had appropriated toward its building; this sum was to be applied toward the new campus in Durham. An appropriation of $100,000, raised by a bond issue, was made toward the expenses of removal and construction. The custody of the Thompson property in Durham was transferred from the Board of Agriculture to the college.

The act also enlarged the board of trustees to thirteen, including the governor, the president of the college, and one alumnus. The other ten trustees were to be appointed for three-year terms by the governor and council. Each councilor district was to be represented, not more than five of the appointive members were to be from the same party, and at least seven were to be practical farmers. The act was to become effective on the day the Thompson executors turned the bequest over to the state, which was done on September 22, 1891.

The election of the alumni trustee, conducted by mail by the trustees, ran into a complication. Of the ninety ballots returned, sixty-four were for George H. Whitcher '81, director of the Experiment Station. He was declared a duly elected trustee. Frederick Smyth thereupon moved: "WHEREAS, The Alumni of this College have elected one member of its Faculty a trustee under the provisions of the law of New Hampshire approved April 10th, 1891; and WHEREAS, It is the opinion of the Board of Trustees that the two offices are incompatible and should not be combined in the same person; therefore be it *Resolved,* That no Member of the Faculty of this College is eligible to the office of trustee; and that the acceptance of the office of trustee shall be construed and held to be a resignation as a member of the Faculty; and the Board shall proceed to fill the vacancy thus occasioned." After considerable discussion the resolution was unanimously adopted.

Upon being notified of the trustee action, Whitcher promptly tendered his resignation as a trustee. Another mail ballot was conducted which resulted in the election of Frederick P. Comings '83, who attended his first meeting on April 18, 1893.

At the 1891 annual meeting of the board of trustees, eleven days after passage of the act providing for the removal of the college to Durham, Lyman D. Stevens was elected president of the board of trustees.* Charles H. Pettee's salary was raised $400 "for extra work as Dean up to the time the college shall be located in Durham and a resident President elected." Pettee and the

* At this meeting, Rev. Samuel Bartlett submitted his resignation as president of New Hampshire College. The resignation was tabled. Thus the trustees preserved their contention that the Dartmouth president had never been in charge of New Hampshire College.

executive committee were instructed to get information on the land in Durham and to make suggestions regarding buildings; the board of control of the Experiment Station was to do the same for the station. It was also voted to raise the admission standards—an indication that academic as well as physical progress was anticipated at the new location.

Dean Pettee moved fast. At the first meeting of the trustees in Durham (in the old library building near the town hall) on June 11, 1891, he showed a plan of the Thompson land and preliminary plans for buildings. The planning was complicated by the location of the Boston and Maine tracks through the center of the projected campus, with both the passenger and freight stations in front of what is now DeMeritt Hall. Plans were made to get the tracks relocated, but it took twenty years to accomplish this. George Whitcher presented preliminary plans for the Experiment Station and a barn.

Pettee estimated building costs at $155,000 and assets at $170,000. He was authorized to purchase land in Durham, "at the lowest price," if considered necessary for the use of the college. Pettee's suggestion that a landscape gardener be retained to advise on the location of buildings was approved.

Meeting in Hanover twelve days later, the trustees set up a committee to negotiate with the Dartmouth trustees about the college property in Hanover. Charles Eliot, a landscape architect of Boston and son of the president of Harvard, was retained to plan location of the buildings at Durham. Invitations to architects to prepare building plans, "free of charge," was postponed until the campus layout was made.

The trustees met again in Durham on August 6. Eliot presented his proposed layout of the campus, which was accepted subject to necessary changes. Purchase of four lots was approved. Dean Pettee had reduced his estimate of the cost of buildings to $140,000, but he had made a more drastic revision of estimated assets. The assets now stood at $130,000. With these figures before them, the trustees voted $50,000 for the main building (Thompson Hall), $25,000 for the science building (Conant Hall), $17,000 for the shop building (Hewitt Hall), and $20,000 for the Experiment Station (Nesmith Hall), barns, and greenhouse. The total of $112,000 did not include heating equipment. Construction of the Experiment Station and farm buildings was assigned to the station's board of control, while the other projects would be managed by the executive committee of the trustees.

Because the architects might not be willing to submit plans free of charge, it was voted to pay one hundred dollars for plans and cost estimates for each of the proposed buildings. The fee would be a down payment to the architect if he was chosen to design the building. A civil engineer, Percy M. Blake, was engaged to give an opinion on the water available from sources recently surveyed by Dean Pettee. The August 6 meeting ended with a carriage trip to Wiswall Mills on the Lamprey River, a possible source of water-powered electricity. At the next trustee meeting, September 2, Blake submitted a plan for a reservoir near the present horticulture farm. The plan was approved and $5,000 voted for necessary land and a dam. Four plans were submitted for Thompson Hall and two for Conant, which were referred to Pettee and the executive committee for study.

Meanwhile the Experiment Station was moving ahead. William M. Butterfield of Manchester was retained to design Nesmith Hall, and George Whitcher himself designed the barn. Trustee Warren Brown saw the barn plans and predicted that the structure would be "the best in the state." By October, bills for the construction of these two buildings were coming in.

On October 9, 1891, the plan of Dow and Rundlett of Concord for Thompson Hall was approved, to cost not over $55,000 exclusive of heating and lighting. In November Professor Albert Kingsbury was added to the committee for Hewitt Hall; Edwin P. Bell of Palmer, Massachu-

Construction begins on Thompson Hall. The cornerstone was laid on the day the class of 1892 came from Hanover for their graduation exercises in the new barn.

setts, was engaged to prepare the plans. The committee for Conant Hall, with Professor Kingsbury a member, approved plans submitted by Dow and Rundlett. Professor S.H. Woodbridge of the Massachusetts Institute of Technology, assisted by Kingsbury, had charge of heating and lighting all buildings; $14,000 was appropriated for this work.

Contracts for Thompson and Conant halls were awarded on April 19, 1892. Lewis Killam of Haverhill, Massachusetts, did the actual building; he also built Hewitt Hall and the attached power plant under a separate contract. Granite used in the construction came from Conway. Brick for Thompson, Conant, and Hewitt halls came from Epping and Hooksett; that for Nesmith and the barn was made in Durham. Dow and Rundlett made a gift of the Thompson Hall clock, made by the Howard Clock Company. The bell was purchased from Meneeley and Company of Troy, New York.

Short of money to complete all of the construction, the trustees were obliged to ask for more

funds. The 1893 legislature appropriated $35,000, adding $15,000 more to pay Dartmouth's liability for Culver Hall. The trustees regarded this last amount as a gift to Dartmouth and not to New Hampshire College.

At the subsequent dedication, the building committee reported that the cost "in round numbers" of the building had been: Thompson Hall, $67,000; Conant, $26,000; Hewitt (including the power plant which supplied heat and electricity to all buildings), $25,000; Nesmith, $13,000; and the barn, $13,000. The barn was soon dubbed "Whitcher's Folly." The trustees described it as "100 feet by 50 feet, with a wing 70 by 40 feet, three stories high and eleven-foot basement; three floors above the basement, with level entrance to each; twenty and one-half foot posts, and [a] gambrel roof . . . ." It also sported three cupolas. They did not glorify the campus long, for the barn burned November 3, 1894. (New Hampshire was not the only state to pay tribute to the agricultural aspect of its state college by a grandiose barn. Kansas, for example, built a "broad cor-

*The foundation for Thompson Hall is at center,
the foundation for Conant Hall is at right.
Ben Thompson's monument can be seen at left.*

*Main Street and Garrison Avenue, about 1893.
Building at left is the Albert DeMeritt House,
later known as Ballard Hall. Across the street is
Dr. Grant's home, now Alumni House.*

30

Built in 1892, destroyed by fire in 1894, the dairy barn was the first College building in Durham. It stood near the present site of Pettee Hall.

Conant Hall (left) was built to house the science departments at a cost of $26,000. Hewitt Hall, the shop building, cost $25,000.

Wrapped in scaffolding and its clockface still blank, Thompson Hall nears completion in the winter of 1892-93.

niced, massive looking stone structure, with numerous wings, towers, stairways, elevators, and offices.")

By April 1893, construction of the buildings was far enough advanced so that the faculty was authorized to pack up for a move during the summer, so that classes could open in Durham in the fall. By this time Durham was not strange territory to most members of the faculty. Their duties in the supervision of construction had taken them there on numerous occasions.

Anxious to have some connection with the new campus, the class of 1892 had asked to have its commencement in Durham. This was allowed, but as the only building far enough advanced to be used for the ceremony was the barn, the class received their diplomas in that truly agricultural setting—doubtless to the satisfaction of the Grange.

Henry G. Jessup, professor of natural history, resigned at the end of the 1892-93 academic year because he did not, at his age, wish to move to a

THE NEW BEGINNING 33

new place of residence. No other member of the faculty resigned, even though the trustees at the April 1893 meeting voted that in view of the finances of the colleges it would be inadvisable to increase any salaries. Even the requested fringe benefit of stocking the new reservoir in Durham with trout was refused the faculty.

The property in Hanover was sold to Dartmouth for $28,000. Satisfied that they had authority to manage Thompson's farm as they saw fit, the trustees also considered the possibility of increasing their liquid assets by cutting some or all of the timber in the woodlot. Advice was sought from the New Hampshire Forestry Commission, which recommended that no timber be cut except blown-down or decayed trees. The recommendation was accepted, resulting in the preservation of the College Woods, to the benefit of the Forestry Department and the delight of countless romantic student couples.

To honor the man whose generosity had resulted in the move to Durham, a monument to him was erected "on an elevation of land" near the present Morrill Hall.*

The academic facilities in Durham were considerably more adequate than those in Hanover, but the town was ill equipped to provide housing for faculty and students. To encourage the faculty to build houses, nineteen lots were laid out on college property and offered for sale. The only lot sold went to Albert H. Wood, associate professor of agriculture, for $250. He built on the site, but left the college in 1894 under unhappy circumstances. For many years this house was oc-

cupied by a Durham physician, Dr. Albert E. Grant. After Dr. Grant's death the building was acquired by the university, and is now the Alumni House on Garrison Avenue.

The most active provider of housing was George Whitcher. He bought several lots and exchanged some with the college. He built houses on Garrison and Strafford avenues, and built a four-story wooden building on Main Street, known for many years as the Pettee Block. He also established a water company. (The Main Street building and the water company both were sold later to Dean Pettee.) Other faculty members built houses on Garrison Avenue, Strafford Avenue, and Madbury Road. A few were housed in available dwellings, such as the Woodman Garrison, which until 1898 stood on the present site of the Oyster River School. Ben Thompson's old house was repaired for use as the official residence of the college president.

Dean Pettee had earlier pointed out that there would not be money enough for both academic buildings and a dormitory. He was not concerned by this fact. Several leading colleges left the housing of students to private enterprise, thus freeing the institutions from the problems not only of construction but of management. Dean Pettee granted that it might prove desirable to have a cottage system of homes for the young ladies.

The private enterprise of the town of Durham was strained to the breaking point to provide housing for three seniors, five juniors, five sophomores, and fifty-one freshmen when classes started on the new campus in the fall of 1893. Two students shared "the bell-boy's room" in Thompson Hall tower, presumably earning their quarters by ringing the bell at appropriate times. Two others had a room in Nesmith Hall. Ten students were residents of Durham; four commuted from Dover. The others had rooms in Durham homes, which had been found for them by trustees Albert DeMeritt and Lucien Thompson, who were residents of Durham. Ten of the students—all freshmen—were women.

---

* In June 1929, the monument was moved to the new Durham cemetery west of town, to be replaced by a boulder and bronze plaque in front of Thompson Hall. At the same time, the Thompson family graves were exhumed. Then-treasurer Raymond C. Magrath recalled the episode in a 1968 letter: "We found Ben Thompson's skull, the name plate for the coffin, and some of the casket, including the metal handles, as well as some of the other bones. They were all carefully put in a metal box and buried in the Durham cemetery." The earlier gravesite had been near the Ffrost Homestead on the Newmarket Road.

6. President Murkland Arrives

In moving to Durham, the college had left behind the president it had shared with Dartmouth. On May 18, 1893, the trustees met in the Senate Chamber in the State House in Concord. Trustee President Stevens submitted several letters he had received regarding the choice of a president. Former Governor Smyth, who had been appointed to the reconstituted board by the governor and council, submitted the name of Rev. Charles Sumner Murkland of Manchester.

After a long discussion, the trustees agreed to stay in session until a president was elected. The secretary of the board presented about seventy-five letters concerning the choice from various Granges. The letters were tabled. Murkland then was elected unanimously; his salary was set at $4,000, and his duties were to start on September 1, 1893. In the first big test, the seven farmers on the thirteen-member board had demonstrated their independence of farm-organization pressure.

Murkland was born in Lowell, Massachusetts, on May 30, 1856. Both his parents were natives of Scotland. After graduating from high school in 1872, he worked for five years as an engraver in the print works of one of the Lowell mills. He entered Middlebury College in 1877, graduating as valedictorian of his class in 1881. From 1881 to 1884 he was pastor of the Congregational Church in Ferrisburg, Vermont, during which time he received the Bachelor of Divinity degree from Harvard in 1883 and a Master of Arts from Middlebury in 1884. During this period he also managed to do some studying at Andover Theological Seminary. In 1884 he became pastor of the Congregational Church in Chicopee, Massachusetts, and remained there until he went to the Franklin Street Church in Manchester in 1886. Middlebury conferred on him a Doctor of Divinity degree in 1900; Dartmouth, a Ph.D. in 1903.

Murkland accepted the appointment on June 12 and resigned as pastor of the Manchester church effective after the first Sunday in July. The trustees then voted to have his salary start July 3, 1893, which officially started his term as the first president of New Hampshire College in Durham.

With a president to inaugurate and a whole set of buildings to dedicate, August 30 was set aside for a ceremony to accomplish both ends. The morning was devoted to the dedication exercises and the afternoon to the inaugural, with Blaisdell's Orchestra furnishing music for both. A nod was given the former connection with Dartmouth by having that institution's new president, William J. Tucker, deliver the opening prayer.

Trustee Charles McDaniel of West Springfield formally delivered the buildings to the state; they were accepted by Governor John B. Smith. Addresses were given by Nahum J. Bachelder, master of the state Grange and secretary of the state Board of Agriculture, and by Joseph B. Walker, who had been a member of the 1866 legislative committee which had prepared the bill establishing the college and who had served on the board of trustees from 1866 to 1868.

In accepting the buildings, Governor Smith foresaw broadening of the college beyond agriculture. Nahum Bachelder took a different view. He argued that the purpose of an agricultural college was not to provide for the sons and daughters of farmers an education they could secure elsewhere, but to provide an agricultural education for *anyone's* sons and daughters. Should the college stray into broader fields, he warned, there would be vigorous protest from the farmers of New Hampshire. He held that the agricultural courses should be intensely practical with all other branches of study contributary thereto.

This remarkable debate continued in the afternoon. Lyman D. Stevens, former president of the board of trustees, emphasized that the college was concerned with more than agriculture by pronouncing its full title. He went on to say:

We are assembled to dedicate these college structures to the cause of "industrial learning," but it is rather for us, the people, to be dedicated to the high resolve that this college shall have a new life of usefulness under its new and improved conditions . . . . I indulge the confident belief that the highest standard in science, culture, morality, and religion will here be set up and persistently maintained; while, on the other hand, I look to see the people insisting upon the most thorough instruction and training, and broad and liberal culture.

In his inaugural address, President Murkland left no doubt about the shape he would seek for the college. He declared: "The desire of an education, and for the best education possible, is almost universal . . . . There will never be too many schools of any grade whose standards are worthy of the age in which they live." Nine to ten thousand young men and women in New Hampshire every year were going without "the advantages that a liberal education would give them." After a review of the ideals of the classical college, Murkland noted the changes that were taking place. "The specializing tendency has made itself felt in our colleges. Whether for good or for evil, and it surely is not altogether for good, the more devoted spirit of learning is forced to give way. And the student, as he receives his diploma, is likely to take it as an emblem of special preparation, rather than as a witness to the breadth and the thoroughness of his culture."

Since students were entering college at a later age, and better prepared, Murkland admitted that there was "less justification for the universal devotion of four more years to the exclusive ideal of culture, however desirable such a practice may be." But he was forthright in arguing that culture still had a place in the curriculum: "The ideal work of the technical college is to send forth, not merely farmers, mechanics, engineers, chemists, but educated men who shall lift each his separate calling to the dignity of a profession, and claim, without fear of denial, the full freedom of the highest intellectual fellowship."

The new president claimed that the farmers were not making use of the college, and he called upon them to have a closer connection with the work of the Experiment Station. He said the college had "one agricultural course, side by side with four other courses, each claiming equal importance with all the others" but that it was probable "that very few students would elect the agricultural course with the idea of returning to the farm . . . . When there shall have utterly ceased the cry of him who says that education has no place on the farm, then the farmer's boy will not feel driven, as he now does feel driven, to choose between farming and intelligence. Until then the mechanical and other scientific courses in the college will be elected by the great majority of the students."

To drive the point home, Murkland warned his audience: "If the occasion should rise, we are not debarred from introducing the ancient languages."

He then discussed various possibilities for reorganizing higher education to achieve both liberal and technical education with economy of time. A preparatory course, post-graduate courses, and a two-year course were cited as possibly desirable. He proposed to "carry some of the benefits of the College directly to the people [by lectures on campus] and some application of the idea of 'university extension.' " He foresaw the addition of more departments and held that "our professors must be well paid, and they must have leisure . . . . With this assured, they must bring to their work—which must not be too voluminous—competence, zeal, devotion, and contagious enthusiasm."

Nor did Murkland hedge on the question of *in loco parentis*: "This college stands for character as well as for scholarship and skill . . . . If we receive boys of the ordinary college age, and of not more than the common development of college freshmen, we must recognize the duty that is therefore incumbent upon us. We can give no guarantee in individual cases. Some students will come here and will return worse than they were before. That is the sad side of all college life. But we will not tolerate vice nor countenance blatant irreligion. This is no sectarian institution. Not one finger shall be lifted to favor one denomination or disparage another."

The reaction was not long in coming. At the next meeting of the trustees—October 11, 1893—they had before them a letter signed by Moses Humphrey and Nahum Bachelder, of the state Board of Agriculture. These gentlemen argued that New Hampshire College "should be chiefly agricultural in its character," for there was "no authority for using funds appropriated or bequeathed for agriculture in establishing a classical school [however] all should receive a good English education." The possibility that the ancient languages might be taught had become a major issue. Trustee Henry W. Keyes, who was not at the meeting, wrote a letter to put him on record as opposed to any courses in Latin or Greek. Those at the meeting, however, voted to send a letter to the state Board of Agriculture, challenging the implication that its position represented the feelings of the farmers of the state. The trustees held that other interests of the state could be served without neglecting those of the farmer. As evidence of Murkland's concern for agriculture, attention was directed to the new "institute course" which he had suggested, and which would make the privileges of the college available to the farmers without restriction. The trustees also stated that, since there was no demand for the introduction of the classics, there was no present plan to offer them. Saying that they would gladly accept any suggestions for making the work of the college more beneficial, the trustees invited representatives of the Board of Agriculture to meet with the curriculum committee of the trustees to propose improvements in the agricultural department. There is no record that the proposed conference ever took place.

The debate continued through 1894. The Hillsboro County Pomona Grange sent resolutions to the trustees criticizing the management of the college. The trustees on January 28, 1895, adopted resolutions in reply:

The Trustees of New Hampshire College . . . deplore the persistent misrepresentation, wilful or otherwise, which has resulted in the resolutions of the Hillsboro County Pomona Grange and in so many similar deliverances.

Emphatically deny . . . that the principles underlying this institution are not being carried out . . . or that the wishes of donors and testators are not being religiously fulfilled . . . .

Condemn as unjust and inimical to the interests of industrial education in the state, the faulty assumptions, the false statements, and the various unworthy methods by which said misunderstanding has been fostered.

Declare our confidence in the people . . . especially in the farmers who have been so persistently besought against their own highest interests by those who antagonize this institution . . . . The intelligence and the integrity of the people do and will demand that [the college] afford every facility for the liberal and practical education of the industrial classes in the several pursuits and professions.

The resolutions were adopted with the intent of sending them to the Hillsboro Pomona Grange and to the newspapers, but on second thought they were. referred to the legislative committee—Lucien Thompson, John G. Tallant, and Charles W. Stone—to use as they thought best. There was good reason for caution. The legislature was in session and the trustees were requesting appropriations for a women's dormitory, a greenhouse, books for the library, and the balance (beyond the insurance collected) of the cost of a barn to replace "Whitcher's Folly," burned the previous November.

Getting money was only part of the battle the trustees faced in the legislative halls. Ever since President Murkland's inaugural address, opposition to his views had been growing. His joining the Scammel Grange in Durham did not make them more acceptable. At the 1894 annual meeting of the state Grange, Master Nahum J. Bachelder made a ringing address, asserting the rights of the farmers in the management of the school. In the discussion which followed, the classics found few supporters. A resolution to sustain Bachelder's contention that New Hampshire College should be nothing other than a school of agriculture was passed overwhelmingly. Not content with resolutions, the college opponents organized to push legislation through the 1895 session.

In January, Representative Edward D. Leach of Franklin introduced a bill which proposed reducing the board of trustees to nine and restricting them closely. The "Leach Bill" prescribed:

That this institution combines physical with intellectual education, in which the graduate of the common school can commence, pursue, and finish a course of study terminating in thorough, theoretic, and practical instruction in those sciences and arts which bear directly upon agriculture and kindred industrial pursuits.

Students shall be admitted to the institution who can pass a satisfactory examination in arithmetic, geography, history, grammar, reading, spelling, and penmanship. In case there be a higher standard for admission, there shall be organized a preparatory course of one year.

The course of instruction shall embrace the English language and literature, mathematics, surveying, agricultural chemistry, dairying, forestry, animal and vegetable anatomy and physiology, the veterinary art, entomology, horticulture, botany, geology, and such other natural sciences as may be prescribed, mechanical and electrical engineering, political, rural, and household economy, domestic arts, moral philosophy, history, bookkeeping, and especially the application of science and the mechanic arts to practical agriculture, including military tactics.

Also there shall be a two-year course of lectures which shall embrace a systematic presentation of the current literature and science of agriculture in their application to practical farming.

A full course of study in the institution shall embrace not less than four years.

There shall be a practical agricultural course of two years, which every agricultural student attending this institution shall be obliged to pursue, supplemented by

a winter course of agricultural lectures covering a period of one month designed especially for farmers.

Not less than two hours of each college day shall be devoted by every student of agriculture to practical labor on or about the farm, during favorable months, while in the winter season such labor as the trustees may arrange for under the guidance of competent instructors, and no such student shall be exempt except from physical disability, while practical work in the mechanical and domestic departments shall be faithfully followed. Only such labor as is of value to the departments shall be paid for, other labor that is purely educational in its character shall be considered instruction.

The required manual labor (which in the beginning had been emphasized by most of the agricultural colleges) got a lot of farm work done but proved to be of so little educational value that it had died out by the time Representative Leach proposed to institute it in New Hampshire. In opposition to the national trend, the New Hampshire Grange legislative committee sent copies of the Leach Bill to all Granges, urging them to petition for its passage. Many such petitions were sent. President Murkland countered by preparing a circular showing in parallel columns what the Leach Bill proposed and what the college *was* doing, the intent being to show that the chief results of the bill would be to reduce the number of trustees and lower entrance requirements.

The *Mirror and Farmer* reported:

The unfortunate controversy that has grown up among the farmers of the state over the policy adopted by the president and faculty of the agricultural college at Durham has made its way into the legislature in the shape of two bills, one reconstructing the board of trustees of the college so as to place it under the management of the opposition to the present policy and the other abolishing the board of agriculture, which, with the Grange, is supposed to be behind the first bill. In other words what may be termed the college party proposed to abolish the board of agriculture because the men who are prominent in the board propose to turn out the collegians.

Before the hearing on the Leach Bill took place, the legislature's Committee on the Agricultural College was invited to Durham to inspect the college. In commenting on the visit, *Foster's Daily Democrat* said:

If Benjamin Thompson . . . could come back to earth his eyes would bulge with pleasure could he behold what was shown a legislative committee . . . . The college's development within a twelve-month has been wonderful and it now ranks with similar institutions of very much older growth. True, its curriculum does not quite meet the approval of that large class of intelligent New Hampshire citizens represented by the Patrons of Husbandry [i.e., the Grange] and kindred agricultural societies. Nevertheless it has made marked progress in the lines of a liberal education and it must hereafter be recognized as an institution to which our state must point with pride and in which the hopes and aims of many of New Hampshire's sons and daughters will be realized.

Other legislators were also in the group. They were shown the buildings, visited classes, listened to speeches on the needs of the institution, inspected the livestock, took sleigh rides out to the College Woods, saw Lieutenant Henry C. Hodges, Jr., put his students through gymnastic exercises, and consumed a "bountiful repast" in DeMeritt (later known as Ballard) Hall. The visitors returned to their homes on the evening trains.

At the hearing on the evening of March 5, 1895, Jeremiah W. Sanborn (once manager of the college farm in Hanover) led off favoring the Leach Bill. He held that the college had no horticulture department, that the agricultural students did not work enough on the land, and that the entrance requirements were too high. For agricultural purposes, Sanborn said, the college was "the poorest equipped of any college of the kind in this country." Albert DeMeritt defended the trustees and declared that, if the legislature would appropriate money for a greenhouse, the college could have a horticulture department. Following DeMeritt, President Murkland charged: "The

whole power of the government of the college is to be taken from the hands of the executive and placed in the hands of a secret society [the Grange] antagonistic to the college and hostile to its purposes. They say we have no horticulture. It is false to say that we have no horticulture department." Murkland admitted that the college did not have "the accessories for a horticulture department" because the legislature had turned down the request for a greenhouse. He declared that the demand for more student labor from the agricultural students would drive them from the college.

Charles H. Burns, a lawyer from Wilton, made an appeal for the bill: "The man who despises and belittles intelligent, honest toil and looks with contempt upon the toiler, is generally himself an ignoramus, too dainty to be decent, and too small to be of any account . . . . The one thing the farmers of New Hampshire do not want is that their college should produce theoretical farmers, who abhor and are ignorant of intelligent, honest labor." Burns claimed that 125 of the 194 Granges favored the Leach Bill.

After the hearing, the Committee on the Agricultural College substituted an act requiring establishment of a department of horticulture and a two-year course in practical and theoretical agriculture. It also specified ten hours a week of practical farm or shop work for those in the two-year course, and for two of the four years of those in any other agricultural course. To cover costs of the specified enlargement of the college program, $2,500 per year for two years was appropriated.

The trustees and President Murkland had won a vital victory. Had the Leach Bill been passed and faithfully enforced, the institution in Durham would have been stifled. Instead, the legislature had determined that the college was to serve all the youth of the state, not merely those pursuing careers in practical agriculture.

7. New Hampshire College Takes Form

The farming interests had criticized New Hampshire College for its high standards for admission. In fact, these standards were rather low. A prospective student was not required to be a graduate of the secondary schools. Attendance at such an institution was *recommended*, but in view of the well-authenticated stories of Dean Pettee's labors in recruiting students, there can be no question that warmth of blood was more important than quickness of mind for passing the entrance examinations.

Beginning in 1897, a year-long preparatory course was offered for the benefit of those who were having trouble with the entrance exams. (Such a course had been one of the provisions of the Leach Bill.) The program of study included algebra, plane geometry, rhetoric, Greek and Roman history, French language, physics, and botany. Once a student had satisfied the conditions under which he had been admitted, he could proceed to take his place in the freshman class.

Except for the General Course, which was intended primarily for women, the four-year programs were clearly technical. They included three options in Agriculture (technical, chemical, and biological) and three in the Mechanic Arts (mechanical engineering, electrical engineering, and technical chemistry). The emphasis given technical subjects can be judged by the makeup of the faculty during the first year in Durham. Listed in order of seniority except for the president, they were:

Charles S. Murkland, A.M., Ph.D., president and professor of philosophy.

Charles H. Pettee, A.M., C.E., dean and professor of mathematics and civil engineering.

Clarence W. Scott, A.M., professor of English language and literature.

George H. Whitcher, B.S., professor of agriculture.

Albert H. Wood, B.S., associate professor of agriculture.

Fred W. Morse, B.S., professor of organic chemistry.

Charles L. Parsons, B.S., professor of general and analytical chemistry.

Clarence M. Weed, D.Sci., professor of zoology and entomology.

Albert Kingsbury, M.E., professor of mechanical engineering.

Herbert H. Lamson, M.D., instructor in plant diseases.

George L. Teeple, M.E., instructor in electrical engineering and physics.

Edwin B. Davis, B.L., instructor in modern languages.

James Hall, instructor in mechanical drawing.

The shop courses were taught by John N. Brown, foreman of machine work, and Allen G. Lowell, foreman of woodwork. Since even the Grangers granted that the agricultural students should receive instruction in the English language, the only faculty members who could be accused of tainting the students with humanistic education were Murkland in philosophy and Davis in languages.

Almost half of the faculty had assignments in the Experiment Station: Whitcher as director, Pettee as meteorologist, Wood as superintendent of the dairy department, Morse as chemist, Lamson as microscopist and photographer, and Weed as entomologist. The staff of the Experiment Station was rounded out by David E. Stone, station farmer; Edward P. Stone, assistant chemist; and Fred D. Fuller, assistant in chemistry.

Courses were offered in agriculture, chemistry, drawing, engineering, English, French, geology,

*Charles H. Pettee rebuilding Main Street
in front of the Experiment Station (Nesmith Hall)
in 1895. Cost per running foot was 63½ cents.*

German, history, mathematics, philosophy, physics, political science, shop work, and zoology. Students registered for sixteen hours of class work per week—and were required to attend chapel seven days a week. Also required was attendance at the half-hour "rhetoricals" which followed chapel on Wednesday.

Provision for instruction in military science was made when Lieutenant Henry C. Hodges, Jr., 22nd U.S. Infantry, reported for duty on September 1, 1894. Beginning in 1895 the catalog listed military science as a three-year requirement for all boys not excused for disability, and elective for seniors. There was one theory class a week, with drill on Monday, Tuesday, Thursday, and Friday from 12:00 to 12:30. The first uniforms were made by B.T. Haley and Company of Newmarket of cloth made in the Sawyer Mills of Dover. They were grey, with black stripes on the trousers and black braid on the blouse cuffs and collar. The letters *N.H.C.* were embroidered

in gold on each side of the collar. A regulation blue army cap was worn. The uniforms cost about sixteen dollars, but "the wearing of such did away with necessity of purchasing a civilian suit for college use." (One of these uniforms, the gift of Edwin J. Roberts '06, is on display in the university museum.)

At President Murkland's suggestion, the trustees had approved a four-week institute course in agriculture to begin February 5, 1894. This course was to "prepare men for an intelligent home study of practical agricultural problems" and was intended for those unable to pursue the regular program. Cost of attendance—including railroad fares, room, and board—was estimated at twenty dollars. The catalog also announced: "The college offers opportunities for post-graduate study in agricultural, scientific, and engineering lines. After satisfactory completion of an appropriate amount of work, advanced degrees will be given." Charles H. Clark, headmaster of Sanborn

Seminary in Kingston, New Hampshire, earned a Ph.D. in 1896. Ned Dearborn, whose thesis was "The Birds of Durham and Vicinity," was granted the D.Sci. in 1901. (No other earned doctorates were awarded until 1957.) The first M.S. degree was conferred on Ralph W. Crossman in 1897.°

To serve the elementary and secondary school teachers, a summer school in botany and zoology was offered in 1894. Fifteen students, including one from Massachusetts and two from Maine, attended.

Although the college had been largely victorious in its battle with the Grange, the catalog of 1895-96 did reflect the pressures of the agriculturalists. Listed, in addition to the four-year course in agriculture, were a two-year course, a ten-week winter course, a four-week dairy school, and a non-residence course. The department of agriculture became "agriculture and horticulture," and for two years there was a requirement that juniors and seniors in the agricultural course work ten hours a week on the college farm. But at the same time the courses in English, history, and drawing were extended.

The move of the college to Durham had a dramatic effect on enrollment. During the final dozen years in Hanover the number of students had varied from thirty to fifty; in the final year (probably due to the preoccupation of the faculty with plans for the move) it dropped to a low of twenty-seven. The first year in Durham there were fifty-one freshmen—triple the typical figure in Hanover. After the first two years the number of freshmen fell off, to a low of nineteen in

1897-98; then it began a steady and unbroken climb. The total enrollment went over one hundred for the first time in the first year of the new century.

The new two-year course did not prove popular. When introduced in 1895-96, it attracted six students, four of them residents of Durham using it as a means of preparing for the four-year course. Only four students registered for the ten-week institute course at the dairy school. There were two graduate students and a like number of special students, requiring the faculty to offer a disproportionate amount of instruction outside the regular undergraduate programs. The load on the faculty was heavy enough in the regular program: the elective system meant that many courses enrolled only one or two students.

The increased attention to agricultural education did not result in a surge of students for that program. In 1898-99 only three upperclassmen—two seniors, one junior, and not a single sophomore—were enrolled in the agricultural program. The technical program in chemistry attracted a like number. The engineering courses were much more popular, attracting thirty-three students out of the forty-four enrolled in the upper three classes. The General Course drew nine upperclassmen and all seven of the sophomore, junior, and senior women.

Four coeds—Carrie A. Bartlett of Lee, Mary B. Bartlett of Epping, and Carrie .L. and Mary E. Comings of Durham—received degrees from New Hampshire College in 1897. They were the first women to have received degrees from the college, and members of the first class to have completed all four years in Durham.

The agricultural troubles of the college were not confined to low enrollment and concern over the possible teaching of the classics. When the college moved to Durham, George Whitcher had retained his post as director of the Experiment Station. Within a year, dissatisfaction with his management of the college farm and with the work of the Experiment Station had caused a trus-

---

° The question of advanced degrees had first surfaced in 1895, when Charles A. Hubbard requested that he be granted the degree of Mechanical Engineer upon presentation of a suitable thesis. Judge Isaac W. Smith investigated the matter for the trustees. The judge reported: "You probably have the same power to confer the degree of M.E. as of B.S. and that may be none at all. If you have the right to confer B.S., why not M.E., and other kindred degrees?" He suggested that to settle the matter the trustees should seek legislation giving them degree-granting authority.

tee to declare that "some radical changes must be effected." A council of seven faculty members, including Murkland, was given charge of all experiments and ordered to report monthly to the faculty and quarterly to the trustees. This did little to help matters, apparently. At the trustee meeting of October 10, 1894, it was voted: "That the services of George H. Whitcher as Director of the Experiment Station and Professor of Agriculture and the services of Albert H. Wood as Assistant Professor of Agriculture be dispensed with on and after November 1st, 1894." Murkland was made director of the station until a permanent director could be found.

Henry E. Alvord was hired to replace Whitcher as professor of agriculture. He started in December 1894 but resigned the following June. Meanwhile he prepared a report labeling the condition of the agriculture department as "deplorable." He claimed that it was destitute of equipment and that there was disease among the cattle; there was so little space, he complained, that many things given the college by the Chicago World Fair had not been unpacked.

On December 2, 1895, a new barn was ready for the college herd. The animals had been sheltered in an old structure, west of the railroad tracks, during the two years since "Whitcher's Folly" had burned. Some of the herd had tuberculosis and had to be killed when the move was made.

Murkland found the burden of managing the Experiment Station too much, and William D. Gibbs was appointed director of the station and professor of agriculture on January 1, 1902. Before Gibbs arrived, another outbreak of tuberculosis was found in the herd, and twenty-two cattle were killed.

The first year of operation in Durham had disclosed other serious lacks in facilities. One of the most serious was the library. The meager college collection—even when supplemented by the town library—did little to offset the loss of access to the library of Dartmouth College. In their annual report of 1894 the trustees said: "The whole income of the college could easily be expended in the purchase of books, and of books almost absolutely necessary. If it is not possible for the state to appropriate such sums as might properly equip this most essential part of the college, may we not hope by some private benefactors our students may be supplied with the best reading?" The college's museum collections did profit from private gifts. The first was of minerals, which had been obtained when the Chicago World Fair of 1893 offered to donate its exhibits in this field to colleges. Murkland had gone to Chicago to get what he could. The second gift, ten years later, was from Mrs. Harriet W. Potter of Portsmouth—a collection of anatomical specimens prepared by her late husband. There was no suitable display place for these exhibits, however.

Another serious lack was in shop facilities. On the basis of a list of needs prepared by Professor Albert Kingsbury, it was estimated that $40,000 was needed for this department. Then there was the matter of housing the women students. "There should be a building, especially designed for the purpose," the trustees said, "accommodating not less than forty girls, provided with convenience for study and demonstration in the various branches of domestic economy, and placed under the care of a competent matron . . . . This Board does desire to give the girls of the state an opportunity for culture and development as great as that afforded their brothers, and at the same time send them forth, womanly not mannish, fit for the positions they may occupy and the activities to which they may be called."

A third request was for a gymnasium, needed for military drill in the winter and for physical education classes. "It is a place where all the students may receive that development of the body without which the best development of the mind is impossible," the trustees argued in their 1894 report.

Of the several requests for buildings, the only

one approved by the legislature was for the women's residence, for which $25,000 was voted. Governor Charles A. Busiel did not share the legislators' concern for the women students, vetoing the bill on March 29, 1895. The trustees decided to repair a dwelling on Main Street—formerly run by Mrs. Warren Foye as a boarding house—as a residence for President Murkland. When Murkland moved out of the Ben Thompson house, it was converted to a women's residence. A few girls moved in for the spring term of 1896; Mrs. George T. Wiggin was matron. Murkland gave high priority to providing a residence for girls: "This is to be the most important matter connected with the girls in the college. A competent matron could do fully as much for them as the whole corps of instructors can do." Unfortunately the girls were soon again without a campus home. The structure burned on December 12, 1897, when it was set afire from a blaze in a nearby building. The $2,000 insurance far from covered the loss.

Private enterprise had helped provide housing for the growing number of male students. In 1894 Albert DeMeritt built what later became known as Ballard Hall, in which fourteen students were housed. Board and room in a heated and furnished suite was $4.50 a week. In another sizeable structure, Q.T.V. Hall, room rent was seventy dollars for the academic year. Other students were helped to find rooms either by President Murkland or Professor Wood, who was secretary of the faculty.

After being rebuffed for their building requests in 1895, the trustees did not again go to the legislature for building funds until 1899. They then asked for a building to house the agricultural and horticultural departments, a modest dining hall to cost $5,000, a new boiler for the power plant, and a new reservoir. They got none of these. The trustees went back to the legislature in 1901, asking $60,000 for an agricultural building, $20,000 for a new creamery, $17,500 for a School of Mines and Mining, and $15,000 toward a wom-

The windmills tower over the DeMeritt House (Ballard Hall) on Garrison Avenue.

en's dormitory "provided with the necessary facilities for a complete course in domestic economy." Apparently the earlier breach with the Grange had been bridged, for in support of the dormitory request it was said: "The local and Pomona Granges throughout the state [have] taken this matter up, and have pledged various sums for the purpose." The trustees said that the top floor of the proposed agricultural building could be used as a drill hall, thus postponing the need for a gymnasium. Of the various requests the only sum voted was $30,000 for the agricultural building. Although this was only half the estimated cost, plans were drawn by J.E. Rundlett of Concord, and construction began in the spring of 1902 on what was to be called Morrill Hall. In November the building was rapidly approaching completion. The contract price, however, did not provide for pipe lines, grading, or a new boiler needed to supply heat. Murkland estimated that

New Hampshire College—all of it—in 1898.

an additional $15,000 would be needed. This time the legislature voted $13,000 to complete the building, plus $5,000 for a new boiler and heat, light, and water connections to the building. For good measure, $7,000 was appropriated for a greenhouse.

With these additions to the physical plant, the value of all buildings was placed at $200,000, apparatus at $20,000, machinery at $6,000, the library at $10,600, livestock at $3,000, and other equipment at $15,000. The campus included 343 acres, of which forty-four were under cultivation and ten were used for experimental purposes. The library had 10,087 bound volumes and 5,200 pamphlets, "exclusive of 800 duplicates."

In their report to the 1897 legislature, the trustees pointed out that the college survived only because of federal money. During the college year 1895-96, the money available to support instruction from federal sources was $21,000 (plus

another $15,000 used exclusively for the Experiment Station). From the state came $4,800 as interest on the federal land grant and $5,500 in direct appropriations. Said the trustees: "The college has practically no resources except those furnished by Congress or the Legislature. We have no investment fund except that of the Conant estate, and the income from this fund is set apart for scholarships to students in one department of the college—the agricultural. We have no income from tuition fees, except such as we receive in a roundabout way through scholarships paid out of the Conant fund." The trustees held that the state was not fulfilling the obligation assumed when the federal money was accepted for running a state college. The way in which the Benjamin Thompson fund was being administered by the state treasurer also was criticized: "It is to be remembered that this estate is constantly producing revenue for the state. If this revenue were computed annually, as in equity it ought to be, it would be seen that the state of New Hampshire, instead of sacrificing aught to the welfare of the institution which is its peculiar charge, is actually receiving, in dollars and cents, more than it is paying out in its provision for the college." The financial situation was related to the academic:

Four years ago there were twelve students . . . . The present enrollment shows a total of ninety-seven resident students. Besides there are the non-resident and short course students to the number of forty-seven. That after so few years of separate existence we have nearly one third of all the New Hampshire students attending college in New Hampshire is not only an indication of its immediate success; it is also an indication of its promise for the future . . . . Whatever outside courses we may provide, our regular courses must be of the grade indicated. Of this there can be no doubt. We have, therefore sought, and shall continually seek, to make the degree of this college, the college of the state of New Hampshire, equal in educational value to the similar degree conferred by any other college in the land.

In spite of this argument, and despite the trustees' foresight in making Governor George A. Ramsdell a member of their finance committee, the state did nothing for the college's operating expenses except to continue the $3,000 scholarship appropriation, and to continue for another two years the $2,500 for the two-year program and the horticultural department.

In January and March, 1899, the college had to borrow money to meet its obligations. This proof of poverty impressed the legislature. Its appropriations were increased in the amount of $5,000, and the 1901 legislature continued for another two years this annual total of $10,500.

With increased enrollment, student activities which had been minimal in Hanover gained new life. In November of the first year in Durham there was a freshman-sophomore cane rush, with victory going to the class with the most hands on the cane at the end of the melee. As freshmen outnumbered the sophomores forty-one to five, it is not surprising that they won. In a move to less-

en the casualties, an inter-class rope pull followed by a track meet was substituted in 1902. This was to be followed by a football game at the end of the season and a debate during the winter term. These more civilized activities did not meet universal approval, and an unauthorized cane rush took place in the fall of 1903. An equally popular event was the picture contest. The freshmen endeavored to have their class officers and as many others of the class as possible gather outside Durham for a class picture; the object of the sophomores was to retain enough freshmen in town to spoil the event.

The Athletic Association was formed in 1893, with departments for baseball, football, and "general" (which included tennis, the most popular sport). Baseball had been played in Hanover. Football was a new enterprise; games were played, and lost, against nearby high schools. Coaching was by former players at other colleges who were hired on a part-time basis for the season. The first NH varsity letters apparently were awarded to the 1897 footballers.

Athletic Association dues were the principal source of support for sports, but in October 1896 the trustees appropriated $200 for the purpose. This was followed by another $200 for athletic equipment in January 1897, providing the money could be found "without creating a deficit." Plans were made for a track team in the spring of 1901.

At an early meeting of the trustees in Durham, three students were given permission to appear before the board to request "a campus for athletic sports." They requested that the field across the street from Nesmith Hall be set aside for the purpose. The real estate committee was delegated to handle the matter, and the trustees authorized work to start in May 1894 on what later became Memorial Field. Over two years, $648 was spent on the project.

The matter of a gymnasium was not so easily solved. At first the second floor of Thompson Hall, which had been designed for a museum, served the purpose. In 1899 this space was cut up into offices and a classroom. Left without indoor athletic facilities, the students started a movement to raise money for a gymnasium. By June 1903 students and faculty had pledged $1,400. In the meantime, the unfinished top floor of Morrill Hall was made available for sports, and showers were installed in the basement. In spite of the uncertain facilities, a basketball team had been organized, the first game being played in Portsmouth on February 16, 1901.

Of the few student clubs active in Hanover, the two most vigorous, the Culver Literary Society and the Q.T.V. Club, transferred their activities to Durham. The Culver Literary Society donated its library of 366 volumes to the college library. One hundred and forty are still on the shelves. In June 1893 it started publication of a monthly journal at first called the *Enaichsee* (NHC). Beginning with the second volume, the title was changed to the *New Hampshire College Monthly,* under which title it continued until replaced by the *New Hampshire* in 1911. The journal contained essays, news of faculty, students, and alumni, and a list of campus organizations with time and place of meetings. The June issue was usually devoted to graduation activities.

The Culver society announced in November 1893 the establishment of a lecture series. In 1895 the society merged with a new student-faculty organization, the New Hampshire College Club, with Murkland as president. Dues were fifty cents a year. This organization did everything from supplying pictures and statuary for the college buildings and flowers for the chapel to securing lecturers and entertainments and sponsoring social events. One of its less noteworthy projects was procuring a stuffed elk for the lobby of Thompson Hall. The animal became a convenient coat rack.

Morrill Hall and the College greenhouses, 1900.

8. The Gibbs Administration

On November 4, 1902, Nahum J. Bachelder was elected Governor of New Hampshire. For ten years he had been a vocal critic of Murkland's policy of making the institution a true college rather than merely a school of agriculture; he also had been a leading candidate for the presidency when Murkland was chosen. Murkland's reaction to the election was not surprising. At a special meeting of the trustees held at the Eagle Hotel in Concord, February 27, 1903, Murkland announced his resignation. He said that he had considered the action for some time, but the trustees had persuaded him to stay on the grounds that the college was not fully established. In his statement of resignation Murkland said: "Some things are settled. It must be a college, nothing less. The standard may be raised; it is not likely to be permanently lowered. The work of ten years is not to be undone."

The resignation was accepted by the trustees—who then moved on to the next item on the agenda, the purchase of a span of horses for the college farm.

Governor Bachelder was a trustee *ex officio*, and was named to the committee to select a new president. The appointment was offered to him, but he tactfully rejected the offer. The trustees turned next to William D. Gibbs, who had been director of the Experiment Station and professor of agriculture in 1902, but who had left for a similar position at Texas Agricultural and Mechanical College. Gibbs was agreeable to returning and was officially elected on August 1, 1903, to assume office on September 1.

Gibbs's background contrasted with that of Murkland. Instead of a classicist, he was an agriculturist. Born in Illinois in 1869, he graduated from the Winchester high school and entered the Agricultural College of the University of Illinois.

During his sophomore and junior years he was foreman of the university farm. Granted the Bachelor of Science degree in 1893, he remained for graduate study, at the same time teaching bacteriology and stock feeding. He received his Master of Science degree and went to the University of Wisconsin for further study. He left there in March 1895 to go to Ohio State University to become farm foreman and assistant in agriculture. Fourteen months later he went to work for the U.S. Department of Agriculture, but he soon returned to Ohio State as an assistant professor of agriculture and was promoted to professor in June 1900. It was from that post that New Hampshire College had first hired him. Although his training had been exclusively in agriculture, it had been secured at land grant institutions where the college of agriculture was part of a comprehensive state university.

Gibbs's inauguration, October 28, 1903, was combined with the dedication of Morrill Hall, the new agriculture building. Governor Bachelder was a speaker, but he took a broader view than he had at Murkland's inauguration. He said that the state should consider New Hampshire College to be "an important agency in state development and a means for securing desirable results, rather than an incubus to be supported." Keeping the emphasis on the practical, he said the state had the right to ask the college president, "What are you giving us for $60,000 annually placed in your hands for supporting it?"*

Gibbs chose as his inaugural topic, "The Mission of the Land Grant Colleges." He said that, as a result of federal support, these colleges had been able "to sound the death knell to exclusive-

---

* Of the amount cited by Governor Batchelder, fully $47,000 was provided by the federal government.

ness and aristocracy in higher education." It was Gibbs's estimate that "at least 3,000 young people enter upon active independent life in our state each year . . . . Would not these thousands of serious-minded young men and women, annually starting out to make an independent living, be more successful as bread winners, would they not get more true enjoyment out of life, exert a wider influence on the community, and take a more intelligent interest in the affairs of the state if more of them had thorough training in the business upon which they enter?" In addition to giving adequate training to these youths, he held that the college should extend its privileges to citizens who were unable to attend its course of study.

The new president advocated a curriculum providing one-third culture studies, one-third pure science, and one-third vocational studies. This would give "depth without narrowness and breadth without superficiality." He advocated continuation of the two-year and the ten-week courses. He also spoke in favor of "a department

of domestic science in which young women may receive instruction in the science, art, and economics of home keeping." Gibbs estimated that about a fourth of the young men and women in the state reaching college age each year were capable of college work, leading to a potential enrollment of two thousand. In conclusion he said: "There should be nothing to hinder [the college's] rapid, healthy growth into that position of influence and power in the state which it deserves and which is demanded by the tremendous interests it represents."

The day before Gibbs's inauguration, the trustees had approved his recommendation that fourteen departments be established: agriculture; dairy manufactures; drawing; English and philosophy; general and analytical chemistry; history and political economy; horticulture and forestry; mathematics; mechanical engineering; military science; modern languages; organic chemistry; physics and electrical engineering; and geology, entomology, and botany.

With the completion of Morrill Hall and a new range of greenhouses, the agricultural course was reorganized. The college herd was improved by selling inferior animals and purchasing better representatives of the Jersey, Guernsey, Ayrshire, and short horn breeds. Substantial progress was achieved in other areas. Ernest R. Groves, a graduate of Dartmouth and the Yale Divinity School, became instructor in English and philosophy and head of the department in 1903. He introduced two courses in education which, together with the course in psychology initiated under Murkland, made teacher preparation a function of the college. Groves soon became well known as a sociologist. In recognition of this, a department of psychology and sociology with Groves as head was organized in April 1911. In the same month, Groves conducted his first annual instruction trip to settlement houses in Boston.

In February 1909, the faculty had voted in favor of establishing a Latin course. Latin courses

Opposite page: Bringing in the hay behind the dairy barn, looking east to Thompson and Conant.
Lower left: Soil physics laboratory, January 1904.
Lower right: Horse judging class in the basement of Morrill Hall, February 1904.

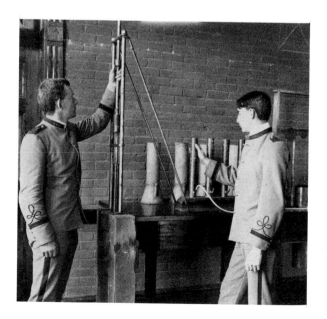

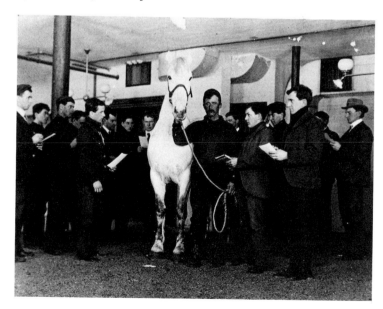

were carried in the 1909-10 catalog—the fourth foreign language to be taught. Whereas the mere assertion by Murkland that Latin was a legitimate subject had raised a public storm, it was added under the agriculturist Gibbs without protest. Not only that, but the treasurer's books show it was paid for by both land grant and Thompson Fund money. In April 1909 the name of the general course was changed to "Course in Arts and Sciences," marking another step toward the establishment of the College of Liberal Arts.

Curriculum changes were not confined to the Arts and Sciences. In 1906 the engineering department introduced an automobile course. In 1907 the two-year course in agriculture was shortened to two fifteen-week terms each year, open to anyone eighteen years of age; ten hours of practical work for the college was a requirement. The following year the ten-week course in agriculture, which had averaged one student a year, was withdrawn, but the ten-week dairy course was continued. A petition signed by 140 students resulted in the trustees voting in 1910 to establish a department of forestry. In September 1911, John K. Foster became professor of forestry. Later the college forest was put in his charge and a department of forestry added to the Experiment Station.

A major reorganization of the entire institution took place in 1911. Three divisions were established. In the Agricultural Division were four courses: animal husbandry, forestry, horticulture, and general. The Engineering Division offered chemical, electrical, and mechanical engineering. The Arts and Sciences Division had a general course and a short-lived "normal manual training" course, designed to train women to teach manual training in high schools.*

---

* Even with this special training, the coeds' financial prospects were not bright. It had been estimated that the average annual income of New Hampshire College graduates was $2,100 for those going into business, $1,600 for engineers, and $1,350 for agriculturalists. Women teachers then averaged $550 a year.

President Gibbs's introduction to Durham had been most unfortunate. All his furniture, books, and manuscripts had been moved into the president's residence when the house and contents were completely destroyed by fire, September 20, 1903. Since the president's salary included rent, the trustees secured a "tenement" for him and his family at a cost of sixteen dollars a month. Replacement of the official residence was estimated to cost $8,500 if wooden, $9,500 if brick. The money was simply not available. President Gibbs, Governor Bachelder, Treasurer Walter M. Parker, and Trustee Rosecrans W. Pillsbury therefore offered to build the house with their own funds. They proposed that the college lease them the site for a dollar a year, pay all maintenance costs, and reimburse them with a rent amounting to five percent annual interest. The trustees accepted the proposal. (On advice of the state attorney general, Parker undertook the venture alone, because the four-man partnership was felt to be unwise.) The resulting building was the brick structure on Main Street which still serves as the president's house. The college was able to purchase it in 1905, using $4,000 in insurance money from the old house and $5,500 appropriated by the state legislature.

Nor was this the only building problem faced by the new president. Enrollment had doubled during the first decade in Durham, rendering many facilities inadequate. In October 1905, Gibbs presented a plan to the trustees by which a library could be built without going to the legislature. Andrew Carnegie agreed to give $20,000 if a like sum could be raised by the institution. Hamilton Smith had bequeathed $10,000 to the town of Durham for a new library; the books of the Durham Public Library and the Durham Library Association were appraised at over $10,000. An agreement was made with the town and the library association. The bequest and the books would be turned over to the college, to match the Carnegie grant, with the college to build a library for the "free use of faculty, students, mem-

Main Street and the original president's house.

bers of the Durham Library Association, and the citizens of Durham." The dedication of Hamilton Smith Library took place on June 3, 1907, although the building was not yet ready for use.°

Because the college had no room in which to store rifles and other equipment, no office for the professor of military science, and no winter drill hall, the U.S. Army did not detail an officer to the college in 1905. For this reason, and to provide a place for other college activities, $25,000 was requested of the 1905 legislature for a gymnasium. The money was voted; the building, designed by Randlett and Griffen of Concord, was dedicated January 26, 1906. The cadets marked the occasion with a military ball. En-

° Hamilton Smith Hall is now a classroom building, with the main university collection housed in Dimond Library. The arrangement with the town of Durham is still in effect. In 1907 it operated to the benefit of the college; today the situation is reversed, and access to the university collection is one of the happier consequences of living in Durham. The town appropriates less than $10,000 a year for the library, all of it used for the support of a children's collection.

larged and remodeled, it now is New Hampshire Hall.

The 1907 legislature appropriated $34,000 for capital improvements, including new boilers and steam lines, equipment for the library, and a women's residence hall. Before her death in 1906, Mrs. Hamilton Smith had promised $10,000 toward construction of a women's residence. In addition, the trustees received $6,000 for the college's interest in the Washington, D.C., residence of Mrs. Smith. With the legislative appropriations, a total of $28,500 was available for building and furnishing Smith Hall. The building was designed by G.O. Totten of the Washington firm which had designed Hamilton Smith Library, and was built by Lewis Killam. After paying the architect's fees and other expenses, $2,569 was left for furnishing, which included a $3.50 potted palm. On the first floor were a kitchen and dining room, living room, and matron's suite. The second and third floors had rooms for thirty-two girls. With Mrs. Marcia Sanders as first matron,

51

*The campus in 1906 (from Thompson Hall) showing
the dairy barn, greenhouses, and Morrill Hall
across the railroad tracks.*

the building opened in September 1908. Women students who did not live at home were required to live in Smith Hall, where rents ranged from $1.25 to $2.00 a week. Board was $3.75 a week at first but in 1910 went up to $4.00.

The boys were still on the town. In 1908 a committee of trustees considered ways of paying for a men's dormitory, and in 1909 Gibbs was instructed to secure cost estimates. Use of the Conant fund to meet the cost was considered but this plan was abandoned, apparently on the basis of an unfavorable opinion from the attorney general. The 1910 trustee report said: "The housing of students has grown to be a serious problem. Several houses in Durham have recently become available as student quarters but many of the rooms are not altogether desirable. While there are many objections to the dormitory system, it will become necessary in a very short time if the numbers of students increase."

The 1909 legislature was asked for $136,000 in plant funds, including $4,000 for a new dynamo. The existing power plant had a capacity of 500 lights, but there were 1,200 in the college buildings. The legislature scaled the request down to $21,890, of which the trustees allocated $12,000

for a new dairy building. (The initial estimate for this building was unusually far out of line, for by the time the building was done in 1911 the cost was $20,789.) Rather than install a new dynamo, it was decided to buy electricity from the Rockingham Power and Light Company at two cents a kilowatt. In 1910, $8,982 was spent for the necessary lines and related electrical equipment. The same year, $1,625 went into the water system and $8,346 was expended on the sewer system.

The physical sciences and engineering had no more space in 1909 than in 1893, yet the number of students had increased by 250 percent. Laboratories, classrooms, offices, and shops were overcrowded. The chemistry department was unable to give more than half of the instruction desired. Many students were refused admission to the chemical engineering program, and those in the general course and in agriculture could not take advanced work in chemistry.

An engineering building to cost $80,000 was the largest item in the 1911 request to the legislature. It was eliminated from the college appropriation bill, but Albert DeMeritt (the Durham representative in the legislature, a trustee, and a farmer) introduced and secured passage of a joint resolution appropriating $50,000 for the building. On hearing this, the students arranged a bonfire celebration to welcome DeMeritt when he arrived from Concord on the evening train. Meanwhile Governor Robert P. Bass vetoed the resolution. DeMeritt got his hero's welcome despite this turn of events; Bass got a satirical lambasting in the 1911 yearbook, and an honorary degree voted in January seems never to have been awarded to him.

A major advance was the removal of the Boston and Maine tracks from the middle campus. The college learned in the fall of 1905 that the railroad planned to double-track the line through Durham. At their winter meeting, the alumni went on record as favoring taking advantage of this development to move the tracks to the western edge of the campus. In January 1908 the trustees voted to negotiate with the railroad to accomplish this goal. The negotiations dragged on until April 1911. In 1912 the college purchased the railroad right of way on the north side of Main Street, thus acquiring title to all the property between Garrison Avenue and the gymnasium. The old railroad station was moved downtown to become Rundlett's store and ultimately the Pizza Den.

Money for current operating expenses continued to be in desperately short supply. The debt for current expenses had grown to about $19,000. "It is of urgent necessity . . . that more teachers be provided before another school year begins," Gibbs wrote. "It also will be necessary to increase the salaries of some of our instructors in order to retain them! . . . During the past year we have lost six instructors mainly because we were unable to pay salaries offered elsewhere . . . . [The college] has demonstrated its usefulness beyond doubt as shown in the great increase in students, the addition of many buildings, and in the important work done by its graduates. The institution is a power for good in the state and its work should not be crippled for lack of funds." The 1907 legislature, to which this plea was addressed, voted the usual appropriation for operating expenses—$13,000 a year including scholarships.

Congress fortunately was more generous. The Adams Act of 1906 increased the Experiment Station budget by $5,000 the first year and $2,000 yearly thereafter, until $30,000 would be reached. The Nelson Act of 1907 increased the amount provided for the general support of the college in similar steps, until the figure of $50,000 was reached in 1912.

In preparation for the 1911 legislature, the alumni for the first time played an active role in supporting the college requests. They paid for the December 1910 issue of the *New Hampshire College Monthly* containing a series of articles on the needs of the institution. New courses were advocated in domestic science, forestry, poultry husbandry, and education, as well as expansion of Arts and Science offerings. It was pointed out that enrollment in Arts and Sciences had increased 300 percent in the past eight years. The need for more money for faculty salaries was noted: professors' salaries ranged from $1,500 to $2,500, and one instructor earned only $833. The alumni also proposed adding a second alumni trustee, who would not necessarily be a resident of the state, and changing the name of the institution to the University of New Hampshire.

The alumni effort was not a great success. The proposal to change the name was snowed under by the agricultural interests. A second alumni trustee was authorized, and Harvey L. Boutwell '82 of Boston was subsequently elected. The $13,000 annual appropriation was continued, but of the other requests only those relating to agriculture were approved: $5,000 for agricultural extension, and $1,500 for printing bulletins of the Experiment Station, $3,000 to purchase livestock, $7,000 for forestry, and $5,000 for a horse barn.

Psychologically, 1911 was not a good year for the college to ask for more money. Since May 1910, it had been receiving in quarterly payments from the state treasurer $31,887 a year as income

Dairy science class in Morrill Hall, 1907.

from the Benjamin Thompson Trust Fund. (The twenty-year period during which this fund was to accumulate had ended on January 30, 1910.) Thompson's will had specified that the trust fund be credited with the value of his estate, excluding the Warner farm in Durham, plus interest at the rate of four percent compounded annually. The value of the assets turned over to the state was $363,823. Over the twenty-year period the interest amounted to $433,358—a total of $797,181. This was the declared value of the fund at its maturity, and it was on this amount that the state began to pay the college a four percent return. This was the bookkeeping aspect of the matter. What had happened in hard cash?

The state treasurer had received securities with a market value in 1890 of $363,823. Some of these

had matured, some had been sold; in 1910 they were carried on the books at a value of $290,551. But the actual market value of the remaining securities was $433,942. During the twenty years, the state treasurer had received $456,942 in cash, from the income from the securities and from those sold or matured. Thus the real value of the trust fund in 1910 was $890,885. Subtracting from this the value of the fund as credited to the college, the state had a profit of $93,704.

Thompson's will had also stipulated that the state set up a second trust fund, into which the state was to put $3,000 a year with four percent compound interest. This account at the end of the twenty-year period showed an accumulation of $92,907. The trustees in 1910 released the state from any obligations on the Benjamin Thompson

State Trust Fund, in view of the nearly $300,000 which had been appropriated for buildings over the years. On this mythical trust, the state might be said to have taken a loss of $208,000. Gibbs wrote in 1910:

The one great danger . . . is that people not familiar with the real financial needs of the institution may think that the income of the Thompson fund . . . will meet all the requirements of the College and that further state appropriations will be unnecessary. It must be remembered first, that the Thompson income *is not a state appropriation and cannot be considered as such in any sense of the term;* it is the income from securities given the state by Benjamin Thompson and is not derived from taxation. Second that the Thompson fund income is not even sufficient to take care of the normal growth made by the College in recent years. Third, that private benefactors should be welcomed as supplementary to state aid, but not to take the place of it . . . . Fourth, that it was never Benjamin Thompson's wish to relieve the state of the expense of the higher education of her sons and daughters, but only to assist and encourage.

It was good to have Gibbs's statement in the public record, but obviously it did not have much effect on the current legislature.

There were a number of changes in the faculty during Gibbs's administration. Professor Groves and some of his contributions have already been mentioned. Arriving the same year as President Gibbs was Frederick W. "Pa" Taylor, professor of agriculture. C. Floyd Jackson was appointed instructor in entomology in 1908, but devoted most of his time to the field of zoology. Another entomologist joined the staff in 1909, Walter C. O'Kane, whose work in the Experiment Station made him a pioneer in what is today called sponsored research.*

New Hampshire College lost one of its most illustrious faculty members when Charles L. Parsons resigned his position as professor of chemistry in 1911, after twenty years on the staff, to become chief chemist of the U.S. Bureau of Mines. He was quoted in the student newspaper as saying that the reason for his departure was the vetoing by Governor Bass of the appropriation for the engineering building. He had brought national attention to the chemistry department by winning the Nichols medal in 1904 for his research on the atomic weight of beryllium. (In 1963, the new chemistry building, Parsons Hall, was named in his honor.) To fill the vacancy in the chemistry department, George A. Perley '08 was appointed assistant professor.

---

* Pa Taylor was named the first dean of the College of Agriculture when the college received its charter as the University of New Hampshire. Professor Jackson was appointed dean of the College of Liberal Arts. Jackson's hobby was dog sledding; the Chinook Kennels at Wonalancet developed from his animals. Professor O'Kane's research eventually became so voluminous that he organized the Crop Protection Institute, housed at the university until 1963, now with its own research laboratory in the adjoining town of Lee. O'Kane also wrote extensively, both in his own field and in others. He retired in 1947, wrote and illustrated *The Hopis* for the University of Arizona Press in 1953, and died in 1973 at the age of ninety-six.

9. Student Life, Student Protest

During the Gibbs administration, the enrollment of New Hampshire College increased from 128 to 307. There was a corresponding surge in student activities.

Fraternities flourished. Not only did they provide sociability; more important, they helped solve the housing problem for male students. Q.T.V., (later a chapter of Kappa Sigma) had been organized in Hanover and requested a building lot when the move was made to Durham. They did not get the lot, but Whitcher built a large house which they rented in 1895. Zeta Epsilon Zeta (later Sigma Alpha Epsilon) was organized in 1895 but did not acquire a house until 1903. Delta Xi (later a chapter of Theta Chi) was formed in 1903 and acquired a house two years later. Alpha Tau Alpha was organized by the two-year agricultural students in 1905 and rented a house the next year. A house was acquired by Beta Phi (later Lambda Chi Alpha) the year it was organized, 1906. The fraternity boom ended with the founding in 1907 of Gamma Theta (later a chapter of Alpha Tau Omega) which rented a house the next year. Casque and Casket was organized in 1905 and promulgated rules for fraternity rushing, known as the "chinning session."

Sororities came on the scene more slowly. The secret W.H.A. society had been organized in Hanover and continued to be active in Durham. It reorganized as a sorority, Alpha Alpha Alpha (later a chapter of Chi Omega) in 1911. A Pi Kappa sorority was organized in 1910 but did not survive.

Not all student interest was directed to fraternal organizations. Formed during this period were clubs for whist, chess and checkers, horticulture, and art. The band was organized in 1906 and a new orchestra the following year. The Student Council came into being in 1907; all class contests and other class relations were placed under its supervision. The council was a men-only organization, so the women founded a council of their own in 1911. Senior Skulls was founded in 1909 to promote athletics, sponsor brotherly feeling among fraternities, students, and faculty, and otherwise benefit the college. There was an Agricultural Club with a meeting room on the top floor of Morrill Hall, containing a trophy case for the awards won by its judging teams.

Student activities received a major boost when the gymnasium was completed. The students helped build it, in fact, when the Boston & Maine Railroad contributed $1,000 in gratitude for their assistance when one of its trains was derailed in Durham. This was the St. John's Express, running more than an hour late and rushing south at about fifty miles an hour, January 20, 1905. At 7:40 A.M. the train left the tracks near where Kingsbury Hall now stands. The last four cars—sleeper, smoker, and two coaches—were badly damaged, tearing up 300 feet of track in the process. There were no fatalities, but eleven seriously injured passengers were taken to Dr. Grant's house or to DeMeritt (Ballard) Hall, then under lease to Zeta Epsilon Zeta. Doctors and nurses were rushed from Dover on a special train.

After the gymnasium was opened, the New Hampshire College Club was reorganized to take charge of the clubroom in the building. Restricted at first to undergraduate men, with dues of $1.50 a year, the club voted in 1906 to admit faculty and graduate students as associate members. That same year the clubroom was connected to the lines of the Newmarket Light and Power Co.: the college plant was unable to furnish current during the spring and summer months.

The gymnasium also provided facilities for chapel and for military drill. Chapel was now

*The Mill Pond and Oyster River Bridge with
the dirt road that is now NH 108 to Newmarket.*

held but once a week—at 11:45 A.M. on Wednesday—and in 1910 its name was discreetly changed to "convocation." The unabashed Protestantism of early days was fading in the twentieth century.

The military drill periods had likewise been reduced, to two a week, each lasting from 11:00 A.M. to 12:30 P.M. Lieutenant William E. Hunt '99 was assigned by the army to New Hampshire College. At his urging, in 1907 senior cadet officers began to be paid for their services. The total compensation, including remission of fees and a small cash payment, was not to exceed $120 for the year. The purpose was to encourage seniors to elect military science.

In 1904 the junior class talked of publishing a yearbook. This did not materialize, but the *New Hampshire College Monthly* carried photographs and brief biographies of the seniors in its June issue. The first issue of the *Granite* was published four years later by the class of 1909. The junior class continued to publish the yearbook annually,

except for an issue missed by the class of 1915. To manage student publications, the New Hampshire College Publication Board was established in 1910 with two faculty and four student members. The next year saw the last issue of the *New Hampshire College Monthly*. It was replaced by a four-page weekly, the *New Hampshire;* Volume I, number 1 was dated September 20, 1911.

The faculty aided athletics in 1904 when they voted to schedule no classes after 3:30 P.M. This action gave the football squad more time for practice. A set of eligibility rules was adopted the following year. Probably little harm was done by the provisions that no member of the college team was to be paid for playing, that a student must play under his own name, or that all players must be registered in the college. More serious was a rule that no student could play who had been officially warned that he was below passing in two or more subjects, or who had deficiencies in eight or more credits. This claimed so many casualties that the students called a meeting on

September 22, 1908. Their protest evidently accomplished little: the football team lost to Brown, Colby, and Maine.

Coaches still were hired by the season, usually a different man each year. Local high schools had disappeared from the schedule, and in 1904 the Athletic Association voted to follow "the lead taken by some other colleges" and not schedule football with either Phillips Exeter or Phillips Andover academies. For a time football and basketball were the only sports in which there was varsity competition, but the freshmen usually fielded a baseball team. Varsity baseball was played regularly beginning in 1907. With the construction of the gymnasium in 1906, and the plowing and grading of the athletic field under the supervision of Pa Taylor in 1908, the college no longer played most of its home games in Dover. A cinder track was added the following year, which led to the addition of track to the varsity competition. Hockey became a possibility with the building of a rink in 1911. At their annual meeting in 1906 the alumni voted to have a "varsity night," later to be known as Homecoming. The first one was observed November 19, 1907, at a home football game.

The early decades of the twentieth century were the heyday of interclass rivalry. The attempt made in 1902 to substitute a field day and rope pull for the cane rush did not succeed, but merely added another battle to the war. The picture contest also continued. Another fracas was added with the freshman poster contest: the poster contained rules for the freshmen to follow, and the idea was for the freshmen to pull it down while the sophomores defended it. Then there were the class banquet contests. Both the freshmen and the sophomores tried to have out-of-town banquets, which the other class would attempt to spoil by kidnaping and other tactics.

In 1912 the banquet contest led to results far weightier than the usual black eyes and torn shirts. The freshmen that year were unusually

alert, and all schemes of the sophomores to get away had failed until they hit on a novel ruse.

At 9:45 A.M. on April 29, the bell in the Thompson Hall tower was rung vigorously. This was the alarm which warned the college and community of fire. President Gibbs, at work in his office on the ground floor of Thompson Hall, looked out for signs of conflagration. He could see none, so he climbed to the bell tower to get information from the ringer of the bell. There he found William Brackett of Greenland, president of the sophomore class and a star baseball player, lustily toiling at the bell rope.

Let President Gibbs take up the story from here, in the words of a letter to Mr. Brackett's father:

Not being able to see any signs of fire I went at once to the bell tower and there found Mr. Brackett ringing the bell. By careful looking I could see a small blaze two or three miles away in the neighboring town of Madbury and I realized at once that the alarm was sounded for the purpose of enabling the Sophomore Class to elude the vigilance of the Freshmen and get away to their Class banquet. I at once asked Mr. Brackett who told him to ring the bell and he replied, "I am ringing it on my own initiative." I then asked him to report to me in my office as he came down. This he failed to do.

Brackett had, of course, slipped out of Thompson Hall to join his classmates at their banquet in Boston. The next morning he was suspended for the remainder of the semester. This action drew a prompt reaction from the students: a committee of sophomores went to see President Gibbs at 9:00 A.M. the following morning. Fortunately a detailed account of the session has been preserved.

The students explained that, other strategems having failed, they had unanimously voted to try the false fire alarm. Brackett had rung the bell as an agent of the class, they explained, not as an individual. They therefore felt that Brackett's penalty was too severe—if any punishment were to be inflicted, it should involve the entire class.

After recounting his version of the affair, Gibbs declared: "Now, nothing you gentlemen have said, and nothing you can say, will change the action of Mr. Brackett." This was the dialogue as it has been recorded:

STUDENT: "We don't think it right that one man should suffer for what the whole class stands back of."

GIBBS: "Then you contemplate a strike?"

STUDENT: "No."

If the student was telling the truth, then the strike which followed was Gibbs's idea. That this was the case is confirmed by John S. Elliott '15, a member of the strike committee. He recalls that, up to the time of this confrontation with President Gibbs, the idea of striking had not occurred to the students.

GIBBS: "Would you be interested to know what would happen if you were to strike?"

STUDENT: "We do not feel that way. We are not planning a strike."

GIBBS: "But would you like to know what would happen?"

STUDENT: "I think we would."

GIBBS: "First thing, everyone would lose his scholarship, which means thirty dollars. You would be suspended and then given a certain length of time in which to come back to college. Then you would be expelled if necessary."

The students naturally snatched up the gauntlet. That afternoon they sent Gibbs a letter demanding Brackett's immediate reinstatement while negotiations went forward. This demand was ignored, so the sophomores stopped attending classes on the morning of May 2. The freshmen, whose rivalry with the sophomores had started the whole affair, now made common cause with them. They joined the strike the same day. Gibbs, with the backing of the faculty administrative committee, made good on his threat and issued the following statement:

Members of the sophomore and freshmen classes who fail to return to their college exercises before May 3, will forfeit their scholarships and will have to re-register and pay $30, one-half annual tuition, before attending classes . . . . Members of the freshman and sophomore classes who fail to return to their college exercises before Tuesday noon, May 7, will be expelled from college and will not receive dismissal papers which would permit entrance to other colleges.

All college exercises meanwhile will continue as usual.

This ultimatum roused the juniors, and *they* joined the strike. They were threatened with the same penalties as the other two classes. This put the seniors in a quandary. With commencement only five weeks away, they decided that the risk of joining the strike was too great. Not wishing to be left completely on the sidelines, however, they sent the following declaration to Gibbs:

As seniors who have carefully studied the present situation at the New Hampshire College, we respectfully offer our services in the settlement of the present difficulties.

The class of 1912 disapproves of the action of the faculty in suspending Mr. Brackett, and furthermore we disapprove of the administration of this college which has led to the present crisis.

The seniors suggested letting all students return to class, with any penalties to be decided later by the trustees. The strikers had, in the meantime, taken their case to the board without much success. One of the alumni trustees, H.L. Boutwell '82, wrote at length to the strikers. Among other things, he told them: "Discipline at the College must be maintained at all times and at all hazards. It is the duty of the President and Faculty to be fair and just on all occasions and it is the duty of the student body to yield a ready and cheerful obedience to all orders, rules and regulations." Boutwell ended by urging the students to return immediately to class, and by offering to go to Durham to help settle the matter.

On Monday, May 6—a week after the fateful ringing of the Thompson Hall bell—the strike was still on, but pressure to end it was building. That morning the heads of all departments met and unanimously passed the following resolution: "We, the undersigned, members of the faculty of New Hampshire College, hereby express our loyalty to President Gibbs in the present crisis." Twenty signatures were appended.

The same morning Trustees Boutwell, Edward H. Wason '86, and Warren Brown, arrived in town. They talked with Gibbs, Brackett, and some of the striking students. The result was the ending of the strike with no penalties being given the strikers; Brackett's punishment was reduced to two weeks' suspension (one week of which had already passed) and probation for the balance of the term.

The following day, President Gibbs wrote to Boutwell:

I explained to you by telephone this morning the conditions under which the strike was settled, and I think we are all very much pleased over the result.

Permit me to express my deep appreciation of the splendid service that you trustees rendered yesterday in bringing the students to see the errors of their ways. I doubt if a settlement could have been effected without your assistance. I deeply appreciate also the support which you gave to the faculty and myself in the position we took regarding the matter.

The students were unhappy that Brackett's services would be lost to the baseball team for the balance of the season, but the trustees refused to intervene further.

This account of the strike is based on the "Notebook" of Oren V. Henderson, long-time registrar of the college and prominent state poli-

tician. Dad Henderson comments: "The 'strike' had reverberations for a number of years and was discussed two years later when I came to Durham. Bill Brackett was the idol of his class and the student body, because of his athletic ability and his carefree manner."

Brackett graduated with his class and served in World War I. He died on June 3, 1921, of an illness attributed to his war service. His name has been perpetuated at the university by the naming for him of the Lewis Fields baseball diamond, dedicated in June 1936.

Gibbs resigned as president during the summer following the strike, and Henderson reports that his resignation was widely assumed to be a result of that difficulty. But Henderson also quotes a letter which gives Gibbs's version of his departure. The letter, to Trustee Richard W. Sulloway, said:

I have thought for several years that I should eventually leave college work and go into business when the right opportunity offered. Soon after Christmas a party of the wealthiest and most conservative business men of Boston conceived the idea of forming a trust company to deal in farm lands . . . and have asked me to be their field manager . . . . I have no doubt I can make a success of the thing, and if so, there will be very unusual opportunities for making money. I feel that enough of my life has been spent in missionary work, and I am going to devote the remainder of it to doing something for my family . . . . The recent strike has nothing to do with the matter, because my going was practically arranged for before the strike.

PART TWO

Liberal Arts to the Fore,

(1913-1947)

Cows grazing in the ravine behind Thompson Hall,
where the university library now stands.

10. The Fairchild Administration

President Gibbs informed the trustees on June 15, 1912, that he intended to leave New Hampshire College on September 1. In his letter of resignation, he summarized the college's growth during the nine years of his tenure—the student body increased to 307, the faculty to 48, the Experiment Station staff to 23, and the number of courses to 276. There were now fifteen buildings on campus. The library collection had increased to 30,000 volumes, "private gifts to the college have amounted to $51,500, expenditures have not exceeded income and the old debt, incurred prior to 1903, has been reduced from $18,000 to $10,000." Gibbs concluded: "Entrance requirements and scholarship standards have been raised, courses of study revised and strengthened and high ideals of college life and work established."

The trustees accepted his resignation at a special meeting on July 30. They then took five ballots on a new president. The candidates were Thomas Chalmers, pastor of the First Congregational Church in Manchester; Dean Pettee; Harvey L. Boutwell, the alumni trustee who had helped settle the strike; and Henry C. Morrison, superintendent of public instruction in New Hampshire. None of them received the necessary eight votes, so Dean Pettee became acting president while the search for a new man went on. A trustee committee was appointed to survey the field and make a recommendation to be brought in at the October meeting. Having failed to find a New Hampshire man who could get the needed votes, the committee looked westward for a candidate.

At their October meeting the trustees elected Edward Thomson Fairchild. His salary was fixed at $5,000, "plus house rent, fuel, lights and water rates." For the preceding six years Fairchild had been state Superintendent of Public Instruction in Kansas; at the time of his election he was president of the National Education Association. Born October 30, 1854, at Doylestown, Ohio, he had received the M.A. and LL.D. degrees from Kansas State Agricultural College. He could not come to his new job until December 1, so Dean Pettee continued as acting president during the fall.

Fairchild's inaugural was set for May 12, 1913. Plans for the inauguration were extensive, having been formulated by a trustee-appointed committee of five members, with eleven faculty members assigned to help with the details. Harold H. Scudder edited an account of the observation.° According to this report the weather was beautiful; all trains—including expresses—stopped in Durham; and the ceremonies went off perfectly, except that Governor Samuel D. Felker was unable to be present. The academic procession, preceded by the college band and a detachment of the college cadet corps, was led from Thompson Hall to the decorated gymnasium by the senior members of the faculty, Dean Pettee and Professor Scott.

The principal address was given by President William O. Thompson of Ohio State University, who said: "New England may not retain the laurels history has so gratefully woven about her unless the agriculture of the region be maintained

---

° Scudder was a Dartmouth graduate who served as chemist in the Experiment Station in 1903-04, left to work a a reporter for the Manchester *Union*, and returned to the college as an instructor in English in 1913-14. He stayed to become professor of English, chairman of the department in 1939, and acting dean of the College of Liberal Arts from July 1941 to October 1943. The semester before his retirement, it was necessary to schedule his course on American humor in Murkland (Richards) Auditorium, to accommodate the 150 students who flocked to take advantage of this last opportunity to take the course.

and developed and unless there be on the farms of New England in the future as in the past a sturdy people whose citizenship is worthy of the pioneer days."

Fairchild devoted most of his inaugural address to the achievements of the agricultural departments of land grant colleges. But he did not overlook the engineering and liberal arts opportunities which such colleges provided: "While we are anxious to return a large number to the farm, we do not believe that all children born upon the farm should stay there. Engineering must receive its full share of support because the mechanical arts lie at the base of all industries." He announced that a full four-year course in home economics would be introduced in the fall, and that if conditions warranted a textile department would be added. (It never was.)

President Gibbs had put a freeze on honorary degrees during the latter part of his administration. This had been due in part to pressure from the alumni. Meeting in Boston in January 1905, they had passed a resolution disapproving the granting of the Master of Science as an honorary degree "except as a mark of excellence and high attainment in scientific learning."[*] This had little immediate effect, as four honorary M.S. degrees were given that year and two more in 1906, plus an honorary B.S. The alumni at a subsequent meeting considered a motion to ask the trustees to award no more honorary degrees unless approved by the alumni, but the motion was tabled. Nonetheless, only one more honorary degree was voted by the trustees during the remainder of Gibbs's administration—that to Governor Bass, which was not awarded.

With Gibbs's departure, the ice jam broke. For the inauguration ceremonies the trustees had voted eight Doctor of Laws and two Doctor of

Science degrees. LL.D.'s went to Dean Pettee and Professor Scott, among others.

Fairchild's administration got off to a good start when the 1913 legislature appropriated $80,000 for an engineering building—sought since 1909. Warren H. Manning, a landscape architect, chose a site on the south side of Main Street, suggested by Professor Hewitt. Construction began in 1913 and was completed the next year. In appreciation of his efforts to obtain this building two years earlier, as well as of his other services to the college, the building was named for Albert DeMeritt.

By September 1914 the departments of mechanical and electrical engineering, physics, and drawing were housed in DeMeritt Hall, freeing all of Conant for chemistry. The expanded instructional space was accompanied by some expansion of offerings. Thompson Hall now housed English, foreign languages, and mathematics (moved to DeMeritt in 1916). Economics, history and political science, and psychology and sociology were on the top floor of the Hamilton Smith Library, while Nesmith and Morrill Halls were used by agriculture and the Experiment Station.

To fulfill a promise in Fairchild's inaugural address, in June 1913 the trustees established a department of home economics and appointed Helen B. Thompson to head it. In addition to being professor of home economics, she was the college's first Dean of Women. At the same time, economics was set up as a separate department with associate professor Guy C. Smith as head. Professor Scott continued as head of a reorganized history department, which also included political science. The department of education was established in June 1915 with the appointment of Charles L. Simmers as its first professor.

The 1911 paper organization of the college into three divisions became operational in April 1915 when Taylor was appointed head of the Agricultural Division, Hewitt of the Engineering Division, and Groves of the Arts and Sciences Divi-

---

[*] In addition to Boston, the Alumni Association now had clubs in Pittsburgh and Chicago, as well as one in Lynn, Massachusetts. The clubs reflected the fact that many graduates—especially in engineering—were finding work outside the state.

sion. Their titles were changed to "dean" in June.

Change of status was not confined to administrators. The trustee by-laws were amended in October 1915 to read: "The faculty of the College shall consist of the president of the College and all instructors who hold full professorships, associate professorships, or assistant professorships, the director of the experiment station, the director of extension work, and the physical director." Prior to this only the president and full professors were voting members of the faculty.

The broadening programs of the institution were recognized in April 1916 when the trustees voted to provide for the granting of the Bachelor of Arts degree. The B.A. would go to graduates of arts and sciences whose majors were other than mathematics or the natural sciences; all others were to continue receiving the Bachelor of Science degree. The first B.A.'s were awarded at the 1916 commencement.

During Fairchild's administration graduate work was offered in agriculture, biology, and chemistry, leading to the M.S. degree. Two professional degrees were also available—Mechanical Engineer and Electrical Engineer—following four years of experience, some graduate study, and presentation of a thesis. Altogether, only seven M.S. and one E.E. were awarded between 1912 and 1917. Nevertheless, the forerunner of the Graduate Council was established when a committee of three, one from each division, was appointed to pass on the qualifications of graduate students and to approve courses of study. Requirements included a full year of residence plus a thesis. Instructors and graduate assistants were allowed to complete requirements in two years.

The Division of Agriculture in 1915 had moved in the direction of insuring that its graduates would have practical farm experience. Candidates for degrees must have lived on a farm for at least two years, after age twelve or to have worked on a farm for at least six months. (At least three of these six months had to be in practical forest work for those seeking degrees in for-

estry.) For some reason, those seeking certificates for the two-year agriculture course must have had two years residence on a farm *before* age twelve; lacking this, they had to have put in four months of practical farm work.

The legislature had appropriated $4,000 a year to be devoted to poultry work. Robert V. Mitchell, assistant professor of animal husbandry, was put in charge. He was promoted to professor and made head of a separate department of poultry husbandry in June 1916. That same year, John M. Fuller joined the faculty as professor of dairy husbandry.

Although the college had conducted agricultural extension work by means of short courses and lectures since its early days in Hanover, the activity gained substance when the 1911 legislature appropriated $5,000 to support extension during the biennium. John C. Kendall '02 was employed as director of extension in September 1911. Soils were tested, experiments carried on with seed corn and fertilizers, and tests made on orchard management. Agricultural reading courses enrolled 207. A Poultry Day, Dairy Day, and Orchard Day were held on the campus, and a Farmers' Basket Picnic and Educational Meeting was held in Durham on August 15, 1912.

The extension work in New Hampshire attracted the attention of the General Education Board of New York City—the first of the Rockefeller foundations. A visit to Durham by David F. Houston, U.S. Secretary of Agriculture, and Wallace Buttrick, Secretary of the General Education Board, resulted in a grant enabling the college to engage agents to work in the counties. The first agents were Charles W. Stone on soil fertility and crop rotation in Rockingham County, M. Gale Eastman '13 in Sullivan County, and A. W. Benner '10 as dairy demonstrator in Grafton County. In 1914 the grant was increased so that clubs for boys and girls could be started. Lawrence A. Carlisle '08 was appointed club leader, and the next year Mary L. Sanborn was made assistant leader.

The Smith-Lever Act of 1914 provided federal funds for cooperative extension work in agriculture and home economics, to be matched by state funds. The federal payment the first year was $10,000, to be increased in subsequent years. By 1917 there were county agents in all counties.

The general availability of secondary education was recognized in 1915, when graduation from high school replaced the passing of entrance examinations as the normal means of qualifying for admission. Any graduate of a high school or academy approved by the State Department of Public Instruction was eligible.

A new attendance rule went into effect for the second semester of 1912-13. One "cut" per credit hour was allowed in each course, except that cuts were not to be taken when examinations were scheduled. If work missed was not made up to the satisfaction of the department head, the student received a zero. To insure that the system worked, each instructor had to send daily absence reports to Dean Pettee. The next year the rule was amended to give a student one semester hour of credit for fifteen unused cuts. This bonus provision worked too well. At the end of three semesters, 333 students had amassed 502 bonus credits; one eager beaver had four to his credit, and eight had three apiece. The bonus provision was repealed in 1915. The next year the whole system was thrown out, and responsibility for attendance was put on the student. One safeguard was instituted: a five-dollar fine for cuts before and after vacations. This effective but unpopular rule was enforced for half a century.

Increasing use of the library was reflected in a decision to have it open every evening, starting in 1913, but it was four years more before the library was kept open during the noon hour. Final examinations were systematized at the end of the first semester in January 1916: a five-day examination period was established with three sessions a day. The following year the traditional letter system was replaced by numerical grades, with 60 the passing mark.

The business operation of the college had now reached such proportions that the rather informal procedures of the past were no longer adequate. At the instigation of Governor Rolland H. Spaulding, two state bank commissioners examined the accounts of the college in 1915. Together with Dad Henderson, at that time business secretary, they installed a new system of accounting that cast more light on what was going on.

The total cost of operations in 1914-15—including permanent improvements, the Experiment Station, and agricultural extension—was $198,482. There was an outstanding debt of $18,500. Of the expenditures, 4 percent went for equipment, 3.3 percent for refunds, 4 percent for extension, 10.8 percent for new buildings, 14.5 percent for the Experiment Station, and 63.4 percent for running expenses. The federal treasury was still the principal source of money, supplying almost twice as much as the state. The breakdown of income was 36.1 percent from federal support, 10 percent from students, 21.4 percent from sales and miscellaneous sources, 13.3 percent from endowment, and 19.2 percent from the state (of which 10.3 percent was for buildings and 8.9 percent for general expenses).

For 1915-16 the state appropriated $178,000, more than doubling its contribution over that of the previous year. But of the state money, $65,000 was for a dormitory—Fairchild Hall—so that for running expenses the state contribution was still less than the federal one.

Fringe benefits for the faculty were a thing of the future. Forrest E. Cardullo, professor of mechanical engineering since 1908 and author of a widely-discussed paper advocating establishment of a textile course at the college, requested a year's leave of absence without pay for 1914-15. He had been offered a temporary appointment in the Harvard Graduate School of Business as a lecturer on industrial administration. His salary would be $800 more than he was then earning, plus expenses for travel and study during the summer. Cardullo pointed out that some universities granted sabbatical leaves and that 1914-15 would be his seventh at the college. The trustees voted not to grant the leave. It would be difficult to obtain a qualified substitute, they argued, and to do otherwise "might establish an unfortunate precedent." (Apparently no one had searched the records. The precedent had been established in 1894 when Edwin B. Davis, instructor in modern languages, had been granted a year's leave on condition that he furnish a substitute at his own expense.) Cardullo, of course, resigned.

Transportation and communications were becoming modernized. In 1914 a garage was built for the president, and the following year Professor Fred Rasmussen of the dairy department was authorized to purchase "an auto milk delivery wagon." The president was not the only one with an automobile. As early as 1913 the *New Hampshire* mentioned a weekend trip by the faculty car owners to the White Mountains to view the autumn foliage. This became an annual event. Pa Taylor organized the expedition of 1916. It got off to a late start but still managed to reach Bethlehem by 5:40 P.M., having traveled by way of Concord, Laconia, Plymouth, and Franconia. Rank determined place in line—an important matter due to the dusty dirt roads—with President Fairchild's car first, followed in order by Dean Pettee, Director Kendall, Farm Manager Stone, Business Secretary Henderson, and lesser ranks. Pa Taylor served as rearguard to render assistance to those disabled by punctures, blowouts, or exhaustion of gasoline. Next day they returned via Gorham, Conway, and Rochester, making a round trip of 278 miles.

A wireless squad, formed in the College Battalion in February 1914, put a station on the air in May. By the following January the *New Hampshire* was getting some of its news items by this means. Durham got its own telephone exchange in 1916; formerly it had been served through Newmarket. The Durham telephone exchange was friendly, obliging, and a good place to pick up current gossip. It was common for a couple

out for an evening of bridge at a neighbor's to receive calls that had been directed to their home number—provided the bridge date had been arranged by telephone.

The old oaken bucket and the out-house were being crowded out of Durham by the growth of the college. In the fall of 1914 the State Board of Health demanded that the college install a septic tank. This was done, and the town of Durham also built a new sewer and a septic tank. The water from the old reservoir, built in 1893, was not fit for drinking, although it was useful for boilers, irrigation, and fire fighting. Drinking water was carried from nearby springs until wells were drilled in 1910. There was a typhoid fever outbreak in the winter of 1911-12, which had claimed as one of its victims the Rev. Telesphore Taisne, pastor of the Durham church and language instructor in the college.

With a large increase in women students expected in the fall of 1914, because of the new home economics program, Smith Hall would no longer have room for the unmarried women instructors and office help who had been living there. Thomas J. Laton, instructor in drawing, had been occupying a college-owned house across Main Street from Thompson Hall. He was asked to vacate so that the building could be used for the instructors and secretaries.

Sixty-four women enrolled in the fall of 1914, double the number of the preceding year. They completely filled Smith Hall. The trustees had no money to build another dormitory, and their authority to borrow for the purpose was questioned. The problem was met by making a lease-purchase arrangement for Ballard Hall. The legislature appropriated $6,200 to buy the building in 1915. This helped the women at the expense of the men: Ballard had been rented by Zeta Epsilon Zeta fraternity. On losing Ballard, the fraternity was able to rent the Cummings house on Ballard Street. Beta Phi fraternity lost the Bickford house in 1916 when it was taken by the college for additional coed housing.

To alleviate the increasingly serious housing problem for men, the college gave some encouragement to fraternities to build new houses. In 1913 Kappa Sigma had asked for a lot on college land. The requested lot was reserved for a future college building, but the trustees agreed to lay out a proposed "fraternity row" and to make long-term leases to fraternities. By January 1915 Kappa Sigma had chosen a lot and was prepared to build—except for arranging the financing. The trustees agreed to take a mortgage for half the cost. They reserved the right to approve the design of the house, which could be used only for a fraternity, and to end the lease at its pleasure upon paying the fraternity for the building. The house was completed in January 1917 and a lease for ninety-nine years was arranged. Three other fraternities and Pi Alpha Phi sorority also requested lots. None was able to arrange the financing, and the trustees did not come forward with assistance.

The enrollment had doubled between 1910 and 1915 (from 240 to 492), and President Fairchild predicted it would double again. The time had finally come to abandon the fiction that Durham could provide sufficient housing. The 1915 legislature was asked to appropriate $65,000 for a dormitory to accommodate one hundred men. The Smith Hall dining room had become too small to care for the women students; to take care of that problem and to provide for the men, $70,000 also was requested for building a common dining hall.

The money for the dormitory was voted. The building was rushed in an effort to get it ready for 1915-16, but the deadline was not met. While waiting for their rooms to be ready, fifty freshmen were housed in the mechanical engineering laboratory in DeMeritt Hall. In October 1915 the trustees voted to name this first dormitory Fairchild Hall. The following fall it was filled to overflowing.

An increasing number of out-of-state students was contributing to the crowding of the campus. For the first time, there was consideration of limiting out-of-state enrollment. In 1916-17 there were fifty-seven students from Massachusetts, sixteen from Maine, eight from Connecticut, and three each from New York, Ohio, and Vermont. In addition there were foreign students from Norway, South America, and Nova Scotia. No action was taken, but the Boston alumni club was sufficiently concerned to go on record in 1916 "as being absolutely opposed to any action by the Board of Trustees or Faculty whereby the students allowed to enter the college be limited to a certain definite number."

11. A New Day for Athletics and Activities

At the beginning of Fairchild's administration, the athletic program was still a hit-or-miss affair. It was inadequately financed and suffered from the practice of relying on part-time coaches—often a different one each season. Tod Eberle, a 1911 graduate of Swarthmore, coached football in 1912 and 1913. In 1912 Eberle was able to get a football training table established at the Utopian Boarding Club. (The *New Hampshire* claimed it to be the first training table in the college's history, but actually one had been in operation back in 1894.) The official football sweater, blue with a V-neck and bearing the letters "NH" in white, was adopted that year. Letters were awarded to thirteen members of the 1912 team. These trappings of intercollegiate athletics did not spell victory: in two years Eberle's teams won four, lost eight, and tied one. The following season the coach was T.D. Sheppard, who had played at Maine and Wesleyan. He could hardly have been a defensive specialist, since Tufts won the first game 83-0 and Colby, the second 66-0. He did not produce much of an offense either, for in nine games the New Hampshire scoring was limited to one field goal and one safety. Three of the games ended in scoreless ties.

Full schedules were played in basketball and baseball. The coaches were different each season, but the results were monotonously bad. A board running track was built behind the gymnasium in 1912. This stirred some interest in track and field, but few meets were held, and in these the results were indifferent. That year also saw the first of the New Hampshire interscholastic track meets, which became an annual spring event.

Efforts were made to establish hockey as an intercollegiate sport, but in five years only three games were played, and those against town teams. Other winter sports fared better, thanks to

the presence of a few expert skiers from Berlin, New Hampshire. These included Carl "Gus" Paulson '15, who single-handedly won third place for New Hampshire in the intercollegiate ski and snowshoe meet in Hanover in 1915; and Walter D. Reid '20, who as New Hampshire College's only entrant won second place in the 1917 Dartmouth Winter Carnival skiing events. A tennis club was organized in 1915 and played some matches in 1917.

Supporting of the teams was primarily the responsibility of the Student Athletic Association. The trustees seldom voted more than two hundred dollars a year for this purpose, so gate receipts and dues from association members were the principal sources of revenue. Gifts were sought now and then for special projects—$250 for bleachers in 1915, for example. The accounts of the 1912 football season illustrate the operations. Expenses were $2,283, of which $500 was paid the coach. Receipts came to $2,159, giving a loss for the season of $123. This presumably was made up out of athletic association dues. In 1916 the dues were raised from three to four dollars a year. In April 1914, 332 students, about ninety percent of those enrolled that term, petitioned to have the college fee increased by six dollars a year, the money to go to a fund to support a department of physical education. The trustees believed that this increase would not serve the welfare of the students and turned it down. The following October, however, they agreed to hire a full-time athletic director if the money could be found. The money was found the next spring, and William H. "Butch" Cowell was engaged.

A new day dawned for New Hampshire College athletics. Cowell arrived during the summer and had twelve men out for football practice a week and a half before college opened. After the

Above: 1917 football lineup in front of the gymnasium.
Below: Women's gymnastics class in Thompson Hall.

start of classes the squad went up to fifty. The result was a season record of four wins and four losses, although a post-season loss to Rhode Island spoiled the even break. Even so it was a vast improvement over what had gone before.

As coaches say, usually during a losing season, "You can't win without the horses." To help recruit athletes, the Alumni Athletic Board proposed that it be given ten in-state and five out-of-state tuition scholarships to dispense. The alumni agreed to match the out-of-state scholarships by five more from their own funds.

Harvey L. Boutwell, then president of the Board of Trustees, asked Dean Pettee for an opinion. The dean replied:

While we necessarily are careful in regard to tuition of non-residents there has already been one precedent in that direction. In accordance with a hint, not a command, from I think the United States Department of Education, the college a few years ago agreed to furnish free tuition to two or three students from outside the United States.

Of course what the Alumni Committee wants is to be able to furnish free tuition to a few non-resident athletes. As this will put them on a par with what they would have if coming from New Hampshire, and since it will be beneficial to athletes when wisely carried out, I favor the scheme.

This opinion, from one not noted for open-handedness with money, influenced the trustees to empower a committee to meet the request. Another device to ameliorate the financial problems of out-of-state athletes was developed unofficially during Cowell's stewardship: a New Hampshire sports fan would "adopt" a promising nonresident youngster, thus making him eligible for in-state tuition and scholarships. It was a simple matter to get a court order establishing a guardianship. (Later, during the Engelhardt administration, the policy was adopted that such guardianships would be recognized only if they were legitimate ones, unrelated to the desire for in-state student status.)

The combination of a full-time coach and financial incentives began to pay off. In 1917 the football team had four wins, two losses and a tie. The basketball team won eight and lost three. New Hampshire joined the National Collegiate Athletic Association in January 1918.

A year after the hiring of Cowell to head the men's physical education department, Elizabeth A. Rollins was appointed to start a similar department for the women. The top floor of Thompson Hall, now outgrown as a site for convocations, was designated a women's gymnasium in 1915. Competitive athletics for women was limited to interclass basketball.

Students and faculty pooled their efforts on November 21, 1916, to improve the facilities on what was later to be known as Memorial Field. Classes were cancelled for the first "New Hampshire Day." Tile drains were installed in gravel-filled ditches. Bleachers, partially prefabricated in the college shops the night before, were erected. At noon the women students served a meal of oyster stew, ham, rolls, doughnuts, and coffee in the gymnasium. Finally there was an evening of entertainment, including a minstrel show, motion pictures, and dancing.

Then as later, winning football teams helped stimulate alumni interest in the college. In addition to their support of athletics, the alumni gave financial support to the interscholastic speaking contest. The College Alumni Athletic Board in 1917 was made an official branch of the Alumni Association. There was no alumni publication, but many kept in touch with the campus through subscriptions to the *New Hampshire*. On March 31, 1917, the *New Hampshire* published a special eight-page Alumni Edition.

The entry of the college into the men's dormitory field had slowed the formation of new fraternities. The only such organization founded during Fairchild's administration was the Delta Kappa chapter of the National Federation of Commons Clubs, in 1914. Four years later it became a chapter of Phi Mu Delta. The fraternities founded earlier were very active in this period, as was the interfraternity organization, Casque

Lunch hour at the commuters' lounge in Smith Hall.

Preparing lunch in Smith Hall kitchen, 1922.

and Casket. Gamma Theta was expelled from the organization in 1912 for breaking the "chinning" rules.

With the increasing proportion of women students, new sororities were formed. Their function was primarily social, since all women students except commuters were required to live in Smith Hall. Pi Kappa was founded in 1910 but did not survive long. Two other new groups, Pi Alpha Phi and Phi Delta, joined Alpha Alpha Alpha in 1914 to found the Sphinx, an intersorority organization. Phi Delta became a chapter of Alpha Xi Delta in 1914; Alpha Alpha Alpha became a chapter of Chi Omega in 1915. As the national sororities required that any campus having two nationals must have a chapter of the Panhellenic Society, Sphinx ceased to function when a local of Panhellenic was installed in 1916. The same year the Pi Delta sorority (not to be confused with Phi Delta), was organized.

Scholarship began to get some attention from the Greek-letter groups. In 1914 the alumni gave

a cup to go to the fraternity with the highest average grades; Beta Phi was the first winner. Alpha Xi Delta donated a similar cup for the sororities the next year. The opening of Fairchild Hall made it less pressing for a freshman to get a bed in a fraternity early in his first year; so, with student and faculty support, fraternity rushing was moved to the second semester, with pledging in May. A student was required to have passed thirteen credits before being eligible for pledging.

Casque and Casket's ball in May challenged the Sophomore Hop as the leading social event of the year. Both were followed by fraternity house parties. In 1916 the first Junior Prom replaced both of these events. The prom and associated activities lasted from Thursday afternoon until Sunday.

In 1912, after twenty bruising years, a freshman-sophomore rope pull was substituted for the cane rush which had survived since 1893. That first year it took the freshmen only five minutes to pull the sophomores into the Oyster River

The freshman-sophomore rope pull in October, 1917, with the class of 1921 in the water.

above the old wooden dam. It was a different story in 1916. At Beard's Creek, just below the Coe's Corner bridge, the tugging went on in heavy rain for an hour and seven minutes without a decision. At that point an unidentified humanitarian swam out and cut the rope in the middle of the stream. The Student Council supervised the numerous interclass contests and made an ineffectual attempt to control hazing.

The Student Council had been reorganized in 1912. It consisted of the president of the college, one faculty member, five fraternity men chosen by Casque and Casket, and two non-fraternity men who had to be juniors or seniors. The two-year students had their own council.

A Women's Council was initiated in 1911. It was given responsibility for drawing up and enforcing rules governing the conduct of the coeds. Callers could be received in the dormitory parlors Friday and Saturday nights until 10:00 P.M. Carriage rides, boating, and similar temptation-laden social activities must be chaperoned. Wom-

en students could attend only those entertainments approved by the dean.

There were numerous events appropriate for the innocent eyes and ears of the young ladies. The Glee Clubs gave Gilbert and Sullivan's *Trial by Jury* in April 1915 and *Iolanthe* in June. The following February the Men's Glee Club, accompanied by a twelve-piece orchestra, toured thirteen communities in New Hampshire, Vermont, and Maine. It made a similar tour the next year. The Women's Glee Club, which had started in 1913, staged *The Japanese Girl* in 1916. That was a big year for the College Dramatic Club. After presenting *The Private Secretary* in January, it began preparations for an April pageant to commemorate the 300th anniversary of Shakespeare's death. With more than one hundred students in a single scene, the pageant was presented in the gymnasium. The audience was served refreshments, prepared by the home economics classes from recipes of the days of Queen Elizabeth I.

Starting in 1912 the college sponsored what

was first known as the Lectures Course, then the Lyceum, then the Lectures and Concerts Course, and finally the Blue and White Series. Among the early presentations were the humorist John Kendrick Bangs, the Ben Greet Players in Shakespeare's *Comedy of Errors*, and former President William H. Taft. Tickets were a dollar for students, $1.50 for others, and provided admission to approximately six events.

Interest in politics was sparked in March 1912. The mid-morning train to Portland stopped in Durham for two minutes to allow former President Theodore Roosevelt, campaigning for delegates in the New Hampshire primary election, to speak from the platform of his Pullman. A Roosevelt club was formed, along with a rival Taft club. The following October a Wilson club made

its appearance. Interest in politics was still greater in 1916 when Wilson was battling for reelection against Hughes. Clubs supporting each candidate were started. In a straw vote, Hughes defeated Wilson 222 to 205. On election night a screen was set up in the gymnasium; returns relayed from *Foster's Daily Democrat* in Dover were flashed on the screen until 2:25 A.M.

Not to be left out of the political activity, the coeds in January 1917 organized a chapter of the National College Equal Suffrage League. (Remember? The nineteenth amendment to the U.S. Constitution, giving women the right to vote, did not become effective until 1920.) There was already a Women's League on campus, for faculty wives and others. It later became the Folk Club.

Working on the athletic field, New Hampshire Day 1916.

12. The College at War

The outbreak of World War I in August 1914 had little immediate effect on the campus. In November an order for one hundred pounds of mercury, placed by Professor James, was held up by the British government. The next month a small donation and a letter of sympathy signed by three hundred students were sent to the King and Queen of Belgium.

The principal impact of the early years of the war on the campus was the rising price level. In 1912 the catalog gave the estimated cost of a year at college from a low of $211 to a high of $335. Although tuition and fees remained much the same, the 1916-17 catalog estimated the cost for students to range from a low of $342 to a high of $442. The faculty were also feeling the pinch. To ease the shock of higher prices, the Durham Cooperative Society was organized about 1915 to buy food and other commodities at wholesale prices.

Federal legislation in June 1916 established the Reserve Officers' Training Corps. Accordingly, the College Cadet Corps was replaced by an ROTC unit in September 1917. Under the new program, freshmen and sophomore men were required to enroll in the basic course, with the advanced course being elective for juniors and seniors—an arrangement that survived until 1964. Graduates of the advanced courses received commissions as second lieutenants, usually in the Army Reserve.

Nor were the women to be caught unprepared by war. Beginning in April 1917, the coeds went on a four o'clock hike each afternoon, to make them physically fit for the national emergency.

The confusion of the war years was compounded by a change in the college administration. Not long after assuming office, President Fairchild began to be bothered by ill health. He was given a two-month leave of absence in 1914. In January 1916 he was given leave for the rest of the college year. He was able to attend the trustee meeting in June, but at that meeting arrangements were made to relieve him of some of his duties. Dean Taylor gave up his teaching assignments and devoted the time to the president's office.

Fairchild died on January 23, 1917. In a resolution adopted by the trustees in Concord next day, it was said: "During the past four years this college has prospered, under his guidance, as never before." Fairchild's salary was paid to his widow until May 1, and she was given use of the president's residence until July 1. The funeral was in the gymnasium on January 26. Those speaking at the services were the Reverend Vaughan Dabney, pastor of the Durham Church, Trustee James A. Tufts of Exeter, and President Lemuel H. Murlin of Boston University.

To replace President Fairchild, the trustees did not start by balloting on local favorites. Meeting in Concord two weeks after Fairchild's death, they appointed a committee of three to search for and screen applicants. Murkland had come from New Hampshire, Gibbs from Ohio, and Fairchild from Kansas. This time the choice fell on a man from Oregon, Ralph Dorn Hetzel. He was elected on June 23, 1917, six months to the day after Fairchild's passing.

Hetzel was born December 31, 1882, at Merrill, Wisconsin. He earned an A.B. and an LL.B. from the University of Wisconsin. On graduation from law school, he went to Oregon Agricultural College as an instructor and later professor of public speaking. He soon became a professor of political science. In 1913, five years after joining the faculty, he was made director of extension, a position he occupied when chosen by New Hampshire. Hetzel was thirty-four years old at the time.

Cadets at attention in front of Thompson Hall.

He took over from Dean Pettee, who had been acting president, on August 17. While his furniture was being placed in the president's house, he decided to go to Thompson Hall for a look at his office. Stopping in the middle of unpaved Main Street, he looked east, then west. Not a wheel was turning, nor a foot shuffling. He asked himself if he had made a mistake to come to an institution so far out in the country.

Hetzel arrived on a campus disrupted by war preparations. Those who normally would have received invitations to an inaugural instead received a printed notice. It announced Hetzel's appointment and stated that inauguration ceremonies, because of the war, would not be held. Thus was started, with a complete absence of public observance, as productive an administration as any in the institution's history.°

° Lack of ceremony was Hetzel's personal style. When he went to Pennsylvania State College in 1927—a prosperous and peaceful time—his inaugural was a simple affair held in connection with commencement, and no visiting dignitaries were invited.

In the spring of 1917 a faculty committee had drawn plans to offer the institution's facilities to the federal government. The trustees were seeking ways to satisfy faculty demand for higher salaries, to help meet the steeply rising cost of living. The 1917 baseball schedule had been cancelled and all formal social activities ruled out.

All classes were cancelled for the week following spring vacation, 1917. During this "preparedness week," the cadets drilled seven or eight hours a day and attended lectures on patriotic topics on four nights. Seniors and other men not in the Cadet Corps did practical work and wrote papers on war topics. Drilling was not confined to the students: the *New Hampshire* reported that thirteen members of the faculty could each morning "be seen faithfully pacing back and forth across the athletic field under the direction of Sergeant Hayes. They are being drilled in the school of the soldier and in squad movements and it is hard to say who is the most proficient. For ambition all honors are conceded Dad Henderson, however."

May 1917: the faculty potato patch was launched under the direction of "Pa" Taylor, seated in the wagon.

While other students were drilling, the band practiced in the gymnasium. Each night a detachment of a cadet officer, three sergeants, four corporals, and thirteen privates stood guard at the gymnasium (or armory, as it came to be called) to keep away unauthorized persons.

The women spent the mornings attending lectures, emphasizing Red Cross work. The click of knitting needles furnished background for the speaker's voices. In the afternoon they had demonstrations on the making of dressings and bandages and the canning of food; at four o'clock they went on their extended hike. A Red Cross chapter was organized under the leadership of Professor C. Floyd Jackson.

The resumption of classes after "preparedness week" did not see the return of normal campus life. More than five hundred students took part in a parade in Portsmouth. Any senior who left campus for military service or war work received his degree nevertheless. Underclassmen were given credit in their courses for the balance of the semester, with grades based on work done to date.

Five members of the faculty were given leaves for war work with the federal or state government. With his usual enthusiasm, Professor Richard Whoriskey, Jr., lectured about the state as often as six times a week. Serving on the state food-production committee were Director John Kendall, Dean Taylor, and professors O'Kane and Charles C. Steck. Recent graduates—Albert H. Brown '11, Oscar E. Huse '12, Ralph J. Bugbee '16, Westley J. Nelson '16, Lewis B. Robinson '16, Albert E. Smith '16, and Victor H. Smith '16 —worked for the state food committee in the counties.

Putting into practice what they were teaching, twenty-eight members of the faculty organized a "Factato Club" to raise potatoes on an acre and a half of land, where the university tennis courts are now. Shares, representing an estimated five bushels, were sold for $2.25 each to cover the cost of seed and fertilizer. Meticulous records, kept by Dad Henderson, showed a yield of 260 bushels at a cost of eighty cents each. (In 1918 the yield went up to 324 bushels.)

The final examination period was eliminated in 1917, and the abbreviated commencement moved up eight days to June 5. From June 18 to 23, the home economics department conducted a school on campus for thirty women to serve the state as home canning demonstrators.

At a trustee meeting on June 23, 1917, Dean Pettee summarized what the war had done to student enrollment. Of 550 students on campus at the beginning of the second semester, fully 322 had left. The departures were for officer training at Plattsburg (28), Harvard ROTC (2), U.S. Navy Reserve (21), U.S. Navy (8), New Hampshire National Guard (3), teaching agriculture (8), Red Cross (1), and of course farming (196 four-year and 55 two-year students). At the end of the second semester, only 130 women and 98 men students remained on campus.

College opened late in the fall of 1917. The war climate was seen in the addition of courses in English history and in military French. A physical examination, provided free of charge by Dr. E. B. Eastman of Portsmouth, was required of every student. The enrollment of men was down dramatically from the previous September, but a gain of thirty women gave an overall enrollment of 562. Campus life was less disrupted than it had been the previous spring. The football team played seven games, two of them with service teams. There were eleven games on the basketball schedule.

It was the fuel shortage that brought the war home to the campus. Beginning in December, the steam to the classroom buildings and the library was cut off at six in the evening until five next morning. The dormitories fared better, being heatless only from 11:00 P.M. to 5:00 A.M. To supplement the coal supply, ties from the old railroad right-of-way were taken up and used in the boilers. By December faculty members were cutting wood for use in their homes. During Christmas vacation students organized a wood-cutting contest to be waged in their home counties, pitting the college divisions against each other.

They cut two hundred cords of wood. The college was about to be closed in January when the arrival of several cars of coal made it possible to keep going. Beginning in February, however, electric power was cut off between 11:30 P.M. and 5:00 A.M.

In January 1918 the college calendar was shortened. Spring vacation and final examinations were omitted, making it possible to advance commencement from June 12 to May 1. The policy of granting full credit for the spring semester to students going on active military duty was continued that year. In a recruiting drive on campus the navy signed up twenty-seven reservists, mostly engineers. Faculty members from President Hetzel down were involved in the Emergency Food Production Committee organized at the state level early in 1918. The Experiment Station prepared twenty bulletins and six circulars on topics such as *War Breads, Meat Savers, Planning the War Garden,* and *How to Raise a Backyard Pig.* A total of 543,000 copies was printed.

To meet military needs for technicians, in April the U.S. War Department organized eight-week courses to be given on college campuses to train auto mechanics, machinists, blacksmiths, draftsmen, cooks, and bakers. New Hampshire College was one of the first to offer this training.

A committee was appointed to take charge of what came to be known as the Vocational Section, the Student Army Training Corps (SATC). Dean Hewitt was general chairman. Other assignments were Dad Henderson, food and lodging; Leon W. Hitchcock, electrician training; Eric T. Huddleston, construction of new buildings; Edward L. Getchell, gas engines and auto mechanics; Harold D. McBride, machinists and blacksmiths; and Lyman J. Batchelder, carpenter training. Eighteen special instructors were engaged to assist the regular faculty.

With commencement on May 1 and the first Vocational Section due May 17, preparations were somewhat rushed. A new kitchen at the north end of the gymnasium was started May 6,

Forge Shop Class of 1917.

New Hampshire College gets a new flag pole, compliments of the army training corps, August 5, 1918.

the work being done by the special instructors and the faculty. The building was completed and the equipment installed so that when the first detachment of 341 men arrived on the mid-morning train, May 16, they were served their noon meal in seventeen minutes.

The college did better in meeting deadlines than did the U.S. Army: the first officers arrived three days after the men. In the meantime Dean Hewitt took command, keeping the men busy with lectures, and assigning them to instructional divisions. Assignment was made on the basis of a questionnaire and an interview with an instructor. Few of the original assignments had to be changed.

The cooks and bakers got practical training in the mess halls. Over two hundred automobiles were repaired by the truck division. The electricians rewired Conant Hall and installed the wiring in Smith Hall Annex, two barracks, and a mess hall. The carpenter and concrete divisions

Top: Army training corps carpenters put the finishing touches on Smith Hall Annex. Center: The first barracks —later known as West Hall— was occupied before it was finished, July 12, 1918. Bottom: The concrete division poses with its instructor Sam Craig (in white shirt).

made the greatest impact, however. A special trustee meeting on June 29, 1918, approved plans for campus improvements to be made by these groups. The concrete division laid 2,742 square yards of sidewalk and poured 1,143 cubic yards of foundation. The carpenter division built numerous small buildings, the annex to Smith Hall, two additions to the shops buildings, and the two barracks. One of the barracks was built in thirty-nine and one-half working hours. It was wired and the plumbing installed so that the second detachment moved in upon arrival. The construction, though speedy, was not flimsy. "A Barrack," rechristened West Hall, was still housing male students half a century later.°

Dean Hewitt devised a novel training program. He suggested to the Boston & Maine Railroad that it put a few railroad cars in need of repair on the Durham siding and furnish the needed material; the carpenter division would repair them. Only one other college adopted this program, but there was a great demand for those who finished the training.

When only six weeks of the Vocational Section program had been completed, a request came for "40 carpenters, 15 gas engine men, and 3 heavy duty truck drivers for immediate overseas duty." The men were sent and performed creditably. Of the first detachment of 341 men, ninety-three were sent overseas by the time they had been in training seven weeks.

The army requested that lectures on morale be given the training detachment. Professor Whoriskey was picked for the task. By July he was giving two lectures a day, three days a week; a month later he was giving all of his time to the lectures and to visiting the men in barracks in the evening. Professor Alfred E. Richards led the men in war songs before each lecture.

In September an influenza epidemic struck.

° East-West halls were finally torn down in 1972. On Homecoming Day, 1973, sentimental alumni paid a total of sixty-two dollars for doors, keys, light fixtures, and other memorabilia from the old barracks.

The training unit was quarantined, entertainments were discontinued, and no one was allowed to walk along Main Street without a pass. Three houses were taken over for infirmaries. In spite of the precautions and care, eleven men died.

Altogether, five detachments were sent to the college. Four were from New Hampshire and one from New York. The breakdown of the total enrollment of 1,269 was as follows:

Auto truck division	308
Concrete division	197
Carpenter division	339
Electricians division	206
Blacksmiths division	50
Machinists division	87
Gas engine division	42
Draftsmen division	7
Cooks and bakers division	17
Clerks division	16

In the summer of 1918, plans were made to train student candidates as officers. A unit of this Student Army Training Corps was assigned to New Hampshire College. It was scheduled to open on September 25, with the civilian students (mostly women) to register October 1. The influenza epidemic delayed the start to the first week in October, while the civilian students did not come to campus until October 22. To adjust to the SATC pattern the college adopted the quarter system, with the summer quarter primarily for the servicemen. The men were housed in Fairchild Hall and in Kappa Sigma and Lambda Chi Alpha, with up to one hundred men in each of the fraternities. The officers in charge had quarters in the Alpha Tau Omega house. The Theta Chi house was reserved as a possible place for the training of war nurses, but it was never so used.

Students in the Collegiate Section, SATC, had drill eleven hours a week; classes fourteen, and supervised study twenty-eight. Courses open to them included English, French, German, chemistry, meteorology, European geography, drawing, descriptive geometry, trigonometry, logarithms, surveying and map making, U.S. history, indus-

Students parade to Dover on Armistice Day.

trial law, military science, military law, and sanitation and hygiene. Faculty members who were not needed to teach their specialties were assigned to other subjects. It had been planned that twenty-year-olds would be in the SATC for three months; nineteen-year-olds, six months; and eighteen-year-olds, nine months. The Armistice changed all that, and the men were discharged in December before they had finished the first term.

The civilian enrollment the fall quarter was 155 women and thirty-three men (of whom all but four were freshmen). But the campus was crowded with 464 in the Collegiate Section of the SATC and about 500 in the Vocational Section. Most courses normally taken by women were offered, but there was little instruction in agriculture. Professor Scott had a stroke during the summer of 1918 and was unable to teach during the fall, so Rev. Donald C. Babcock was hired to teach history to the SATC. While preaching in Somersworth he had become acquainted with President Fairchild and Dean Groves, who knew that he wanted to teach. Babcock recalled that the SATC men were not eager students, since the most capable were transferred to Plattsburg for officer training.

Others who began a long association with the institution that fall were Heman C. Fogg '18,

graduate assistant in chemistry; James H. Marceau, assistant professor of modern languages; Henry B. Stevens, assistant emergency demonstration agent for Rockingham County; Horace L. Howes, professor of physics; and M. Gale Eastman '13, assistant professor of agronomy.

With the delayed registration and a variety of programs, the campus had hardly settled into a routine when official verification of the Armistice on November 11 caused everything to change. President Hetzel and Major Stanley G. Eaton, commanding officer, declared a holiday to start at 10:00 A.M. The festivities began with a bonfire, after which all gathered around the flagpole. Professor Whoriskey presided, Sergeant Jack White led the songs and cheers, and President Hetzel spoke. It was voted to parade to Dover after lunch, with the women students riding in army trucks. The procession was met at Sawyer's Mills by the Dover band, which led it to the city hall. There was a thanksgiving service, followed by refreshments served by the city. Then there was the long walk back to Durham. Classes were resumed the next day, the shortened term coming to an end for the civilian students on December 14; the military units being disbanded the following day. The regular winter quarter was scheduled to start following Christmas vacation.

13. Hetzel Forges a University

When classes resumed in January 1919, the campus was almost back to normal. Coach Cowell, who had been on active duty as a lieutenant of field artillery, was home again and planning an athletic program. The fraternities too were back in business. They had conducted unsupervised pledging the previous fall, though with only thirty-three men on campus the competition must have been intense. Two local fraternities had gone national and a chapter of Phi Mu Delta had been organized, for a total of nine nationals on campus. The first postwar rushing season was held in the fall of 1919. Alpha Tau Alpha, down to three members, was able to pledge eighteen new brothers. The sororities were also expanding: in 1919, Delta Kappa (later a chapter of national Kappa Delta) was established and Pi Delta became a chapter of Phi Mu.

Changes even more remarkable were coming to the men and women living in the college dormitories. Upon the initiative of President Hetzel, Fairchild Hall was placed under student government in February 1919, with a proctor on each floor. Even the females had been given some responsibility for the preservation of their honor. In the spring of 1917, the rules were relaxed to allow the senior women to go riding, driving, motoring, and boating without chaperones.

The no-smoking tradition had been dealt a crippling blow by the invasion of the campus by the military during World War I. In recognition of the wishes of Benjamin Thompson, and also of John Conant, the catalog from 1893 had carried a statement that scholarships would be withdrawn from those using tobacco or intoxicating liquors. In 1905 the faculty had softened this rule by voting that it should be "interpreted as meaning that no student receiving money for any scholarship shall use tobacco on the street or in public places." Compliance was universal—for faculty as well as students. President Fairchild, who loved his pipe, would on occasion transfer a conference from his office to his home across the street so the participants could light up. But the times were now changing.

One of the first student organizations to revive when the campus returned to normal in 1919 was the Athletic Association. It was still responsible for the financial support of athletics, except for the salaries of coaches. Its funds had come from dues and gate receipts, but in the spring of 1918 the students had voted a yearly increase of five dollars in the student fee, the increase to go to the Athletic Association. In return each student got a ticket for admission to all home games, which formerly had sold for four dollars.

"The greatest and most successful football eleven that ever played a game for the Blue and White" was the way the *Granite* characterized the 1919 football team. It won seven games, losing only to Brown and Maine. The first string, with Dewey Graham as captain, included "Smiles" Leavitt, "Gad" Gadbois, "Doc" Bell, "Buck" Harvell, "Batch" Batchelder, "Ham" Anderson, "Ted" Butler, "Mac" McKenney, "Ducker" Davis, and "Dutch" Connor. Substitutes were Ernest Christensen, Earle Farmer, "Pete" Lovejoy, Clarence Waterman, "Merk" Haseltine, Carl Lundholm, and Charlie Reardon. The basketball and baseball teams were not quite so good, but both had winning seasons. In track Gordon T. Nightingale was the national intercollegiate cross-country champion and holder of the national indoor two-mile title.

At the first annual alumni meeting after the war, a memorial was proposed to honor the alumni who had lost their lives in the conflict. Meeting

with Hetzel in November 1919, the alumni decided to raise $25,000 to rebuild the athletic field. By the end of June pledges amounted to $10,000, but only $4,000 in cash had been received. In January 1921, when Coach Cowell said he had to have definite word on the project so he could plan his track and football activities for the coming year, pledges were $16,000 and cash on hand was only $6,700. Nevertheless, Cowell was told to plan on the new field: "Somehow—some way—we're going to get that money."

Memorial Field—now the women's athletic field —was dedicated on June 10, 1922. The alumni purchased a bronze tablet with the names of the war dead and placed it at the entrance to the field. The first game played there was the final one of 1922—a 56-7 victory over Massachusetts. It was an auspicious beginning for the new facility and a fitting close to the season. Under the leadership of "Dutch" Connor, the football team had opened its regular season with a 10-7 victory over the powerful Army team. A loss to Dartmouth and a tie with Springfield were the only setbacks of the year.*

In its first major fund drive, the Alumni Association had amassed a total of $27,885. The organization then went on to raise money for a series of memorial scholarships, also to honor the war dead. These tasks were eased by the fact that, in 1921, the trustees voted to authorize an alumni publicity manager and field representative. Professor Perley '08, a faculty member in the chemistry department since 1911, undertook the job as a part-time assignment. He started the

Above: Stalwarts of the Class of 1920 prepare for the freshman-sophomore rope pull; the cross-country team poses for its photograph.
Facing page: At work on the baseball field, 1921; a cane rush at Memorial Field.

---

* Football was not the only sport in which New Hampshire College was becoming a power. At Lake Placid in December 1923, the ski team took third place while its star, Gunnar D. Michelson of Berlin, N.H., won the Marshall Foch Trophy for the best jump. Another New Hampshire skier, Stewart Weston, won the Marshall Foch Trophy in 1924, and Ernest D. Pederson won it in both 1926 and 1927. The New Hampshire men were Eastern Intercollegiate champions in 1925. The following season they claimed undivided supremacy in winter sports—which, in those days, included snowshoeing and skating as well as skiing.

The serving line in Commons dining hall, 1922.

tecture and drawing. Professor Eric T. Huddleston was its head.

The Agriculture Division added agricultural engineering to the majors already available. For a short time, an eighteen-month program in forestry was offered for veterans.

The Arts and Science Division increased the number of quarter-term credits required for graduation from 204 to 216, at the same time raising the required grade in major subjects from 70 to 75. By 1922 each department was obliged to spell out its major and minor requirements in the catalog. Also in 1922, a year-long freshman course was introduced as a prerequisite for all courses in history, sociology, education, and economics. Titled "Introduction to Social Science," it would eventually evolve into "Introduction to Contemporary Civilization." History was moved from the social science to the humanities group. The B.A. degree was now awarded only to those majoring in the humanities group, with all others receiving the B.S.

With the authorization, given by the trustees in June 1921, to grant the Master of Arts degree, new regulations governing advanced degrees were adopted. The faculty committee on advanced degrees was charged with passing on the qualifications and the proposed plan of study of all candidates. About two-thirds of the work, including credit for a thesis, was to be in the major department and one-third in a minor department. Fifty-four quarter hours were required, of which at least eighteen must be in regularly scheduled classes. Up to half of the work could be transferred from another institution. An oral examination was required.

Although some summer courses for teachers had been offered before the turn of the century, it was not until 1922 that a regular six-week summer school was instituted under Dr. Herman Slobin, who had been hired as professor of mathematics in 1919. The enrollment of 107 the first year went up to 144 the second, including forty-eight teachers and school superintendents,

New Hampshire Alumnus, the first issue being dated March 1924.

Enrollment increased rapidly in the postwar years. The 607 students registered in 1918-19 had doubled to 1,230 within five years. With a plentiful supply of students, the faculty began to press for higher admissions standards. The trustees agreed to higher qualifications for out-of-state applicants, but voted to continue the policy that any New Hampshire graduate of a high school approved by the state Board of Education would be admitted. Since 1918, when vocational subjects were introduced to the high schools, this rather liberal policy had included graduates with as much as half their secondary-school work in such subjects.

Internal reforms came more easily. In the Technology Division, architecture was organized as a separate program in 1920-21, and the department of drawing was renamed the department of archi-

of whom ten were working for advanced degrees.

With the enrollment doubling, priority in campus construction had to be given to places for the students to sleep and eat. The 1917 legislature had appropriated $100,000 for the Commons dining hall. Professor Huddleston had been told to draw plans for it—the first of many campus buildings he designed. (In 1963 the Commons was renamed Huddleston Hall in his honor.) The plans were approved by the trustees in October 1917. Because of rising costs it was found necessary to eliminate the east wing. The revised plans were approved in January 1918 and contracts for the construction let, but a steel shortage held up progress. The building finally was ready in September 1919 and soon six hundred students a day were being served there. Men and women were not allowed to sit at the same table. A twenty-one meal ticket, with second servings allowed, sold for six dollars. The ground floor cafeteria seated 200, the main dining room 288, and the President's dining room on the second floor seated 25. Rooms on the third floor, originally intended for men, housed twenty-eight girls. Women students were required to eat in the Commons, but no such regulations applied to men until 1926. The dining hall was open seven days a week, fifty-two weeks a year, until it finally shut down for the Thanksgiving vacation in 1923.

Housing for men was provided in the barracks built by the SATC. Under the direction of Lyman J. Batchelder, woodworking instructor, wallboard partitions were erected to make double rooms for 160 men. Closets in the rooms were back to back; the residents soon cut holes in them to facilitate room-to-room visiting without bothering to go out in the hall. Heat was provided by a row of steam pipes which ran the whole length of the buildings. Shut-off valves were in the last room in each row, giving the occupants of that room the power to control the comfort of their mates down the row. The barracks remained in this condition until 1926, when the wallboard partitions were replaced by lath

Above: Faculty procession at the 1921 commencement. Bottom: Prof. Huddleston teaches a women's art class in DeMeritt Hall.

and plaster, and radiators were installed in each room. At this time the buildings were renamed East and West halls. Even with improvements the buildings were still considered "temporary."

Even though the women had taken over the top floor of the Commons, there still were not enough beds for them. The first women's dormitory, Smith Hall, had been made possible by a bequest from Mrs. Hamilton Smith. Her will had also provided that half her estate should, upon the death of her daughter, go to the college as the Alice Hamilton Smith Fund, the income to be used for the general purposes of the institution. The money became available in 1919. Although the trustees could not use the capital of the fund for building, they were able to borrow from it and did so to erect another women's dormitory, named Congreve Hall after Mrs. Smith's first husband. To rebuild the fund, $3,000 a year from the room rents of the dormitory were repaid to it. The new dormitory was ready for occupancy a few weeks after the opening of the college in September 1920. It was expanded by adding the center section in 1922.°

Hetzel did not leave the campus dotted with new buildings, although there were substantial gains in student housing. He left, instead, two great legislative victories. The first of these was the change in the name of the institution in 1923; the second was the millage act in 1925.

In the early days, agricultural enthusiasts were unhappy that "Mechanic Arts" was included in the title of New Hampshire College. The two major benefactors of the college, John Conant and Benjamin Thompson, sought to support agricultural education and accepted related disci-

plines as unavoidable evils. Still, it was the related disciplines that grew most vigorously. The alumni in 1910 had proposed that the name be changed to the University of New Hampshire, and this proposal was endorsed by the trustees. A bill to effect the change was actually introduced in the 1911 legislature, but was buried under the protests of the agricultural interests.

Twelve years later the situation had changed. The college had grown and expanded into many fields; of its three academic divisions, Arts and Sciences had shown the most dramatic growth. Both the students and the alumni were strongly in favor of university status. On January 10, 1923, the trustee minutes record that "The question of change in the corporate name of the college was referred to the Legislative Committee of the trustees, with power." House Bill No. 385, "An Act Relating to the New Hampshire College of Agriculture and the Mechanic Arts and Establishing the University of New Hampshire," met little opposition in either branch of the legislature. It was signed into law by Governor Fred H. Brown on April 23, 1923, to become effective on July 1.

Hetzel returned from Concord later that day and was met at the station by the student body. He was transported down Main Street in the Tom Thumb coach, followed by a parade of students carrying a banner with the legend "University of New Hampshire."° As the class of 1923 would graduate before the change in name became official, Hetzel arranged to have their diplomas carry a statement that the college became a university in the year of their graduation.

July 1, 1923, fell on Sunday, so the trustees held the organizational meeting of the new university in Nashua the next day. The two senior members of the faculty in terms of service, Dean Pettee and Professor Scott, were invited to be

---

° If housing was tight for the students, it was even worse for the faculty. Professor Babcock recalled that he was obliged to live in Somersworth when he was hired in 1918. He took a train shortly after 6:00 A.M., reaching Durham in time for the eight o'clock class; he returned to Somersworth by the 6:15 P.M. train. When a vacancy opened in Durham, "it was dog eat dog." Hearing of a rental, Babcock telephoned the owner and secured the place, to the chagrin of a colleague who had made his plea by mail.

° The coach, made in England, was given to Mr. and Mrs. Tom Thumb by Queen Victoria. It was later acquired by a Walpole, New Hampshire, couple who gave it to the college in memory of their son, Maxwell Smalley '17. The coach is now in the Ford Museum in Dearborn, Michigan.

Jubilant students give President Hetzel a carriage ride as NHC becomes UNH—April 23, 1923.

present. Hetzel read the act establishing the institution, the full name of which was the University of New Hampshire and the New Hampshire College of Agriculture and the Mechanic Arts. (This title was carried on the university catalog for the next twenty years, and until 1939 duplicate sets of minutes of the trustees were kept.) A set of bylaws and a university seal were adopted. President Hetzel, the faculty, and all other employees of the college were elected to the same positions in the university.

As part of the transition, the finance committee of the trustees was instructed to study the status of trust funds. In October 1923, the trustees voted that all funds appropriated for the New Hampshire College of Agriculture and the Mechanic Arts—and all bequests, receipts, and other funds held by the college, except for the Benjamin Thompson fund—were to be held and used as funds of the University of New Hampshire.

The change in name did nothing to improve the institution's financial situation, which had become progressively worse during the early years of the Hetzel administration. The growth of en-

rollment and war-induced inflation both contributed to the difficulties. Small grants from the state's contingency fund during the 1917-19 biennium were not sufficient to enable the institution to meet day-to-day demands. Federal payments for the army units were insufficient to meet costs and had to be adjusted. (Two federal auditors came to the campus in the spring of 1919 and made satisfactory adjustment of the college claims. After they left, Dad Henderson sent a sizeable check to a grocery firm in Boston in settlement of its account and was shocked to be informed that there was over $5,000 still due. A bill for the amount claimed, on paper somewhat smaller than the others, had stuck to another bill and had been overlooked. Henderson caught the auditors at Dartmouth and was successful in getting an adjusted claim accepted.)

By July 1919 the college had borrowed $30,300. An increased appropriation by the 1919 legislature still did not keep up with the enrollment and inflation.

The faculty was feeling the pressure of the rising cost of living, and a committee headed by Professor Walter C. O'Kane had requested increased salaries. Even though they did not know where they would find the money, the trustees promised substantial raises. The year before, the trustees had established $3,600 as the top salary for a dean or director and $3,000 for a department head; when the new salary scale went into effect July 1, 1920, increases averaged over twenty percent.

In September 1920, tuition went from $60 to $75 and fees from $30 to $36. Room rents were also increased. The next year, out-of-state tuition went to $150 and fees for all four-year students became $50. For the two-year agriculture course tuition was $50 in-state and $100 out-of-state with fees for both at $35.

These rising student expenses combined with the rapidly growing enrollment put pressure on the institution's resources for financial aid. The annual legislative appropriation for free tuition had grown to $6,000. It was out of this that the Grange° and Senatorial scholarships were paid. Since the institution exercised no control over the awarding of these, the result was that some of the scholarships were going to students with little need while there was nothing available for other students with much greater need. In April 1921 the regulations were changed. The Granges and senators, instead of awarding the scholarships, henceforth made recommendations on forms supplied by the college. The college authorities then made the awards on the basis of the student's financial requirements. At the same time, the college dropped the traditional provision that scholarships would be forfeited should the student use tobacco or intoxicating liquor. Also in 1921, the legislature decreed that the scholarships going to juniors and seniors should be not outright grants but loans to be repaid with interest after graduation. The repaid money was to go to a student loan fund.

° In 1904 the trustees had voted that each subordinate and Pomona Grange in the state could annually appoint one student to receive from the college a full-tuition scholarship ($60).

A deficiency appropriation of $112,318 by the 1921 legislature—to which the governor and council added another grant of $18,720—finally enabled the college to clear up its debts. Beyond this appropriation, the 1921 legislature voted $638,705 for college operations over a two-year period. The generosity of the legislature did, however, have its limits. The 1923 session was asked for a classroom structure and additions to the Commons and Congreve Hall. No money was voted for buildings, and the operating appropriation was only $600,738. The governor and council, from their emergency fund, provided $20,000 for improvements.

It was becoming increasingly obvious to Hetzel and the trustees that a more stable means of state support would need to be found to replace the unpredictable biennial appropriations of the legislature. When the college opened its doors in Durham, there was one student for each 6,272 of the state's population. When it became a university in 1923, there was a student for every 503 of population. Nearly three-quarters of the students earned some or all of their college expenses. Low-cost education was essential to them.

As early as 1920, the trustees had investigated the mill tax as a means of support. In his 1924 report Hetzel stated: "A ten-year program based on a millage tax allowance, which would be adequate to care for the maintenance of the institution and at the same time make available a certain sum for the development of the physical plant, would be both economical and statesmanlike." In lieu of an adequate millage tax, he suggested a state bond issue for buildings.

The estimated needs for the 1925-27 biennium totaled $844,555. Governor John G. Winant, a strong supporter of the university, was in attendance at a trustee meeting in Concord on January 16, 1925. A resolution was adopted which said in part: "An extreme emergency exists . . . because of the serious lack of . . . classroom buildings and dormitories." Hetzel and a committee were authorized to submit a plan to the legislature for future support and development.

In his statement of the plan, Hetzel said in part:

In view of the educational traditions of our people, the increasing importance of higher education, the growing need for scientific investigation, [and] the decreasing opportunity for collegiate training in the endowed colleges of the country, the maintenance and continued development of the University on a sound and conservative basis is imperative . . . . [The trustees] have estimated that within a period of fifty years, the University will have an enrollment of 2,000 to 2,500 . . . .° The trustees . . . have laid out a plan for the development of the physical plant . . . . It would be sound public policy for the legislature of the state to provide for the maintenance of the University and for its development in accordance with such plan . . . . This could be done in any one of several ways, but probably best by following a plan now in effect in several of the states, by which there would be set aside each year from the income of the state an amount of money bearing a definite ratio to the assessed valuation of the property of the state . . . . It is estimated that an allowance at the rate of approximately one mill on a dollar would provide sufficient funds . . . . Such a policy would seem to represent an economical, efficient procedure, and would have the additional virtue of representing a policy of pay-as-you-go.

Both major political parties were in favor of making adequate provision for the university, as were the state Grange, the state Federation of Women's Clubs, the Women's Christian Temperance Union, the Legion Auxiliary, the Parent-Teachers Association, the League of Women Voters, and many other organizations. Governor Winant recommended that the legislature make a survey of the university. A committee made up of members of both houses was authorized to make the survey; the result was House Bill 403: "An Act providing for a fund to be known as the 'University of New Hampshire Fund' and regulating the enrollment of students at the University of New Hampshire."

° The enrollment reached 2,000 in thirteen years. In September 1973, with two years still to run on Hetzel's forecast, the campus at Durham had an enrollment of 9,755.

There was little opposition to the bill, which was signed into law by Governor Winant on April 22, 1925. It provided that there be credited to the fund, each year, an amount equal to one-tenth of one percent of the assessed valuation of all property in the state. With the consent of the governor and council, the trustees could borrow for building, up to $100,000 in a fiscal year, but this had to be repaid the following fiscal year. Any income received by the university from other sources was to be retained by the institution. The new law also provided that, beginning July 1, 1925, new out-of-state students would be limited to twelve percent of the preceding entering class—eight percent from Maine, Vermont, and Massachusetts, and four percent from elsewhere.

The income from the millage law was not munificent, but it was substantial and predictable. The first year it amounted to $585,422, out of which was to come both operating and building costs. The year before the legislature had appropriated $370,513 for operating costs and nothing for buildings. The law's great virtue was that it enabled the university to plan ahead for development of its academic programs and buildings.

The county extension agents were not supported out of the "mill tax" income because, in the same session of the legislature, a law was passed that they be paid jointly by county, state, and federal funds. The state made an appropriation of $36,000 to cover its share. This new base of support made it possible for New Hampshire to be the first state to have agricultural, home economics, and club agents in every county. The Experiment Station, which did receive a small part of its support from general university funds, profited when in 1925 the Parnell Act was passed by Congress. This provided the station with an additional $20,000 the first year, with increases each year thereafter until the annual contribution reached $90,000.

14. Building for the Future

The new charter in 1923 and the mill tax law in 1925 did not come about by accident. Adrian O. Morse, who worked closely with Hetzel in Durham and who later served as his provost at Pennsylvania State College, has recalled how shrewdly Hetzel campaigned for these landmark pieces of legislation.

In those years, the typical legislator considered his prime function to be the keeping down of taxes. The New Hampshire legislature was encouraged in its thrift by lobbyists—especially those for the railroads—who kept asking why the state should pour money into the Durham campus when it already had Dartmouth College. Nor did the agricultural interests give the support that might have been expected. Many farmers did not see the need for "scientific" agriculture.

To overcome this reluctance, Hetzel carried on a vigorous campaign to acquaint the legislators with the institution. In 1925, for example, a legislative committee or delegation was entertained on campus every Friday, arriving in Durham on the morning train. The first stop was for coffee and doughnuts at the Faculty Club, a small wooden building originally intended as a recreation center for the World War I training units. Here Clement Moran photographed the group. A tour of the campus followed, including examples of the best and the worst buildings. At the dairy building the visitors received an ice cream cone; at the greenhouse they were presented with a carnation. After dinner at noon there was a convocation, with the legislators seated on the platform, and selected members of the delegation were asked to speak. The first speaker would be a friend of the institution. He would be followed by one or two of doubtful attitude. Gazing down on the attentive faces of the assembled students—who had been briefed beforehand on the importance of exemplary behavior—these men would invariably be inspired to pledge support in the future. More coffee and doughnuts would follow the convocation. Just before the departure of the five o'clock train, Moran would give each legislator a print of the group photograph he had taken on their arrival.

Hetzel's remarkable accomplishment in advancing the University of New Hampshire had not gone unnoticed around the country. At a special meeting of the trustees on September 20, 1926, he announced that he had been offered the presidency of Pennsylvania State College and would soon be leaving Durham.

Of rather severe mien, Hetzel had not generated among students and faculty that feeling of warmth that is associated with popularity. Professor Babcock characterized him as "a young man in a hurry." But he was fair, approachable, and considerate in his dealings with those on campus. His promises were as good as gospel, and he had come to be held in great respect. The trustees had unlimited faith in him. Upon learning of his resignation, they set up a special committee with power to do anything possible to keep him, but the offer from Penn State proved beyond the means of New Hampshire to match. Hetzel's departure was set for January 1, 1927. In accepting the resignation, trustee president Harvey L. Boutwell wrote:

During your nine years as president, our University has prospered to a far greater degree than any of us had reason to predict . . . . I am sure that every trustee will agree with me in saying that you are primarily entitled to the credit for the greater part of the prosperity which has come to our University during your administration. You have at all times had the confidence and esteem not only of the trustees, but also of the faculty, the student body, the alumni, and the people of New Hampshire.

If growth is a measure of prosperity, Boutwell was correct to say that the institution had prospered under Hetzel. When he left, the student body numbered 1,784—triple the enrollment when he had come to Durham. The fifty-six faculty members had become 103. Even more significant was the change in baccalaureate degrees granted at the first and last commencements of Hetzel's presidency:

	1918	1926
Agriculture	23	25
Technology	13	41
Liberal arts	31	133

The college had become a university in fact, and one clearly dominated by the liberal arts. A department of philosophy and psychology had been added in 1925. Teacher training in manual arts had been transferred to technology, which in turn had been strengthened by the addition of a civil engineering department in 1926. Work in home economics was expanded. "Prescribed curricula" were instituted in women's physical education, pre-law, pre-medicine, and pre-architecture. A business program had been added. By 1926-27, special teaching methods courses were offered by eleven departments in all three colleges. These were followed by practice teaching under the direction of the education department. A modest start in what is now called "continuing education" was made in 1924 when Professor John W. Twente of the education department offered a credit course in Laconia during the fall term.

The summer school continued under Professor Slobin's direction until 1927, when Professor Justin D. Wellman of education took over. Beginning in 1926 students could earn credits by joining the European Study Tour under Dr. Hamilton F. Allen of the language department. Thanks largely to the summer school, the enrollment in "short courses" (which included two-year agriculture) had swollen to 666 by the time Hetzel left the university.

Even more heartening, there was evidence that the quantitative gains were eventually to be matched by qualitative ones. In April 1926, the trustees finally yielded to faculty pressure and voted that, starting in 1927, officers of the university were "authorized to put into effect a selective process for the admission of students, residents of the state, similar to the process used . . . in selecting out-of-state students."

The faculty were less successful in lobbying for their own welfare. In his 1924 report Hetzel had said: "No provision has been made . . . for retirement allowances to those who have given their life's work to the institution. The University has now reached the point where this question is acute." He proposed that the question be studied and suggested that a good plan would be one in which the University would contribute to faculty annuities through the Teachers Insurance and Annuity Association. The trustees appointed a committee to study the matter, but no plan was adopted until the Engelhardt administration.

The need for such a program was highlighted by the situation of Professor Scott, who had started his career with the institution in 1876. Following a stroke in 1918, having no other means of livelihood, he had returned to teaching in January 1919 although he was nearly blind and deaf. He was able to read his lectures but was not aware of what was going on in the class. Professor Babcock went to Scott's class on the top floor of Hamilton Smith one day, to discover that the boys had reached out the windows to get icicles off the eaves, which they were tossing about the room. Babcock entered by a side door and chided the students for taking advantage of a man who could not defend himself. The class quieted down, and Babcock left without Scott's knowing he had been in the room. In 1925 Scott was given an undemanding appointment as university historian and relieved of part of his teaching.

Hetzel also favored establishment of a policy on sabbatical leaves. A plan prepared by the faculty committee on educational policy and

The student body massed in the "ampitheater," 1924.

method was submitted to the trustees in May 1925. The only result was that a year later the trustees went on record in favor of any action Hetzel might take to encourage the faculty to pursue graduate study.[*] To improve their status, in February 1925 the faculty formed a chapter of the American Association of University Professors.

Although the growth of the student body had stimulated most campus activities, it proved fatal to one. The eighth and final New Hampshire Day was held in 1924. These occasions had contributed an annual cleanup and countless improve-

[*] Always one to exhort by deed as well as word, Hetzel himself had arranged in 1922 to have a year's leave of absence. He wanted to pursue courses in the administration of higher education offered by the University of Chicago. Upon applying for admission to the Chicago program, he received a reply saying that the university had been unable to find a competent instructor for the courses, and asking Hetzel to teach them. He declined the invitation and canceled his leave.

ments to the campus: building cinder and concrete sidewalks, planting eighteen maple trees to honor students killed during World War I, constructing and improving numerous sports areas, painting fire equipment, building a log cabin in the College Woods, and clearing an amphitheater behind Hamilton Smith Library. In 1921 the Fox newsfilm company had sent a crew to cover the event. But by 1924 the willing hands were so numerous that the university could no longer provide enough tools to keep them all busy.

Among the sports facilities constructed by New Hampshire Day volunteers was a ski jump on Beech Hill in the town of Madbury. The activities of the second winter carnival were centered there. The carnival, a one-day event first sponsored by the forestry club in 1922, proved such a success that the Outing Club was organized the following year to take charge of it thereafter.

In 1926 the student body adopted the wildcat as the official mascot of the University of New Hampshire. The same year saw the first campaign to elect the "Mayor of Durham," the honor going to Laurence V. Jensen '27. In 1926, too, the automobile emerged as a significant part of undergraduate life—and a significant headache for university officials. A rule was adopted that year which read: "No student in the University will be permitted to operate any motor vehicle during the time the University is in session without written permission from the Executive Secretary, such permission to be based on already indicated necessity and subject to revocation at any time. No permits will be granted to minor students except on the written consent of parent or guardian." The executive secretary at that time was Adrian O. Morse. Unhappily for students who flouted the rule, "Tony" Morse doubled as dean of men and as judge of the Durham municipal court.

Two more fraternities, Phi Delta Upsilon and Sigma Beta, were added to the Greek world. Consideration was given to allotting university land for fraternity houses, as had been done in the case of Kappa Sigma, but in 1925 building lots became available on Madbury Road. Sigma Alpha Epsilon, Theta Chi, and Theta Upsilon Omega purchased lots, thus establishing the present "fraternity row."

The first sorority to build a house was Alpha Xi Delta. The university trustees helped matters along in January 1924 by voting to guarantee a $10,000 loan to the sisters; Professor Huddleston designed the house, and it was ready for occupancy in December. Mortgage loans were later guaranteed for Chi Omega, Mu Alpha, Theta Upsilon Omega, Phi Mu Delta, and Sigma Alpha Epsilon. In the 1930s, however, these mortgage guarantees posed a problem for the trustees, and since that time the university has left fraternities and sororities to handle their own finances.

The Greek-letter building boom helped ease the university's perennial housing shortage. By

Above: The cabin in College Woods (destroyed by the hurricane of 1938).
Below: The mascot and its keeper.

May 1925, however, the situation was still so tight that the trustees voted to construct another men's dormitory, named for President Hetzel even before plans for it were completed. A new power plant was authorized in 1926. The water tower behind Nesmith Hall was completed in 1924, when the university began to supply water to the town on an informal basis, pending the working out of a permanent cooperative arrangement. The negotiations were speeded by the events of February 15, 1924, when a spectacular blaze destroyed the Pettee Block in downtown Durham. This five-story frame building contained Gorman's pharmacy and other stores on the first floor, with student rooms on the upper floors. Mrs. Gorman discovered the fire in the middle of the night, made her way up the fire escape, and roused the sleeping students in time for them to escape. The near-tragedy was an impetus for the town and the university to cooperate in matters of water

supply and fire protection, as they have done ever since.

One major academic building was started in 1926 but not completed while Hetzel was on campus. Shortly before former president Murkland's death in November 1926, he was informed that the new building would be named for him. Murkland Hall was the first building on campus to be built to house the liberal arts.

In building as in organizational structure, what Hetzel did was to lay the groundwork for the future. During his administration five large tracts of land were purchased and added to the university campus. In April 1924 a landscape architect, Bremer W. Pond of Boston, was engaged to prepare plans for future development. And Hetzel himself drew up a five-year building plan, complete with the rationale for each building, its probable cost, and the expected source of the funds with which to build it.

Campaigns for "Mayor of Durham" were a regular feature on campus from 1926 to about 1960.

15. Lewis and the Great Depression

To perform the duties of the president between the departure of Hetzel and the arrival of his successor, the trustees set up a seven-member commission. The commission in turn established a two-man executive committee consisting of Trustee James A. Tufts and Executive Secretary Adrian O. Morse. Tufts was not on campus much, so in effect Tony Morse was acting president.

The interim administration did not have an easy time. Governor Huntley N. Spaulding liked the university, but he liked the taxpayer more. In the 1927 session of the legislature two bills were introduced to cut the university's income. The first, in the Senate, would have cut the rate under the mill tax formula to three-quarters of a mill. It came before the Senate on March 29 with a favorable committee report, but was tabled on a roll call vote. A week later it was sent back to committee. When the bill came out of committee again on April 13, it proposed to cut the mill tax rate not to three-fourths but to seven-eighths. It was killed by a voice vote.

In the House the attack came from a different angle. The House bill provided that, from the annual payment to the university under the millage law, the state would deduct the interest paid on the trust funds it held in the university's name. In addition to the original Land Grant Fund ($4,800 a year), there were the Benjamin Thompson Fund ($31,895), the Valentine Smith Scholarship Fund ($400), and the Samuel S. Whidden Fund (about $800). Other trust funds, such as the Conant, were held by the university, and would not have been affected.

The fight for this bill was led by Rep. Joseph A. Rogers of Rumney, who was the governor's righthand man in the House. The fight for the university was led by Morse, with assistance from Dad Henderson (who was serving his first term in the legislature) and from the growing body of alumni. The committee reported the bill as inexpedient, but Rogers came to the floor with a minority report. When the vote was taken, his lonely voice was overwhelmed by the supporters of the university.

Early in 1927, Walter M. Parker died. He had been treasurer of the institution since 1898. Governor Spaulding advocated the election of the state treasurer as the university treasurer also, thus concentrating the financial affairs of the institution in Concord. Some of the trustees thought this was a good idea, but others believed it would make the university subservient to the politicians in the State House.

Tony Morse and the others backed Raymond C. Magrath for treasurer. Magrath had joined the staff as chief clerk in 1922 and had become the business secretary in 1923.

At the April 1927 meeting of the Board of Trustees the election was held. Magrath and two others were nominated. On the second ballot Magrath was elected by a one-vote majority. Spaulding did not take his defeat lightly and refused to reappoint three trustees who had actively opposed him, and whose terms expired while he was governor.

At the same meeting Edward Morgan Lewis was elected president of the university. Born at Machynlleth, Wales, on December 25, 1872, Lewis had come to this country at the age of nine. He earned a Bachelor of Arts degree from Williams College in 1896 and a Master of Arts from the same institution in 1899. Although foreign-born, he took so readily to the great American sport of baseball that he pitched for the Boston Braves from 1896 to 1900 and for the Boston

A class in quantitative chemistry, Conant Hall.

Red Sox the following season. A religious man, his contracts provided that he would not be called upon to play on Sundays. From 1897 to 1901 he coached the Harvard baseball team.

Lewis was appointed instructor in elocution at Columbia in 1901, and in 1904 he returned to his alma mater as instructor of public speaking. He was promoted to assistant professor before going to Massachusetts Agricultural College as dean in 1911. At Massachusetts he served at various times as head of the department of languages and literature, head of the humanities division, acting president, and finally president. He was president from 1926 until he left to take over at the University of New Hampshire, September 1, 1927.

Lewis started his administration with a financial prospect more promising than any enjoyed by his predecessors. Murkland Hall was just completed. The fight against reduction of the millage formula had been won earlier in the year, promising a modest amount of money for future construction. At the meeting in April at which Lewis had been elected, the trustees had voted

that the next construction should be a new power plant and an addition to Congreve Hall.

Impressed by the reputation the chemistry department had attained under Professor Charles James, Lewis believed that it should have more suitable quarters. Consequently, at the first meeting of the trustees attended by Lewis, the earlier vote to add a wing to Congreve Hall was rescinded in favor of a new chemistry building to cost an estimated $386,000. The new structure was to be west of DeMeritt Hall, to match Murkland to the east, so it was necessary to move the greenhouses then on the site. For new greenhouses, $55,000 was voted.° The chemistry building plans—the joint effort of "King" James, Professor Thomas G. Phillips, and architect Eric Huddleston—were approved in January 1928, with work to start in the spring.

Professor James did not live to see the new facility. He died in Boston on December 10,

° The greenhouses were completed in 1929 at a cost of $60,222. They were to be moved again twenty years later to make way for Kingsbury Hall.

*Dairy barn under construction in 1931, with
tree on ridge pole to bring good luck.*

1928, from pneumonia following surgery. Born in
England, he had joined the faculty in 1906 as an
instructor in chemistry. He was an internationally
recognized authority on rare earths, having been
awarded the Nichols medal in 1912—the second
time this honor had come to New Hampshire College. When Professor Parsons left in 1912, James
had succeeded him as chairman of the
department.

Lacking adequate laboratories and with limited
financial support, he nevertheless attracted superior graduate students who helped carry on his research. His correspondence with scientists around
the world was filed in what his colleagues called
a three-dimensional system: piles of letters on a
desk. When the desk top was filled, he made
new space by placing a board across the
pulled-out writing extensions on the front.
Wanting a certain item, he would quickly select
the pile in which it was located, reach in at the
proper height, and pull it out.

King James was thesis adviser for Bradford

McIntire '25, who has provided this recollection
of him:

In spite of being a giant physically and intellectually,
he was a very sincere and extremely down-to-earth
gentleman, warm and genuine . . . . At the beginning
of a final exam period he entered the room and said,
"Gentlemen, I am about to finish another separation of
praseodymium and neodymium, which I have been
working on for a long time. I am going to leave
you—knowing that you will all take this exam without
help or communication." He never used the word
"cheat." During the unmonitored exam period no one
violated his confidence.

He was an inveterate pipe smoker, and Jim Gorman,
who ran the local drug store, imported for him a tobacco called Craven's Mixture. Of course, we all decided
to smoke just that. He had a sly and cute habit—on a
new student—to request some tobacco. He would produce a very small pipe, and then when you handed
over your tobacco can, he would produce a huge-
bowled pipe that would consume at least half a can of
your prized tobacco.

When an edict came down . . . that there should be
no smoking on campus, classrooms and offices in-

cluded, we were in a real dilemma . . . . After lab at four or four-thirty we would gather in the upper office for consultation, a chat, etc.—Dr. Fogg, Professor Smith, and I. On occasion the "King" would join us. One afternoon came a knock on the door as we were all enjoying our pipes. In walked Dr. Hetzel. Professor James greeted him cordially and after a short discussion the President left. Whereupon "King" James said, "Gentlemen, I am proud of you. No one tried to hide his pipe." We waited for repercussions which never came.

While the bell of the Durham church was tolling for James's funeral, the steel ridgepole of the new chemistry building was being lowered into place. At their meeting in January 1929 the trustees named the building Charles James Hall.

The $487,040 spent on James Hall absorbed so much of the funds available through the millage law that no major construction could be planned for 1930. A number of minor projects were authorized, however. These included a new practice house for home economics, a new dairy barn, a sewage disposal plant on the banks of the Oyster River, some remodeling occasioned by the relocation of departments following completion of Murkland and James halls, and a tunnel for steam lines along Main Street. The steam lines were roofed over by a sidewalk warm enough to melt snow which fell on it. In connection with this project, the heating system was changed from steam to hot water.

The first major gift from an alumnus provided a modern infirmary, Hood House, with accommodations for thirty patients plus a suite of guest rooms. Charles H. Hood, the only member of the class of 1880, and his wife gave $125,000 for construction of the building and an additional $75,000 for its maintenance. At its dedication on June 12, 1932, the principal speaker was Ray Lyman Wilbur, M.D., Secretary of the Interior.

By January 1932 the financial situation was healthy enough that it was possible to attend to the acute dormitory shortage, relief of which had been shelved when it was decided to build James Hall. Instead of proceeding with the plan to add a wing to Congreve Hall, a new building to house 120 women was authorized. It cost $140,000 and was named for Professor Scott, whose half-century of service to the university had ended with his death on May 8, 1930. He had been one of the chief advocates of coeducation in the old days at Hanover.

By the time Scott Hall was completed in the fall of 1932, New Hampshire was beginning to feel the impact of the Great Depression. On December 15 the trustees held a special meeting in Concord at which the state comptroller presented figures to show the need for "rigid retrenchment." He urged the trustees to aid the state's financial crisis by a moratorium on building. The trustees had little choice but to suspend building and to vote that "a sum equivalent to 20 per cent of the millage fund established by state law be appropriated during each year of the next biennium to the State Treasurer for the use of the State, provided, however, that no alteration of the existing millage law is effected by legislation."

In the four years beginning July 1, 1934, only $26,000 of state money went into construction and improvements. By September 1933 there was the prospect of securing federal funds for construction. Seventeen projects were considered; the number was finally reduced to seven, including recreational fields ($133,000) and a new water supply ($67,000). Civil Works Administration funds were secured for construction of the playing fields and a new reservoir.

The alumni agreed to raise $15,000 to buy materials for a stadium on the new playing fields. The trustees loaned this amount to the Alumni Association from the general investment funds of the university, to be repaid with interest in two or three years. The loan had to be extended because at the end of three years only $10,497 had been raised to repay it.

Before the financial crisis became severe, the university had purchased several parcels of land which became important in later development of the institution. In 1930 Professor O'Kane sold most of the former Albert DeMeritt farm, 110 acres, to the university as a site for agricultural activities. The next year George G. Hoitt sold the old DeMeritt-McDaniel farm of 125 acres on Mill Road. This is now the site of some of the buildings on College Road, south of the ravine, and of the faculty housing development.

Building was not the only phase of university operations affected by the Depression. In the 1932-33 budget the trustees did not provide for the usual salary increments. The income from the millage formula had been about $620,000 a year up to June 30, 1933; for each of the next two years it dropped to $413,568. The chairman of the House Appropriations Committee requested the university to reduce salaries, as was being done in other state departments and institutions. For the 1933-35 biennium all university salaries over $1,500 were cut ten percent. When the millage income went up to $439,749 a year in the next biennium, the salary cuts were reduced to five percent. The millage income was restored to its former level in 1937-38, and salaries went back to their 1932-33 level.

In April 1928 Lewis had secured authority to "grant instructors short leaves of absence for professional improvement provided they can be taken without additional expense to the State." This policy was liberalized in June 1930 to provide up to six months' leave with full pay, once every seven years, for those with the rank of assistant professor or above. Each case was to be decided on its individual merits. Often the candidate had to arrange with his colleagues to assume part of his load, since hiring a replacement at additional expense was not permitted. Even this carefully guarded arrangement was suspended during 1932-33, "in view of the depression and its attending problems and difficulties."

In his 1929 report Lewis made a strong plea for the establishment of a retirement system. He noted the plight of "several members on our staff who have literally given their lives to the institu-tion and who, as compared with colleagues in other institutions, are forced to labor to the limit of strength." He called attention to the program of the Teachers Insurance and Annuity Association and suggested, as an alternative, a form of group insurance with an estimated cost of $6,000. It was not until 1934 that his efforts resulted in a trustee-faculty conference to try to work out a policy. Lewis did not live to see any tangible results of the deliberations.

Prior to the market crash of 1929, tuition had been increased. The in-state rate had gone from $75 to $150 and the out-of-state rate from $150 to $250. The apparent doubling of the in-state tuition was actually an increased cost to the student of $20.50, because most former fees were absorbed in the new tuition rate. The actual increase for out-of-state students was $45.50. The only fee retained was five dollars for a diploma. In 1929-30 room rents varied from $63 to $120, and board at the Commons was $215. Total cost for a year at the university for an in-state student was estimated to run from a low of $453 to a high of $655.

The number of tuition scholarships was increased to 225 in 1928-29 and to 250 the following year. By 1933-34, the general economic situation was so bad that the amount available for tuition loans was increased to $32,500, and $10,000 was taken from general reserves to be used for employment of students on special campus projects.° Federal funds for student labor became available in February 1934, and by the end of the

---

° Although the university tried to help its students remain in college, there still were hardship cases. Gordon O. Thayer '32 could not find a job when he graduated and so had stayed on to work for an Ed.M. Near the end of the first term he met President Lewis in the corridor. Lewis asked the lad how he was doing. Thayer replied that he would have to drop out for the second term because he could not raise the money for room and board. Lewis invited him to his office and personally loaned him $100—later increased to $150—without interest. Dr. Thayer returned to the administrative staff of the university in the 1960s to play a major role in the development of the Merrimack Valley Branch.

year $7,148 from this source had supplemented the university funds. As many students were finding it impossible to get summer jobs, the trustees set aside $15,000 for student summer employment on campus projects.

In the 1936-37 academic year, 953 students received a total of $147,805 in financial aid. This was broken down as follows: $38,409 in university student labor funds, $26,673 on National Youth Administration jobs, scholarships totaling $30,933, and loans to the amount of $51,389.

The plight of the students encouraged private gifts to augment the loan fund. The largest contributors were Dr. James B. Erskine of Tilton, $8,000; Mrs. Mary D. Carbee of Haverhill, $19,000; and Huntley N. Spaulding of Rochester, $15,000. Beginning in 1932 the Cogswell Benevolent Trust of Manchester started an annual gift of twenty scholarships of $200 and ten of $100.

The loan program was very important in helping students finish college. Graduating seniors who had borrowed from the fund ranged from forty-two percent in 1932 to fifty-seven percent

in 1936. The repayment record was excellent. Setting up a sliding schedule for the repayment of student loans was a new idea when it was instituted at New Hampshire in 1928. The program attracted so much attention that Treasurer Magrath was retained as a consultant by the Harmon Foundation of New York City when it was planning a student loan program.

Student financial problems during the Depression were fraternal as well as personal. In April 1933, to help the chapters, the trustees ruled that no student would be granted a degree until he had satisfied his fraternity board and room bills. In 1934 a faculty committee was appointed to look into the business operations of the fraternities and sororities. By the end of the 1934-35 academic year one sorority and one fraternity were in such condition that it was recommended they liquidate; two other fraternities were in almost the same state. As a result the trustees ruled that no new chapters were to be formed and that no new houses were to be built. By 1936 some of the fraternities were unable to meet their

"Hell Week" initiates prove themselves worthy of Theta Kappa Phi fraternity.

mortgage payments. An association of faculty advisers was set up that year, giving alumni considerable supervision of fraternity finances. A quota system for pledging was also established in an effort to distribute the candidates, so that each house would have enough members for efficient operation.

The enrollment had grown rapidly during the previous administration. Hetzel was intent on getting the people of New Hampshire acquainted with their university, and he believed that an important means of achieving this goal was to enroll as many New Hampshire students in the institution as possible. Therefore he was not receptive to faculty members who urged that the admissions standards be raised. In 1924 selective admissions had been put into effect for out-of-state applicants; in 1926 a similar program was authorized for New Hampshire applicants. But it was not until after Hetzel's departure that the faction striving for higher standards was able to gain any significant ground.

At the trustee meeting of April 1927—the same meeting which had elected Lewis to the presidency—a committee was appointed to study limitations on enrollment. This resulted in a vote the following year to restrict enrollment to 1,600 for 1928-29. Although only a small reduction over the number of students on campus when the vote was taken, it was a significant decision nevertheless: the only time in the history of the university that the policy of admitting all qualified in-state applicants was abandoned. At the same time, the number of out-of-state freshmen was to be held to eight percent of the preceding freshman class, instead of the twelve percent allowed by law.

Lewis was requested to formulate a selective admissions policy. The policy adopted could hardly be termed severe: to "investigate" those applicants who were in the bottom quarter of their graduating class, as well as any others whose preparation seemed questionable. For September 1928, only fifteen of the fifty-one students thus investigated were denied admission.

The admissions committee included Dean Pettee. After his early experience of scouring the state for enough students to make New Hampshire College look respectable, Pettee found it difficult to reverse his thinking—especially if the applicant was an athlete. The other committee members were Professor Wellman of the education department, who took a middle ground, and Adrian O. Morse, who was committed to raising standards. On one occasion when a number of questionable applications (some of them from athletes) were ready for review, Dean Pettee was confined to his bed with illness. Tony Morse took advantage of the situation to call a meeting of the committee. Not to be bypassed, Dean Pettee asked to have the meeting in his bedroom. On his way to the meeting, Morse realized that he had been defeated when he saw Coach Cowell leaving the Pettee residence. The athletes were not rejected.

In any event, the desire to limit enrollment was more than satisfied. Only 1,515 students were registered when classes started in September 1928. This was 118 under the previous fall and was due primarily to the shrinkage of the freshman class. It was the first time in ten years that the enrollment had dropped, and the first time that out-of-state enrollment was under the legal ceiling. In explaining the drop, Lewis wrote:

Some of the known factors are the following: the publicity given to the desire of the administration to keep numbers down; the increase of yearly tuition by $20.50; the quite common but wrong inference that the tuition had been doubled, resulting from the fact that fees have been abolished and their amount consolidated with tuition; the reduction of the number of out-of-state students by twenty more than that required by law; the actual rejection of fifteen [New Hampshire residents] and the fear of rejection by others; discouraging advice of school principals; competition of normal schools and junior colleges; and the financial depression in our textile centers. Most important of all is the fact that we are probably at about the crest of the wave of increase in college attendance which has swept the whole United States since the war. About half the colleges reported decreases in attendance this year.

16. Better Studying, Better Teaching

The decline in enrollment did not seem to distress Lewis. His slogan for 1928-29 was: "Better studying and better teaching." In his first annual report he spelled out his reasons for this novel attitude:

Educational progress is too often today measured by mere bulk. In the last analysis it depends upon quality, quality of effort and of work on the part of teacher and pupil . . . . [Quality] should underlie the thought of teacher and taught alike not only this year, but next year, and serve as a guiding principle of conduct to all college campuses. It is the general impression that at New Hampshire we have experienced all along the line as serious an effort to do good work during the past year as we have ever done.

Lewis's concern with scholarship was made known to the students. The editor of the 1929 *Granite* observed: "[Lewis] has set out to place the University of New Hampshire among the leading educational institutions in the country, and with that purpose in mind, he has made his first step in raising the scholastic standards to a high level."

Eliminating weak students, by increasing the proportion dropped for scholastic failure, was not part of the drive for better scholarship. Dr. George N. Bauer, who had joined the mathematics department in 1924, was in October 1928 appointed officer-in-charge-of-freshmen. He was "to study and advise the entering class how to best make their college adjustments so as to meet their scholastic demands most effectively." The year before Bauer's appointment ninety-eight students had failed. By 1930-31 this number had been reduced to eighty-three, and the following year it went to sixty-eight. Selective admissions went into effect the year Bauer started his work with freshmen, so it is impossible to tell how much the improvement was due to his efforts

and how much to elimination of the weakest candidates. Lewis attributed part of the improvement to "the reasonable plan of demanding adequate secondary-school preparation on the part of applicants for admission." In September 1931, the New Hampshire freshmen averaged four and a half points better than the average of 45,000 freshmen across the country who took the same scholastic aptitude test.

In 1932-33 the scholastic probation rules were tightened. Under the former rules, a student remained in good standing if he maintained an average of 60. The new rules placed a student on probation—with attendant loss of eligibility for financial aid and extracurricular activities—if he did not pass two-thirds of his work and obtain a grade of 70 in at least half of it. The trustees apparently were concerned that standards might be going up too fast. In January 1931, while the new rules were under consideration by the faculty, they passed the following resolution: "the Trustees desire herewith to express the opinion, without thought of encroaching upon the powers and policies of the Faculty, that consideration might be given to the extension of the trial period for freshmen beyond the first term, possibly until the end of the freshman year."

Honors courses had been introduced by the department of zoology in 1926-27, with history and French following in 1927-28. Honors students were relieved of some of the prescribed work, substituting for it seminars and the writing of lengthy papers. The honors courses were not offered after 1933-34, however.

Lewis involved students by asking the Student Council and the Women's Student Government to make a joint report "on problems pertaining to housing and scholarship." In his 1928 report he said the students "deserve great credit for a thorough and comprehensive statement characterized by good temper and fair dealing." The student report recommended abolition of a time-unit system of determining academic credits, adopted in 1926-27, terming it "entirely unsatisfactory." They also favored "lighter schedules for students in Liberal Arts in order that they may concentrate on their major fields, and the inclusion of more cultural subjects in the Technology courses."

The faculty took until 1933 to agree that the time-unit system should be abandoned, setting the requirement for a degree at 216 quarter hours instead of 600 time units.* The following year the liberal arts requirement was reduced to 192 quarter hours. In connection with the abandonment of the time-unit system, the question of going back to a semester calendar was discussed. With liberal arts in favor, technology divided, and agriculture opposed to a change, Lewis put off a decision in the hope that further discussion would bring the colleges closer together on the question. There was agreement to offer year-long courses running through all three terms. These started in 1933-34 and continued until the university changed to the semester plan in 1936-37.

Lewis sponsored study of the curricula from the beginning of his administration. As a result, in agriculture the freshman and sophomore years were made uniform for all majors, and one elective course in the humanities was required. Because many students in the College of Agriculture were preparing to be scientists and not farmers, students majoring in agricultural and biological chemistry, botany, and entomology were not required to have a period of practical farm experience before graduating. In 1929 the summer work in forestry was concentrated in the White Mountain Forestry Camp in the Passaconaway Valley. It was also decided to separate the business operations of the college farm from

* For each course the number of hours of preparation per week was estimated and then added to the hours spent in class or laboratory. This sum became the number of units assigned the course.

Zoology laboratory in Thompson Hall, 1935.

the instructional aspects. The two had always been closely related. Dean "Pa" Taylor was reassigned as Director of Commercial Departments and relieved of all responsibility for instruction. Professor Eastman of agricultural economics was made Associate Dean and Director of Resident Instruction, to "have full charge of the courses of study, teaching, personnel and all matters pertaining to budgets of the college which concern instruction and maintenance."

The most noteworthy work of the Agricultural Experiment Station at this time was that of the animal nutrition laboratory, supported in part by the Carnegie Institute. Research Professor Ernest G. Ritzman conducted experiments in the metabolism of farm animals that, in 1929-31, attracted scientists from Germany, Switzerland, Angola, Scotland, Japan, France, the U.S.S.R., Czechoslovakia, Puerto Rico, China, and Sweden to study under him. Ritzman had also been carrying on a project to breed multiple-nipple ewes to increase sheep production. This research had been started by Alexander Graham Bell. In 1924 Bell's flock was given to the college so that the work would be continued.

The College of Technology made the work of the freshman and sophomore years less specialized by combining the several beginning courses in chemistry into a single broad course to serve all students. Instead of following the recommendation of the students to include more humanities in the technology programs, the college instituted a special course in the contributions of scientists and engineers to the field of engineering; it was offered to physically disabled students to make up the credits they would otherwise have earned for physical education and military science. A special English course for technology seniors was also established, "to stress the fundamentals of composition rather than emphasize the subject matter as in the past." Signs of the times were the addition of a course in aeronautics and the substitution of work in radio for that formerly offered in electric railways.

To do for industry what the Agricultural Experiment Station had been doing for farmers since 1888, and to stimulate research by the technology faculty, technology Dean George W. Case advocated the establishment of an Engineering Experiment Station. The trustees voted in 1929 to establish the station, but it did not begin operations until January 1933. Industries in the state were invited to submit problems to the station for study, but routine testing was to be avoided. In general no charge was made for the services; contributions were encouraged, however.

In liberal arts, the freshman survey course in social science was moved to the history department in 1931-32 and renamed "Introduction to Western Civilization." Associate Professor William G. Hennessy of the English department introduced a course in the appreciation of art. In 1934-35, curricula in social service and in public health nursing were introduced; the latter did not survive.

C. Floyd Jackson, who succeeded Albert N. French as dean of liberal arts in July 1930, instituted the practice of appointing a student committee to advise on college policy and to assist with freshman registration. Upon recommenda-

tion by this committee, a "vagabonding scheme" was established which allowed students with honor grades to visit classes for which they were not registered.

In 1928 a Marine Zoological Laboratory was established under Jackson's leadership on Appledore Island, one of the Isles of Shoals off Portsmouth. Jackson personally bought two old buildings on the island and furnished them free for use by zoology summer school courses. The university leased the island for $800 a year. Students contributed the labor of moving supplies and equipment, with water transportation supplied by Jackson's motor boat, the *Shankhassick*. An old automobile was taken to the island for hauling supplies from the pier to the buildings.[*]

Graduate study achieved its present administrative pattern in January 1928, when the trustees approved creation of a School of Graduate Study under a dean and with an executive committee known as the Graduate Council. The first dean was Professor Herman L. Slobin, who continued to hold his post as chairman of the department of mathematics. Through subterfuge or innocence, the trustee minutes indicated that this development would entail "no additional expense." In April a proposal by Lewis for tuition scholarships for in-state graduate students was approved.

In 1927-28 there were thirty-two graduate students, enrolled in the following departments: agricultural and biological chemistry (3), botany (3), chemistry (3), education (4), entomology (1), history (3), horticulture (3), mathematics (2), physics (1), political science (2), philosophy and psychology (2), and zoology (5). The next year the graduate enrollment was fifty, and the Master of

---

[*] The restrictions of World War II ended the venture. University officials inspected the buildings on Appledore in the fall of 1946 to see if they were suitable for reoccupancy. The inspectors were not impressed, and there was no further development in this field until 1968. In that year the university started construction of the Jackson Estuarine Laboratory, located on Adams Point in Durham, at a cost of $631,223. The new facility is primarily a research station, whereas Professor Jackson's primary interest on Appledore was instruction.

Education degree was added to the M.S. and M.A. already offered. Lewis reported: "This graduate work was carried by the faculty members concerned in addition to their full loads of undergraduate instruction." A normal teaching load was then fifteen hours a week. He added: "I have also stressed that our graduate program cannot become the dominant interest of any department." Eight years after the establishment of the M.Ed. degree, master's degrees were authorized in civil, electrical, and mechanical engineering, with a third of the credit to be in courses and two-thirds in thesis.

Lewis's interest in student activities became apparent soon after his arrival. To strengthen student leadership, several changes were tried in the composition of the Student Council. In 1927 only the president of the council was elected by the student body; the other twelve members were the presidents of campus organizations or the editors of student publications. The next year the representation—all male—was by class. In 1935, to reduce the alleged influence of the fraternities, all council members were elected at large by the student body. Lewis reported that the council was becoming "an increasingly influential factor in the guidance and conduct of certain phases of student life" and would "inevitably take over a still larger share of leadership and responsibility."

Accompanying these changes in student government were changes in student personnel officers. Professor Norman Alexander was appointed dean of men in 1929. Mrs. Elizabeth DeMeritt, the highly regarded dean of women, retired in September 1931 and was succeeded by Dr. Ruth J. Woodruff.

To give major student organizations a sound financial base, a student activities tax—$3.65 for men and $4.50 for women—was instituted in 1935. Associated Student Organizations, under the control of Professor Arthur W. Johnson as treasurer, had been started in 1930 to systematize the finances of those organizations. In 1933-34 Ballard Hall was renovated and much of the space made available for offices of student organizations.

As would be expected of a former major-league pitcher, Lewis took an active interest in athletics. This did not, however, result in outstanding records for the Wildcats during his administration—except for the baseball team of 1936, which Jere Chase '36 captained to a thirteen win, one loss record. Lewis attributed the mediocre sports results in part to "the overambitious athletic mind so common among undergraduates and alumni everywhere," which had led the teams to arrange difficult schedules. At his suggestion, an Alumni Advisory Committee on Athletics was set up in 1934; four members were appointed by the president of the university and four by the directors of the Alumni Association. The director of athletics served as chairman.

The interest of the alumni was not confined to athletics. Lewis met with the alumni directors frequently, suggesting projects ranging from the building of a student union to a fund to restore old athletic trophies. Growing out of these discussions was the Alumni Fund plan. This was approved by the trustees in June 1934 after it had been presented to them by Frank W. Randall '07. Under the plan, dues for the Alumni Association were abandoned in favor of an annual gift "for specific or unrestricted purposes of such an amount as the graduate's resources allow." Ten percent of the annual contributions were to go to support the work of the alumni office. Harry O. Page '27 was alumni secretary at the time.°

Another innovation in alumni affairs was the establishment of the Alumni Meritorious Service Awards in 1933. Five awards were to be given the first year and three in succeeding years. The recipients of 1934 were Charles Harvey Hood '80,

° Page also ran the Bureau of Appointments, a job-placement service started by Alumni Secretary Edward Y. Blewett in 1929. Opposition from department heads—who wished to place their own graduates—delayed formal establishment of the bureau until 1934, when the Depression made job-hunting so difficult that the department heads were willing to cooperate.

George Arthur Perley '08, Albert Huckins Brown '11, Rohl Chase Wiggin '17, and Christopher James O'Leary '20. The presentations were made by Lewis at the annual alumni banquet in June.

The first outdoor commencement in the institution's history was held in 1934. Since 1906, commencement ceremonies had been held in the gymnasium, but with the growth of the graduating classes the facilities had become too limited. Although the location of the ceremony was changed, the graduates received the old style, large diplomas tied with a blue ribbon. The book-size diploma was introduced two years later.

President Lewis was in poor health for some months before undergoing surgery in Boston in the spring of 1936. He was unable to attend the April 17 meeting of the Board of Trustees and died at his home just after midnight on May 24. The university was closed all day for his funeral, which was in the Community Church of Durham.

Lewis had viewed the new athletic fields, completed in 1936, as offering facilities for an expanded intramural sports program. At their first meeting after Lewis died, the trustees voted to name the fields after him.

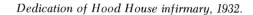

Dedication of Hood House infirmary, 1932.

17. Engelhardt Makes Decisions

The trustees held a special meeting on the day of Lewis's funeral. After designating Roy D. Hunter, president of the board, to be interim executive officer, they named a committee of five to search for a successor. Although no faculty were on the committee, they were asked to suggest characteristics of the man they would like. Ability to make decisions headed the list. Their desire was fulfilled when Fred Engelhardt, professor of educational administration at the University of Minnesota, was elected at a special meeting of the trustees on December 10, 1936. Engelhardt took office the following April 1.

Engelhardt was born April 15, 1885, in Naugatuck, Connecticut. His parents were German immigrants of limited means, but he was able to attend the Sheffield Scientific School of Yale on a scholarship. He graduated in 1908 as a physics major and stayed on the next year as an assistant. For several years he was a teacher and principal in public high schools in New York and in private schools in Illinois and Pennsylvania. He was awarded the Master of Arts in 1915 and the Doctor of Philosophy in 1924 by Teachers College of Columbia. During World War I, as a major in the Coast Artillery, he was inspector of instruction for officers at the heavy artillery school at Fort Monroe, Virginia.

The trustees had scheduled a dinner at the Commons and a reception for the faculty on the day the Engelhardt's van of furniture arrived from Minneapolis. The unloading was not finished when the time arrived for the dinner, so Engelhardt sent his wife on ahead while he stayed behind to supervise. It was a black tie affair. Mrs. Engelhardt had not had a chance to unpack her formal clothes, so she wore an informal dress she had brought in her suitcase. Engelhardt appeared in a dark business suit.

Word spread quickly through the faculty homes that the new president and his wife were not sticklers for formality.

The interim administration under Roy D. Hunter had not been a stagnant period. A fully equipped operating room was installed in Hood House infirmary as a gift of the Hood family. Six thousand dollars was voted to construct shower and dressing facilities under the new stadium. A new rate was approved for the sale of water by the university to Dean Pettee's Durham Spring Water Company. To replace dying trees along Main Street—tradition says they were planted by Ben Thompson—$1,500 was voted. (Fortunately, in view of the recent ravages of Dutch elm disease, Professor Lewis Swain's suggestion was followed that some of the new trees be Canadian maples instead of elms.) The dining halls in the Commons were enlarged. A poultry nutrition laboratory was built. Plans were drawn for additions to the Hamilton Smith Library. For a faculty housing development, located on the De-Meritt-McDaniel farm purchased from George Hoitt, a price of four cents a square foot was set for lots on Mill Road and three cents for those elsewhere. Faculty members who built houses for their own use were to get a half-cent discount. No lot could be resold without consent of the university, and commercial operations were barred.

September 1936 saw the return to the semester system and the institution of new requirements in the general curriculum of the College of Liberal Arts, including a proficiency test in a foreign language. In the first football game on the new Lewis Field the UNH Wildcats smothered Lowell Textile 66 to 0, but the story was different when the field was dedicated on October 10, the University of Maine winning 27 to 6.

The first trustee meeting attended by Engel-

The men dining at Commons—with waiter service.

hardt was that of April 16, 1937. It might be said that several eras ended at that meeting, for it was voted to make Charles H. Pettee Dean Emeritus and University Historian, effective July 1. Pettee had joined the faculty in 1876. In addition to teaching, he had vigorously recruited students to keep the college alive in the early days, had supervised the move to Durham, and had thrice served as acting president. The university having no retirement plan, Pettee was to receive such compensation as the trustees from time to time agreed upon.

Engelhardt put a retirement plan high on his agenda. On July 1, 1938, a little more than a year after his arrival, the Teachers Insurance and Annuity Association program was put into effect. The university matched faculty contributions of two, four, or five percent of salary, depending on age.° Faculty members in service before July 1,

° The plan has been improved from time to time, so that by 1968 faculty and university each contributed 5 percent of a salary up to the limit covered by Social Security with the faculty contributing 7 percent and the university 10 percent on amounts beyond that point. Social Security coverage in addition to the TIAA annuity had become effective for the faculty in 1955.

1938, were required to retire at sixty-nine, those coming after that date at sixty-five.

Other faculty personnel policies were improved as well. Leaves with pay for professional improvement were made more generous, and provisions for attending professional meetings were broadened. Regulations on appointment, promotion, and tenure were adopted in 1939.

On May 21, 1937, a new faculty senate was established as the legislative body of the faculty. Composed of representatives of the departments and some administrative officers, the senate, "under the leadership of the president and subject always to the approval of the board of trustees" had "legislative jurisdiction in all matters of student government and educational policy." The senate held its first meeting in November. In addition, there was a university council composed of administrative officers and six faculty members to advise the president and to act on urgent matters between meetings of the senate.

The staffs of the experiment stations and extension service, which formerly had been separate, were amalgamated with the other faculty and given appropriate faculty rank. The unified list-

An emotional moment in Cowell Stadium, 1939.

ing appeared for the first time in the 1938-39 catalog. This catalog also gave a very brief biography of each member of the faculty, thus putting subtle pressure on those whose academic background was minimal. The *Faculty Handbook,* issued in July 1939, spelled out the new faculty organization and policies. A companion *Student Handbook* detailed the rules and regulations affecting students.

Engelhardt believed that every college graduate should be prepared to earn a living, and that those likely to go into teaching should be thoroughly prepared for that profession. On the grounds that most of them would end up as college teachers, all graduate assistants were required to register for a year-long course in higher education, taught originally by Edward Y. Blewett; such a course was a novelty at the time. The reaction of some departments, and students, was actively unenthusiastic. Engelhardt, although formerly a professor in a college of education, supported local sentiment in favor of keeping education a department in the College of Liberal Arts, instead of setting up a separate college of education. The intent was to involve the aca-

demic disciplines closely in the preparation of teachers.

In an attempt to correlate work in the biological sciences, a Biological Institute was organized in 1939 with C. Floyd Jackson as director. To replace Jackson as dean of liberal arts, Engelhardt appointed Edward Y. Blewett '26, at the time assistant to the president. (Blewett served in the post for twenty years—at that time by far the longest term for any college dean at the university—until he resigned to become president of Westbrook Junior College.) The departments of bacteriology, botany, and zoology were combined into a department of biology in 1941, with each of the former departments as a division.

A unique plan replaced the traditional freshman English course in 1939. Students whose performance was found to be satisfactory, on the basis of tests, were excused from instruction in English. Others were taught in small groups or individually until they achieved an acceptable level of competence. A writing laboratory was established on the top floor of Murkland Hall where members of the English department were available to give help to students seeking it. All instructors in the university were supposed to judge the writing of their students and to remand to the English department those whose written work was unsatisfactory. Referrals by the faculty were uneven. On occasion Mrs. Lucinda P. Smith, who was involved in the program, would procure a batch of written work from a department and go through it herself to find students who should have been remanded. (The plan was abandoned in 1946, and freshman English again became a requirement until 1969, after which it was not required of students with satisfactory College Board English examination scores.)

Majors in political science were given an opportunity to work as interns in some branches of the state government. A Bureau of Government Research was established. The department of philosophy and psychology was dissolved, courses in philosophy going to the history department and those in psychology to education. A department of the arts was established in 1942; all courses dealing with art were transferred to the new unit, which was headed by George R. Thomas, reassigned from the department of architecture. Instruction in pottery became a feature of the new department. This had started on campus in 1939 as a joint venture of the university and the New Hampshire League of Arts and Crafts. Edwin Scheier, who together with his wife Mary gained an international reputation in the field, had become the pottery instructor in 1940.

Another contribution to the arts was the establishment in the summer of 1938 of one of the first Writers' Conferences. Directed by Professor Carroll S. Towle, this flourished for years.

To serve the important resort industry in New Hampshire and neighboring states, a four-year curriculum in hotel administration was established, the only one east of Cornell. In 1939-40 a five-year cooperative nursing program became available, the first two years on the campus and the last three at Elliot Hospital in Manchester. Four years later an occupational therapy curriculum was inaugurated.

In the College of Technology, curricula in architectural engineering and in building construction and marketing replaced the architectural curriculum. To the chemistry curriculum was added an option in chemical engineering. A curriculum in physics was made available.

The two-year program in agriculture, which since 1895 had been taught by regular faculty members, was reorganized with a new staff of its own, to qualify as a vocational agricultural course eligible for federal aid under the George-Dean Act. One of the first teachers was Philip S. Barton '28, who became director of the unit in 1941. It was then termed the Applied Farming Course; in 1953 it was to become the Thompson School of Agriculture, and in 1963 the Thompson School of Applied Science.

Since he had arrived on campus in 1915 as the first full-time coach in the institution's history, William H. "Butch" Cowell had run the athletic department through the agency of the Athletic Association. In 1921 some restraints had been put on the department's fiscal independence. While Hunter was acting president in 1936, a committee of trustees had been appointed to look into the athletic situation. As a result, the athletic department was put under the same control financially as the other departments, and its director was made directly responsible to the president. Engelhardt was to hire a new football coach. (The man hired was George H. Sauer, a former All-American who had played with the Green Bay Packers in 1935 and 1936. Selected as his assistant was Charles M. Justice. Their first season, 1937, resulted in seven wins and one loss. Sauer left the university in 1941 for service in World War II. Justice coached football for the six-game 1942 season, winning all games for the first time in the university's history.) The position of associate director of physical education, reporting directly to the president and responsible for all instructional activities of the department, was created. Carl Lundholm '21 was given the post as of September 1, 1938. Six weeks later he was made acting director because Cowell's health was failing; in June 1939 Lundholm was named director, a position he occupied until he retired in 1963.

The Alumni Advisory Committee on Athletics was abolished. Some alumni did not like this, nor did they share Engelhardt's convictions on intercollegiate athletics. These, set forth in his report of 1938, stressed the value of sports for the development of the individual, called for the elimination of athletic scholarships, and advocated complete separation of the coaching staff from fiscal authority or responsibility. He held that "if athletics are operated as they should be no one college can or should win all its games all the time."

The Athletic Association went out of existence in May 1938. Determination of athletic policies, awarding of letters, and approving of schedules was turned over to a faculty committee, of which the director of athletics and physical education was a member.

If alumni were unhappy about the new athletic policies, they were more unhappy about the treatment accorded Cowell. Groups of alumni and students started a campaign to have the new stadium or the field house named for Cowell. The trustees denied the requests on the grounds that the playing fields already had been named for Lewis, that they should not be further broken down, and that the field house had already been officially designated the University of New Hampshire Field House.

The Cowell issue influenced the vote for an alumni trustee in June 1940 when the second four-year term of John S. Elliott '15 expired. In a three-candidate election Ernest W. Christensen '23, formerly an assistant to Cowell, received twenty-six more votes than the runner-up, Elliott. (Bradford W. McIntire '25 ran a respectable third.)

Cowell died in Dover on August 28, 1940. At their October meeting the trustees voted $350 for a memorial plaque to be placed in the Field House. At the same meeting they turned down re-

quests from three alumni groups to name the Field House for Cowell.°

The fourth annual alumni drive in 1938 failed to meet its goal but went over $4,000 for the first time. This virtually paid up the $15,000 loan made to purchase materials for the concrete stands which were to become Cowell Stadium. Freed of this obligation, in 1939 the alumni fund was devoted to endowing the Charles Holmes Pettee medal. This medal was created "to honor selected native sons and daughters of New Hampshire or others who may have rendered a unique service to this state comparable with that expressed by the life of the late Dean Pettee." Engelhardt advocated the establishment of the award as a replacement for honorary degrees; he did not believe in honorary degrees, and none was awarded during his administration. The first Pettee medal was bestowed on Supreme Court Justice Harlan Fiske Stone, and the second on Mrs. Marian Nevins MacDowell.

Before Engelhardt arrived it had been decided to enlarge the library, and in June 1937 plans were approved for the addition of two wings. Approval had also been given for construction of a field house. The construction program was to be rounded out by a fire house—the fire equipment was kept in a former barn, which also housed the agricultural engineering laboratory and the forestry department. What should never happen to a fire department happened on the night of July 12, 1937. The barn burned.‡ Engel-

° Cowell's friends continued to press for his recognition, and finally, in 1952, the football stadium was named for him. The Field House was incorporated into a greatly enlarged physical education facility in 1967. The indoor running track was named for Paul Sweet, the main gymnasium for Carl Lundholm, and the swimming pool for Henry C. Swasey.

‡ A fire engine was rescued by two summer school students, John J. Lorentz and Bernard Robinson. The young men reasoned that the machine was without a home, that it would have no further duties that night, and that it owed them something for rescuing it; they therefore decided that it would be a proper conveyance to take Lorentz to visit his girl friend in Massachusetts. They were turned back by three stern state policemen in Newmarket.

New Hampshire Hall before it was remodeled in 1940.

Thompson Hall in 1936.

hardt, who was vacationing on Cape Cod, rushed back and had plans made by Professor Huddleston for a building to replace the barn. This was approved by the trustees at an estimated cost of $92,000, ten days after the fire. At their October meeting the trustees named the building for Dean Pettee, who died on March 23, 1938, before the building was completed.

The new wings to the library were finished in February 1938. Murals were painted in tempera on the interior walls by the Federal Arts project in New Hampshire, many cases of eggs from university hens going into the work. Before the furniture was moved into the new space, it was the scene of a two-day exhibit of antiques which attracted over 1,500 visitors from New Hampshire and nearby states. When the new reading rooms were occupied, the space vacated on the second floor was arranged for an art exhibit area, an art library, and music listening rooms.

With the new field house nearing completion in the fall of 1938, application was made for Works Projects Administration funds to remodel the old gymnasium. The altered building, rechristened New Hampshire Hall, was ready for use late in 1940. It provided improved facilities not only for women's physical education but also for dramatics, concerts, and lectures. Offices and a small chapel were provided for the campus religious organizations.

The addition of two wings to Nesmith Hall and consequent remodeling of Morrill and Thompson halls, together with the construction of Pettee Hall and the revamping of New Hampshire Hall, resulted in the reassignment of space for most of the departments in the colleges of agriculture and liberal arts. Such shifting invariably results in a spate of campus politicking, and a cautious president appoints a committee to handle the matter. But Engelhardt was not one to shrink from controversy. He called in the chairmen of the affected departments and detailed the moves that were to be made. He then asked for comments. There was silence until Professor Babcock said, "Mr. President, as you say everything is settled, there doesn't seem to be much use in giving our opinions."

With the easing of the Depression, enrollment began to rise to the point where student housing again became an acute problem. A study in 1937 showed that dormitories could accommodate 917, chapter houses 499, and private residences 241; commuters numbered 144. As a general rule, undergraduate women were required to live in dormitories or sororities, so their number had to be limited to the accommodations available. To meet the need for more housing for women, in January 1938 the trustees voted to construct the wing on Congreve Hall which had previously been proposed but set aside for other projects. Money was borrowed from the Alice Hamilton Smith fund, as had been done in the case of an earlier addition to this building, and part of the remaining cost came from W.P.A. funds. Bickford House, caring for twenty-two women, was rented. In 1939 a $250,000 state bond issue made it possible to complete Congreve by building the wing known as North Congreve. Houses on Garrison Avenue were bought for dormitories.

The growth of the campus caused a parking problem, of course. Additional space was provided in front of Nesmith and near the power plant. Engelhardt reported to the trustees: "the parking problem, which is becoming a difficult one, would adjust itself." The adjustment has yet to be completed.

The hurricane of September 21, 1938, did considerable damage to the College Woods. A road and bridge were built to make the area accessible, and a saw mill was put up. By the end of the winter nearly a million board feet had been salvaged. Enough was sold to recover the cost of the operation, and much was stored for future university use; the beams and paneling in the alumni room of New Hampshire Hall came from this source.

The state payments on the millage formula were restored to their full value beginning with the 1937-38 fiscal year, when $548,431 was received. (Income from the federal government was $268,332.) The theory of the millage formula was that assessments through the state would grow at about the same rate as enrollment at the university, thereby giving a relatively stable income per student. Reduction in property values, due first to the Depression and then to the 1938 hurricane, upset the theory in one direction; the unexpected growth of enrollment upset it in the other. In his 1938 report, Engelhardt pointed out that the $434 per student yielded by the millage income in 1925-26 had dropped to $280 in 1938-39. Meanwhile the cost of resident instruction had grown to $445 per student. As a result, compared to other state colleges and universities, New Hampshire's $250 out-of-state tuition was twelfth highest and its $150 in-state tuition, eighth highest. Engelhardt concluded his discussion by saying, "a large number of worthy youth are denied the opportunity to go to college because of the fact that the charges are much too high."

To help students meet the costs of their education, the university continued the financial aid program which had been greatly expanded during the Depression. There was a change in terminology, which was merely that. Starting in Engelhardt's administration, awards based solely on financial need were termed "tuition grants," and only those coming from endowed funds or based on significant accomplishment were termed "scholarships." During Engelhardt's administration, also, the university accepted its largest scholarship gift up to that time. Frank S. Lord of Conway willed an estate valued at $300,000 to the university, effective upon the death of his immediate heirs, with the money to benefit students from Carroll County. (The fund became active in 1951.)

With the economic recovery following America's entry into World War II, the financial plight of the students eased. In almost all categories of student aid, a peak was reached in 1940-41 and then fell off sharply. The class of 1941 borrowed

Governor Robert O. Blood and Engelhardt cutting the cake for the 75th anniversary, 1941.

$56,024 from the student loan fund, more than any other class. In subsequent years the university invested a large part of its loan fund in U.S. war bonds, since the students did not request it. In work programs, too, the demand was dramatically reduced. The student wage rate was raised from thirty cents to thirty-five cents an hour. Despite this increase, the problem now was to find students to fill all the available jobs, rather than finding jobs for those who needed them.

The University would have its seventy-fifth birthday in 1940-41 and the directors of the Alumni Association proposed that the event be observed with a year-long celebration. At its meeting in January 1939, the Board of Trustees adopted the suggestion and authorized the organization of a number of planning committees, with Huntley N. Spaulding as general chairman. The stated objectives of the celebration were "to appraise the development of the 75 year period; to demonstrate the present possibilities of service to the people of the state; to illuminate the program for development in the future."

Many organizations—state and national, student and adult—accepted invitations to hold annual or special meetings on campus in 1940-41. There were special dramatic and musical presentations. Following commencement there was a ten-day series of meetings, each day being concerned with a topic such as the home, the community, social controls, religion, or the university's future development. Another major event was a convocation in the Field House on Benjamin Thompson's birthday, April 22, attended by notables from governmental and academic circles, and featuring an address on Benjamin Thompson by Professor Harold H. Scudder. And on the evening of March 14, before an audience of six hundred diners, Lowell Thomas broadcast his radio news summary, which in those pre-TV days reached an audience of millions.

Although the institution had possessed three official historians—Lucien Thompson was appointed to that post in 1893, Professor Scott in 1925, and Dean Pettee in 1937—no historical record had ever been published. This lack was remedied for the anniversary celebration. A committee consisting of Donald C. Babcock, Harold H. Scudder, and Philip M. Marston was appointed to oversee the work. The general editor was Henry B. Stevens. John P. Hall '39 did much of the writing, and the editorial staff included Marion Boothman '39, Anthony J. Nebeski '39, Phyllis R. Deveneau '43, Cornelia Constable '43, and Elizabeth Norton '43. The book was published in 1941 as *History of the University of New Hampshire, 1866-1941.*

116

18. The War and Its Aftermath

Even before the end of the university's anniversary year, shadows of World War II reached the campus. In October 1940 the faculty participated in the registration of male students twenty-one to thirty-six years of age for selective service. Shortly thereafter the students conducted a vote which showed 630 out of 763 in favor of conscription; to help Great Britain 545 were in favor and 118 opposed. At the same time a presidential preference poll was taken, Wendell Wilkie getting 455 to Franklin Roosevelt's 295.

In September 1941 the number of men in the upper classes was down a little, but more women registered. The freshman class was slightly larger than the year before. That there was discussion among the students of the threatening war was evidenced by a headline in the *New Hampshire:* "Durham Pacifists Hold Wild Sesssion over Nonviolence." The usual horse show was held in October and plans were made for a student musical, *Katy Cadet.*

The attack on Pearl Harbor came on December 7, 1941, bringing death to Ensign Edward B. Cloues of Warner, who had been a freshman at the university in 1935-36 before transferring to Annapolis, from which he had graduated in 1940. (A year later the Congressional Medal of Honor was conferred posthumously on Captain Harl Pease '39 of Plymouth. The Air Force Base in Newington is named in Pease's memory.)

The Student Council appointed a defense committee. Air raid wardens were selected and began a training course. A student-faculty University Defense Committee began to make plans for the institution's role in the war. One of its first recommendations was that a student entering military service after December 7 be given full credit for courses in which he was passing. In contrast to the exodus of World War I—when three-quarters of the men left campus the semester war started—the students were urged to continue their education until ordered into service. These calls soon began to come, for both students and faculty. The first semester was shortened by eliminating the final examination period and substituting tests during the final week of classes.

Two hundred enrolled in a first aid course. Blackout drills were held. The Carnival Ball was held early in the second semester, but the sophomore Spring Hop was canceled. Clara Knight '44 was chosen to edit the 1944 *Granite,* the first woman to hold that position. Registration dropped the second semester, especially in the Graduate School. Commencement came early in May.

Registration for the first semester of 1942-43 was almost equal to that of the previous year, and the freshman class was larger. Many young men graduating from high school were anxious to start college before they were drafted or called up by the reserves. During the second semester, forty-eight selected high school boys were admitted as freshmen, their schools agreeing to award them diplomas when they completed the semester's work. Male students were subject to the draft except for pre-medical, pre-dental, and pre-veterinary majors; upperclassmen in engineering fields; and those in the advanced ROTC program. Most U.S. Army reservists were called up before they began the second semester; reservists in the Navy, Marines, Air Corps, and Signal Corps were allowed to continue. The Air Corps reservists did not get far, however, for they were called up in February. Altogether, male enrollment dropped from 1,230 the first semester to 830 the second.

In March the university contracted to conduct an Army Specialized Training Program (ASTP) unit. The purpose of ASTP was to give qualified enlisted men some specialized training before ordering them to active units or to officer candidate schools. The university had programs in engineering and pre-medicine. The men were under military discipline, were allowed no cuts, and were graded every two weeks.

Initially the ASTP students were housed in East and West halls, which had been built by and for the training units of an earlier war. And the Alpha Tau Omega house, which had served as headquarters for the World War I program, was assigned to the same purpose for the ASTP. All other fraternity houses were taken over by the university to be used as dormitories or for other purposes, for at its peak the ASTP program occupied not only East-West but also Hetzel, Fairchild, and Commons.

In April a related program came to the university—the Specialized Training and Reclassification (STAR) unit for the northeastern United States. This was a screening agency for ASTP.

Men came to Durham by the trainload to be tested, interviewed, and assigned. University faculty members participated in the testing and interviewing. It was expected that juniors in the ROTC would be classified through the STAR unit, but instead they were ordered to Fort Devens to proceed with their combat training.

Even before the United States had entered the war, the university had begun an Engineering, Science, and Management War Training program. It ran from January 1, 1941, until June 30, 1945, under the direction of Professor Leon W. Hitchcock. Altogether, forty-five courses in twelve locations were offered to 3,506 students. The shops were scheduled almost twenty-four hours a day. Many of those who received their training in this program were employed at the Portsmouth Navy Yard.

During 1943-44, fifteen coeds completed a training program offered by Pratt & Whitney and were later employed by the aircraft company as

ROTC juniors return to campus from Fort Devens after induction into the U.S. Army, April 17, 1943.

engineering aides. To give preliminary flight training, a Civil Aeronautics Authority program was started by Professor E. Howard Stolworthy; at first the classes were held in Durham with flight training in Portsmouth. Later the program was transferred to Laconia Airport and the Tilton School.

As had happened during World War I, the women's physical education department instituted a physical-fitness program. Several newsreel companies filmed it, and *Life* magazine ran a feature story.

By September 1943 the civilian enrollment at the university had been cut nearly in half. Only 1,083 students—779 of them women—were enrolled in the regular curricula. The campus was crowded nevertheless. There were 1,101 young men in the ASTP, plus a floating population of men being assigned by STAR. They did not have time for student organizations. The *New Hampshire* suspended publication in 1943-44, and the 1944 *Granite* was likewise omitted. Intercollegiate sports were also canceled.

To enable the civilian students to accelerate their work, two six-week summer sessions were offered in 1942. By attending both a student could complete almost a semester's work. In 1943, a full semester was scheduled between May and September, the fall and spring semesters having been shortened by eliminating exam periods and condensing vacations. The ASTP meanwhile was operating on a quarter-term plan. This so confused the schedule that none was printed in the 1943-44 catalog, and the following year no catalog was published. Another result of the intensified program was that tuition was charged by the credit hour instead of by the semester. With tuition set at $4.50 per hour for in-state students, and with 140 hours required for graduation in all three colleges, the cost of a degree was about the same as before.

In the midst of the war activities, Engelhardt was stricken by cancer. He carried on his duties for a time despite his illness. He was unable to attend the trustee meeting in January 1944, however, and on February 3 he died. At a memorial service in New Hampshire Hall, Roy D. Hunter quoted from the trustees' resolution: "Dr. Engelhardt put his dream for the university in these words, 'to assist all the people in the state all the time.' It was a dream that could come out only from a good and brave man."

Hunter, as president of the board, was once again appointed interim executive officer. The trustees established a novel precedent when they asked the faculty to name a special committee to help select a new president. Having consulted with other members of the faculty, this committee drew up specifications for the position and reported to the trustees on March 18, 1944. By this time there already were thirty-nine nominations. To succeed the gentle scholar Lewis, the faculty had asked for a man who would make decisions; in Engelhardt their desire was generously fulfilled. Now they wanted a man with scholarly recognition.

Advice came from other quarters as well. The Agricultural Conference of New Hampshire advocated the appointment of an agriculturalist. Unswayed by this plea, the trustees elected Harold Walter Stoke on August 10, 1944, from a field of eighty-four nominees.

Stoke, the son of a minister, had been born in Bosworth, Missouri, May 11, 1903. He graduated from Marion College in Indiana in 1924 and earned a Master of Arts degree from the University of Southern California in 1925 and the Doctor of Philosophy from Johns Hopkins in 1930. He was professor of political science at the University of Nebraska when, in 1937-38, he became supervisor of training in public administration for the Tennessee Valley Authority and lecturer at the University of Tennessee. The following year he was an educational associate of the Institute of Local and State Government and visiting associate professor of political science at the University of Pittsburgh. In 1939-40 he was dean of the graduate school of the University of Nebraska; the next year he moved to the University of Wisconsin as professor of political science and assistant dean of the graduate school. He was the author of two books and several articles on political science.

When Stoke arrived for the first semester of 1944-45, the university was still on a war basis. His inaugural consequently was kept simple. There was an afternoon convocation on December 17, to which delegates from selected organizations and colleges were invited. The civilian enrollment that semester was just over 1,200, three-quarters of them women. But the Allied armies were advancing toward Germany and the United States was soon to destroy the Japanese naval power. The changing fortunes of war were symbolized on campus when Everett B. Sackett, chairman of the University Defense Committee, was given a new assignment—the Postwar Problems Committee.

There were to be problems. Congress passed the "GI Bill," providing educational benefits for veterans and portending an unprecedented surge in college enrollments at the war's end.° At the University of New Hampshire, where registration had never been appreciably over two thousand, Sackett's committee estimated a registration of 2,938 for 1946-47, rising to 3,969 the following year, then turning down again. The estimate for the peak year was miraculously close to the mark. But the sudden capitulation of Japan, and the rapid demobilization that followed, pushed the registration for 1946-47 far beyond the figure that had been estimated. Enrollment for the first semester was 3,478, of whom 2,235 were under the Veterans' Administration and the GI Bill. (The sharp drop in registration expected after 1949-50 never did materialize. The registration did fall, reaching a low of 2,899 in 1953-54. Then,

partly as a result of a new GI Bill for Korean War veterans, it turned up again.) In spite of the squeeze, the university was able to boast that it admitted every qualified in-state veteran who applied.

The policy for September 1946 was to consider out-of-state alumni children if they could be squeezed in. These plus returning students kept the out-of-state enrollment at about a quarter of the total; it had been a third during the war years. By April 1947 students were being urged to attend summer school to take required basic science courses, because even by scheduling evening sections some laboratories could not accommodate the potential enrollment. In spite of the crowding, the trustees decided to admit twenty-five to fifty out-of-state women in September 1947, to achieve a better balance between men and women and to accommodate the daughters of alumni.

The veterans coming to campus were not the bright-eyed lads fresh from high school the university was used to dealing with. (The bulk of the veterans were men, of course, but there were a few women among them.) They had been engaged for months or years in pursuits anything but scholarly. Many of them had not planned on college and were not properly prepared for it, but with the GI Bill available they wanted to give it a try.

To handle the admissions and readjustment problems of the veterans, the University Senate in 1944 had established a Postwar Education Service. The idea had been proposed by Sackett and by William A. Medesy, a veteran of the North African campaign who had succeeded Norman Alexander as dean of men. The new service was to counsel veterans, test them, and arrange for refresher instruction. The staff of the service, in addition to the student personnel officers, included faculty members from each college to advise on selection of courses. To the extent possible, review courses of six or seven weeks duration preceded the start of each regular term. By

° Maurice F. Devine, a Manchester attorney, as a member of an American Legion committee had a major part in designing the GI Bill. Devine in 1949 became a UNH trustee, a post he held until his death in 1969. Devine Hall was named for him.

November 1945 the service had interviewed more than one thousand veterans; of these, about four hundred were denied admission. (During the life of the Postwar Education Service, July 1944 to June 1946, Medesy estimated that he interviewed 3,500 veterans and wrote to unestimated thousands.) With the end of the war the university contracted with the Veteran's Administration to operate a counseling center to give vocational and educational advice to all veterans wishing it, whether they were planning to attend the university or not. The counseling procedures followed were essentially those of the Postwar Education Service.

As it turned out, the veterans proved very capable students. Those who had been in the university before their military service raised their academic average about an entire letter grade. Some who had been suspended for academic deficiency returned to make the dean's list. A number of students coming straight from high school complained that the veterans made the competition for good grades too severe. As the *Granite* said: "courses were now [fall of 1946] more difficult, and professors were liberal with assignments."

Addressing the New England Association of Colleges and Secondary Schools in Boston, December 1946, Stoke said: "Veterans have brought new elements into the classroom and new anxieties to complacent and unchallenged teachers. Education will have to reflect more than it now does a variety of interests and talents which its enlarged clientele will bring to it."

The main desk at Hamilton Smith Library

Veterans camping out in New Hampshire Hall.

College Road housed an influx of married veterans.

19. The Campus under Stoke

Plans to house the postwar jump in enrollment had started to take shape in the spring of 1945. In April the enrollment forecast was presented to the trustees; in May they were shown a chart of housing needs at the university. One need, that never before had been of concern, was the accommodation of married students.

The war continued until mid-August, so dormitory construction was not possible in time for the 1945-46 academic year. The first semester was no problem with an enrollment of 1,416. More than five hundred veterans were expected for the second semester, however· and during the 1945 Christmas vacation Stoke sent a letter to all students and their parents, warning them of the anticipated crush. To ease the situation, students living within twenty miles of campus were required to commute. The commuting radius included such substantial towns as Dover, Portsmouth, Somersworth, Rochester, and Exeter. Married students were expected to live in Wentworth Acres (now known as Seacrest Village)—a government housing development near Portsmouth, built originally for workers at the Navy Yard—with transportation provided by two war-surplus buses. On the Durham campus, dormitory rooms would be crowded beyond normal capacity.

By December 1945, Professor Huddleston had prepared plans for three permanent dormitories, each with an optimum capacity of 100 but capable of housing 165 with three men in a room. Construction began as soon as the ground was frost-free, with completion scheduled for mid-September; the buildngs were to be named for William D. Gibbs, Fred Engelhardt, and Roy D. Hunter. Stoke presented to the trustees plans to house the 838 women and 2,375 men students expected in September 1946. He was authorized to proceed with plans for a fourth men's dormitory (Alexander) and a new women's dormitory (Sawyer) to be built the next year.

The "quadrangle" buildings—Engelhardt, Hunter, and Gibbs—were not ready when the university opened in September, even though the opening was delayed a week. Nearly six hundred cots were borrowed from the U.S. Army and set up in New Hampshire Hall and the Field House. In New Hampshire Hall were 338 men; in the Field House, 169 single men plus 70 married veterans waiting to move with their families into the apartments then being assembled on College Road. Morrill Hall was opened evenings to provide study space. The dormitories—complete except for doorknobs and locks—were finally occupied on October 17.

The College Road apartments were wooden barracks from the Davisville Seabee station in Rhode Island. They were sawed into sections, brought to Durham on trucks, and erected by the federal government under provisions of the Lanham Act. There were 252 apartment units altogether, with those in Z Building set aside for faculty families. The university spent more than $30,000 to provide utilities and otherwise prepare the site. The faculty apartments were provided with hot water heat from the university system, but the original oil heaters were retained in the student units—a constant source of worry to local fire officials. Wooden fire escapes were provided for the second-floor units, and the wallboard partitions were marked where they could be broken through to allow escape into adjacent apartments. The student units were ready earlier, but it was not until late October that the faculty families were able to move into Z Building.°

° Z Building was torn down in 1957 to make way for Devine Hall. The last of the student apartments were demolished a few years later, upon completion of the first phase of the Forest Park housing development.

Longer-range faculty housing was made available in the Mill Road area, where a faculty development had been approved in November 1945. Within two months, twenty-three faculty members had selected lots. Little building was done before the fall of 1946 because of the difficulty in finding contractors and building materials.

The need to house students and faculty took precedence over academic construction. In 1945, the legislature approved a $350,000 bond issue "to forward a building program." The money went for major maintenance and alteration projects. The only new buildings to appear on campus other than dormitories were two surplus structures moved in sections from military bases. One of these, identified as a Q-3 building was erected on what is now the Bookstore parking lot and served to house the forestry department. The other was a USO building from Ayer, Massachusetts, to serve as a temporary student union.

Tight scheduling made it possible to handle a doubled enrollment in the prewar academic buildings. In those leisurely days almost nothing had been scheduled after 12:00 noon except laboratories; few laboratories had met in the mornings. Now lecture sections ran until 5:00 P.M. and laboratories started at 7:30 A.M., with a few in the evening. Student traffic in Murkland was so heavy that signs were posted in the corridors urging students to keep to the right, so that the traffic would move fast enough for classes to begin on schedule.

The 1947 legislature was asked to approve a bond issue to construct an academic building costing $1,200,000. This figure was increased to $2,000,000, and approved, so that in April the trustees authorized Stoke to proceed with plans for a new technology building (Kingsbury Hall).

The increased enrollment naturally resulted in budgetary problems. Fortunately the GI Bill provided that the Veterans' Administration would pay the *cost of instruction* of the veteran students. Restricted operations during the war had resulted in a substantial increase in the university's financial reserves. But it was clear that the university could not continue to function effectively on the original millage formula. The enrollment had gone up much faster than had been estimated in 1925, the yield from the mill tax had actually gone down. During the Depression, $598,000 in mill tax funds had been withheld by the state. Of this amount, $496,000 would have gone into buildings, which the university now was faced with constructing at higher cost.

Stoke presented an analysis of the problem, together with some suggestions for its solution, to the trustees in October 1945. After some months of consideration, it was decided to go to the 1947 legislature with a request that the $598,000 withheld during the Depression be appropriated for buildings, and that the millage allowance be raised to one and a half mills. Stoke explained the situation to the university faculty on October 14, 1946. He pointed out that, whereas college enrollment in the country had experienced an eight-fold growth since 1900, the University of New Hampshire had grown thirty-fold. The university was "now [because of the GI Bill] very largely, perhaps dangerously, dependent upon the federal government," he said. He suggested that New England, of all regions, had the lowest proportion of its college-age population in college because it charged the highest fees in its public universities. "Young men and women of New Hampshire will constantly meet and measure arms with young men and women educated elsewhere," Stoke declared.

The statement read to the faculty was widely distributed around the state in a pamphlet entitled *The University of New Hampshire in the Service of the State.* With little opposition, the 1947 legislature increased the millage rate to one and one half mills. The university did not press its case for the funds withheld during the Depression, however.

A few weeks after arriving on campus, Stoke had read a paper to the University Senate.° This document, entitled *Policy Making in a University*, was later mimeographed and sent to all members of the faculty. In it Stoke described a university as a complex of faculty, staff, students, and parents, plus peripheral groups. In those days before the advent of student power, he saw university governance as a three-way tug of war between the administration, the faculty, and the trustees, with students and alumni providing an occasional push or pull. He argued that a university should be governed by consensus, not by separation of powers, and urged that the University Senate be more active.

As a means of encouraging faculty involvement, Stoke suggested at the next meeting of the senate that it create two new committees. The first, a standing Faculty Welfare Committee, would concern itself with housing, social, intellectual, and financial matters. The second was to be an *ad hoc* Senate Personnel Committee to study employer-employee relations.

The personnel committee, chaired by Professor Clifford S. Parker, took its work seriously. In December 1945 it presented a lengthy report dealing with such matters as appointments, tenure, and the selection of department chairmen. It advocated abolishing the policy that there should be no more than one full professor in a department. Also proposed were visiting, exchange, and endowed professorships. It opposed three other ideas: rotating department chairmanships, rating faculty by either colleagues or students, and involving faculty committees in personnel decisions.

Stoke in turn asked for a longer non-tenure

period for instructors and assistant professors, and that three-year appointments for department chairmen be substituted for the current indefinite ones. The University Senate voted to keep the tenure rules as they were, but agreed to the three-year terms for chairmen.

In January 1946, the Board of Trustees acted on these matters. Provision was made for more than one full professor in a department, for visiting and exchange professors, and for endowed professorships. As the positions became vacant, chairmen were to be appointed for three-year terms, although there was no limit on the number of terms a chairman could serve. Standards for appointment and promotion were included in the new statement of policies.

At the same meeting, the trustees approved a reorganization of student personnel services. Under Everett B. Sackett as dean of student administration, the new arrangement consolidated responsibility for student health, counseling, living arrangements, employment service, extracurricular activities except athletics, and financial aid; admission, conduct, and scholastic standing; record keeping; and veterans' education.

The Senate Personnel Committee soon turned its attention to improving salaries. This was not a new thought for the faculty, lagging salaries having been a concern since the start of World War II. A report of the committee in March 1946 termed the salary situation "chaotic." The committee reported that the highest-paid instructor and the lowest-paid professor were both earning $3,000 a year. The range for assistant professors was from $2,200 to $3,700, for associate professors from $2,500 to $4,000, for professors $3,000 to $4,100. The committee agreed that merit should be the principal factor in determining salaries, but held that upper and lower limits for each rank should be set. The proposed minimums were $2,000 for instructors, $2,800 for assistant professors, $3,600 for associate professors, and $4,400 for professors. It was also requested that the typical annual increment be in excess of one hundred dollars.

No substantial improvement having been achieved a year later, the faculty presented Stoke with a petition for higher salaries. The petition was pointedly addressed to the Board of Trustees. The trustees replied that such matters should be handled through established administrative channels. However, a cost-of-living adjustment, which until then had not figured in retirement contributions, was made part of the regular salary.

Money was not the only matter on which Stoke and the faculty did not always agree. The president was given to inquiring unobtrusively into faculty reading habits, and he once proposed a series of dinner meetings at which there would be scholarly lectures. In these and other indirect ways, the faculty got the impression that Stoke thought the level of scholarship in the university community was not all that it might have been. This opinion had one welcome side effect. Beginning in the summer of 1945, a small fund was made available to assist faculty members who wished to engage in summer study or other professional activities.

The rating of faculty by students continued to be an issue. At a January 1947 meeting of the University Senate, Stoke presented sample rating forms for consideration. After discussion the matter was referred to the Faculty Council. In February the council recommended that faculty members be required to use a rating scale "which may voluntarily be submitted to a faculty committee for analysis for future recommendations." By a close, show-of-hands vote the matter was referred back to the council where it was interred.

The trend under Engelhardt to add new programs and break down the lines between departments was reversed during the Stoke administration. As a result of a study of the architectural program by Dean Lauren E. Seeley of the College of Technology, the trustees accepted Seeley's recommendation that the curriculum be eliminated. At the same meeting, in January 1946, the trustees voted to admit no more students to the two-year program in secretarial studies. The trustees did vote in May 1946 to establish a department of agricultural engineering, but this was more a housekeeping matter than an expansion of offerings.

Differentiation in the number of credits required for degrees in the three undergraduate colleges was voted by the University Senate in December 1945. The new scale set 128 credits for liberal arts, 136 for agriculture, and 144 for technology.

The combined biology department, created in 1941, was split into its original components—bacteriology, botany, and zoology—in July 1947. The department of botany was transferred from liberal arts to the College of Agriculture in September 1947. One thing accomplished by the combination of the departments had been the creation of a basic course in general biology, required of nearly all students in liberal arts. To retain the interdisciplinary nature of this course, an interdepartmental committee was set up to conduct it.

A move to relax the tight faculty control of athletics, established when the sports programs were transferred from the Athletic Association to the department of physical education, was made in May 1946. The University Senate proposed that its athletic committees be abolished. In their place would be an Athletic Council to set policies on intercollegiate sports. The proposal eventually passed, after assurance was given that the council would report periodically to the senate. Each college was to elect one faculty member to the body for a six-year term, with other members to be the director of athletics, the dean of student administration, and the alumni secretary. This returned to the alumni a part of the voice in athletic policy they had lost in 1938 with the abolition of their advisory committee on athletics.

Athletics, in hibernation during the later years of the war, showed signs of life in the fall of 1945 with the organization of a four-team intramural touch football league, in which East Hall won the championship. Intercollegiate athletics returned with the 1945-46 basketball season. The 1946 *Granite* loyally pointed out the record—3-11— was not as bad as it seemed, for moral victories had been scored in some games which were lost by only a basket or two.

George Sauer had returned as head football coach, following his discharge from the Navy in October 1945. He resigned in January to become head coach at the University of Kansas. To succeed him, Stoke picked James W. "Biff" Glassford from a field of seventy-two candidates. Glassford, an All-American tackle at Pittsburgh, had been a line coach at Manhattan College, Carnegie Tech, and Yale. His appointment was heralded in the *New Hampshire* under the heading "Surprise Move by Prexy." Before the *New Hampshire* story was published Glassford had arrived on campus for a meeting with football candidates and had even started spring practice.

Other campus activities were picking up, but it would be inaccurate to say that they were returning to prewar normalcy. "Joe College" had gone off to war, to be one of those who did not return. As an editorial in the *New Hampshire* put it: "The veteran is a hard person to sell anything to . . . . Campus activities must be made attractive to him or he will ignore them. At present [his] chief interests are focused upon the problem of housing, studying, obtaining books, and a number of small details which were not to be coped with previously. So it stands to reason any social organization must be made doubly attractive."

The veterans established a cooperative in a university room to sell staples. An apartment on College Road was turned over to them to establish a child care center for their preschool youngsters.

The thirteen fraternities had a rushing season in March 1946, each chapter being allowed to pledge five men in anticipation of the time when their houses were turned back to them. Although veterans did not display much enthusiasm for some of the frothier aspects of fraternity living, the fraternities did offer a place to sleep and eat and so did not lack for members.

Early in the war, the alumni had proposed raising funds for a student union building as their memorial to the soldiers. Money came in slowly. The drive was loosely organized, plans for the building were vague, and there was controversy about its location. The site originally proposed was on Main Street adjacent to New Hampshire Hall. Later the location was changed to Bonfire Hill. This did not meet with universal approval, but when the university acquired the abandoned USO recreation building it was trucked to the campus in sections and reassembled on the Bonfire Hill site, between Hood House and East-West halls. Stoke offered a twenty-five dollar prize for a suitable name. "The Notch" was declared the winner, in honor of the cut which had been blasted through the lower part of the hill, when heating pipes and a sidewalk had been laid from Thompson Hall to the Commons. The building opened in May 1947 and served as a student activity center until it was demolished to make way for the present Memorial Union.

PART THREE

Everybody's University

(1948-1971)

*Posing for a recruiting brochure, this couple
symbolized the golden postwar years.*

20. Adams Improves the Image.

After only three years in Durham, Stoke resigned in August 1947 to become president of Louisiana State University. In his final report to the trustees he reviewed the problems facing the university. To raise standards and communicate enthusiasm, he suggested that it hire a handful of well-prepared, widely-experienced, and sophisticated individuals for key departmental and administrative posts. For much the same reason, he urged improvements in the academic plant and in the dormitories. In what must have been a reference to East-West halls, he commented: "While I would not for a moment disturb the distinctly utilitarian and even ascetic spirit of the University, certain improvements in convenience and taste would be highly desirable."

Stoke noted that the drive for memorial union funds had not enjoyed much success ($150,000 had been raised to date) and warned against a building too small. He suggested joining the union to the president's house, thus achieving economy in construction, while at the same time removing the president and his family from the center of campus. "Students wandering in at 2:00 A.M.," he pointed out, "wish exuberantly to greet the president and occasionally make the evenings quite long."

Stoke also recommended that the students assume more responsibility for their own affairs, and that they be taught how to manage them better. In closing, he handed a bouquet to the trustees:

The great factor which has made the administration of the University a pleasure for me is the belief that the single criterion which has governed the Board has been an *objective interest* in the welfare of the University. Matters of personal preference and interest, and of pressures from outside sources have all been subordinated to what the Board believed would pro-

mote the finest development for the University. So long as this spirit governs, the State will have few anxieties about the work of the University.

Carrying on between presidents was becoming a way of life for the Board of Trustees. The board president, Frank Randall, served as interim executive officer with the help of committees appointed from the trustees and from the university staff. Randall, however, was still active in business. Consequently Dean Lauren Seeley of technology, chairman of the faculty advisory committee, in effect became the acting president.

Thanks to a $2 million bond issue voted by the 1947 legislature, there was considerable planning for construction during 1947-48. The principal projects were Kingsbury Hall, a million-gallon standpipe and other improvements for the water system, and an expansion of the heating plant.

Since August the trustees had been considering a successor to Stoke. The faculty was asked to elect a committee on presidential qualifications, to report to the trustees by October 18, and a committee of two from each college was elected. Randall also asked the faculty to nominate candidates for the presidency. During the fall a number of candidates were invited to come to Durham for interviews by the trustees. Among those at a meeting on November 22 was Dr. Arthur S. Adams, provost of Cornell University. On January 17, 1948, he was unanimously elected on the trustees' first ballot.

Adams was born in Winchester, Massachusetts, July 1, 1896. Upon graduation from the U.S. Naval Academy in 1918, he was assigned to submarine duty which left him seriously ill. He was retired and sent to a sanitorium in Colorado. By 1922 he was teaching mathematics and science in the Denver public schools. In 1926 he earned a

*Walking to class
on the heated sidewalk
through "the notch."*

master's degree at the University of California, then returned to Colorado to study at the School of Mines, which awarded him the degree of Doctor of Science in 1927. He stayed there as assistant professor, professor, and finally assistant to the president. He went in 1940 to Cornell as assistant dean of engineering. In 1942 he was recalled by the Navy to take charge of its V-12 college training program. He returned to Cornell as provost in 1945. At the end of his war service he was awarded the Legion of Merit with a citation reading: "You were a central figure in planning and administering the Navy V-12 program, under which more than 150,000 officer candidates were enrolled in colleges and universities and more than 50,000 were qualified for commissions during the war."

Giving an early indication of his policy to build up the public image of the university—not only in the state but in the nation—Adams planned his inauguration in connection with a three-day symposium. It would bring to the campus outstanding leaders of contemporary thought in the fields of activity in which the university was engaged. Professor George R. Thomas, chairman of the department of the arts, was made general chairman to plan the event for October 7-9, 1948.

Speakers during the three-day event included Oliver C. Carmichael, president of the Carnegie Foundation for the Advancement of Teaching;

Charles E. Saltzman, assistant secretary of state; John L. Sullivan, secretary of the navy; General Lewis B. Hersey, director of selective service; Charles E. Gratke of the *Christian Science Monitor*; Charles E. Kellogg of the U.S. Department of Agriculture; Max W. Ball of the Department of the Interior; Sumner H. Slichter, Lamont Professor of Economics at Harvard; Albert W. Hull of the General Electric research laboratory; Alfred C. Neal of the Federal Reserve Bank of Boston; and Admiral Lewis L. Straus of the Atomic Energy Commission. As an inaugural it was rivaled only by that of Murkland in 1893, when the four original college buildings in Durham were dedicated and the speakers had joined issue on the future direction of the institution.

The next event observed—Founders' Day in April 1949—was a lesser affair. Adams and Dad Henderson addressed students who gathered around the Thompson Hall flagpole. Adams recorded messages commemorating the event, which recognized Ben Thompson's birthday, to be played at meetings of alumni clubs around the country on April 22.

The new building for the applied farming program (named in honor of George M. Putnam, long-time president of the New Hampshire Farm Bureau Federation) was dedicated on December 10, 1949. At the one-day symposium Governor Sherman Adams brought the greetings of the

132

state. Other speakers included Senator Styles Bridges; Arthur L. Deering, dean of agriculture at the University of Maine; Jessie Harris, dean of home economics at the University of Tennessee; Senator Edward J. Thye of Minnesota; and Sir James Turner, president of the Farmer's Union of Great Britain. More than six hundred attended.

The following November 11, there was a cornerstone laying ceremony for the new technology building. Cornerstone ceremonies had been held for Culver Hall in 1870 and for the Agricultural Experiment Station building in 1888, but this apparently was the first such event since the move to Durham. The trustees had earlier received a letter from Lewis H. Kenney '99, asking the university to give recognition to Albert Kingsbury, who had been professor of mechanical engineering from 1891 to 1899. After checking with senior members of the technology faculty, the trustees voted to name the engineering building for Kingsbury.

At the dedication ceremonies, Kingsbury's five daughters were on the speakers' platform. The event was made the occasion for a two-day symposium on "Technology in the Service of Mankind." Speakers included Ralph D. Paine of *Fortune*; James Phinney Baxter III, president of Williams College; Spofford English of the Atomic Energy Commission; Senator Ralph E. Flanders of Vermont; Governor Sherman Adams; Dean William C. White of the American Society for Engineering Education; and Claude Putnam, president of the National Association of Manufacturers. Worcester Polytechnic Institute presented Kingsbury's test apparatus, which it had in its possession because Kingsbury had gone there upon leaving New Hampshire College. The most important item, the original model of the Kingsbury thrust bearing, was made by him while he was at New Hampshire.

During his first summer in Durham, Adams retained Raymond F. Howes, secretary of Cornell University, to make a survey of the public relations program of the university. As a result, the trustees voted in September 1948 to create the post of director of public information. Francis E. Robinson '31, then university editor, was appointed to the position. A full-time assistant to handle athletic news was also authorized, and the budget for publicity was increased. The expansion, coupled with the noteworthy speakers brought to the campus, had results. Newspaper clippings in which the university was mentioned went from 237 in June to 1,955 by October. By the fall of 1949 clippings were running over 2,100 a month. °

To handle the details of all-university functions, entertain important campus visitors, coordinate scheduling of events, and oversee official publications, Adams suggested that the post of university secretary be established. In October 1949 Dr. Herbert J. Moss, then an assistant professor of sociology, was appointed to the position. University ceremonies, such as commencement, had already become somewhat formal under Stoke. Now they were planned with military precision. Each participant was furnished a mimeographed script, complete to the exact wording to be used; deans, in presenting candidates for degrees to the president, were instructed to tip their mortar boards.

The improvement of the public relations program did not result in a rush of state funds to support the university. In preparation for the 1949 legislative session, the trustee planning committee met on November 17, 1948, to discuss needs for buildings and operating funds. The trustees believed it was useless to go to the legislature with

° There were two other factors bringing press attention to the university. One was a controversy over political speakers, which is treated in a later chapter. The other was the filming of *Lost Boundaries*, produced by Louis de Rochmont and starring Mel Ferrer. The movie was based on the story of Albert C. Johnston, Jr., a UNH music major from Keene, whose Negro family had "passed" as white for many years. The filming took place on campus in the spring of 1949. A number of Durham residents appeared in the movie, as did the university choir under Professor Karl Bratton.

a request for another increase in the millage formula. This left an increase in tuition the only likely source of more money, together with a larger proportion of out-of-state students.

President Adams discussed the university's financial situation with Governor-elect Sherman Adams. The new governor attended the January 1949 meeting of the trustees, and at his suggestion the board voted to send a statement of the university's activities and financial situation to the members of the legislature. In March President Adams was invited to present the university's case before a joint session of the legislature.

Despite these efforts, the legislature made deep cuts in the university's appropriations. The 1949-50 budget was precariously balanced by deferring campus improvements and by reducing expenditures for travel, supplies, and instructional equipment. Little could be done to improve faculty salaries, but a cost-of-living adjustment made in 1948 was continued.

An added financial problem was the shrinking income from the GI Bill. For the veterans, the government had paid at various times either out-of-state tuition or a computed cost-of-instruction. In 1949 the Veterans' Administration refused to pay the new $450 out-of-state tuition; in addition the VA insisted that other federal funds received by the university must be deducted from the cost-of-instruction computation. This latter ruling affected all land grant institutions. In the fall of 1949, Adams was elected president of the Association of Land Grant Colleges and Universities. He took a leading role in the successful effort to guide new legislation through Congress to reverse the VA ruling. The new legislation helped some but not enough.

Adams reported to the trustees in February 1950 that the preliminary budget for 1950-51 had a deficit of $250,000, and that faculty salaries were $500 to $700 below the average of other New England land grant institutions. Further work reduced the estimated deficit, and in March the budget was approved "in principle" with the hope that additional money could be found to balance it. Governor Sherman Adams promised that he and the council would transfer $150,000 to the university from their emergency fund during the biennium.

The budget did provide improved salaries. Cost-of-living increments were made part of the base pay; the faculty received a $200 across-the-board increase, with fifty-three of them receiving merit increases as well. The basic stipend for graduate assistants was raised to $1,000 for the academic year. When Adams reported to the April 1950 University Senate meeting that his recommendation of a general salary increase for the coming year had been approved by the trustees, he received a standing vote of thanks.

Two steps were taken to seek a solution to the university's financial problems. The legislature established an interim commission to study future needs of the institution, and the university prepared A Summary of Financial Information for distribution around the state. The brochure showed that in 1948-49 the university's income had been a shade less than $4 million. Of this total, student fees had contributed $1.1 million as the largest single source of income, some $40,000 more than the amount appropriated by the state.

A list of needs for the next decade was presented to the interim commission in November 1950. At the top of the academic list was $200,000 for improvements in the salary scale; in this category also were an addition to the library and new buildings for liberal arts, the creative arts, the dairy department, and the home economics department. Heading the list of non-academic needs were two dormitories for women and three for men at a cost of $1,250,000, to be repaid from income. Other non-academic needs were a student union building, an armory, and physical-education improvements including an addition to the Field House, an indoor swimming pool, and an artificial ice rink.

21. Free Speech: Round One

Adams's concern for the university's image was put to its severest test in the area of what has come to be called "academic freedom"—the right of faculty and students to inquire freely, even if this means challenging the standards of the larger society. Though the issue was most intense in the postwar years, it was nothing new in the history of the institution.

Early manifestations concerned religion, not politics. There had been no problem in the early days when the dominance of Protestantism was taken for granted. In Hanover the college rented a pew in the Congregational church and contributed to the salary of its minister. Ezekiel Dimond, in effect the college's first executive, was nominated for his post by a Protestant pastor. Charles Murkland, the first president in Durham, was himself a minister; in his inaugural address he warned that blatant irreligion would not be tolerated on campus. President Lewis in 1929 secured trustee approval for a credit course in the history and philosophy of religion, to be taught by a Congregational minister. Also during the Lewis administration, the university began to make an annual contribution to Christian Work, Inc., and the University Senate elected faculty members to serve on its board of directors. Although this organization was open to Catholics (though hardly, it would seem, to Jews) they did not join. Learning of the university contribution, Rev. J. Desmond O'Connor, Catholic chaplain from 1938 to 1966, asked for proportionate contributions to the Newman Club (Catholic) and the Hillel Club (Jewish). When Father O'Connor's request reached the trustees in 1947, they wisely stopped contributing to any religious group.

Professor Donald C. Babcock, an ordained minister and for thirty-eight years a teacher of history and philosophy, has recalled that early complaints about courses also focused on religion. Father O'Connor objected to a text used in the required freshman history course, and advised Catholic students against registering in certain courses. And Governor Francis P. Murphy once had occasion to complain to President Engelhardt· "What is the matter with [Professor] Babcock? Is he anti-Catholic?" In recent years an ecumenical atmosphere has prevailed, while conflict has shifted to the political arena.

Politics emerged as an issue in the mid-1930s when compulsory ROTC was first seriously questioned. In the spring of 1934, the campus Progressive Club sent delegates to an anti-war conference at Smith College. At the same time, two sophomores canvassed student sentiment against compulsory ROTC. Members of the Progressive Club formed a new organization called the Student League for Industrial Democracy. President Lewis took the ROTC matter up with the trustees, and in June 1934 they voted that cases of "so-called conscientious objection" should be referred to Lewis. That fall, four students were reported as excused from ROTC. Nearly all of the students cut their eleven o'clock classes on a day in April 1935 to attend a "strike against war" rally in the gymnasium. The New Hampshire Daughters of the American Revolution, who had contributed money to the university's student loan fund, protested that they did not want their money helping to support such students. As a result, the trustees voted "to authorize the treasurer to return to the New Hampshire Daughters of the American Revolution the entire principal of funds contributed to and administered with the University Student Loan Fund."

President Engelhardt, upon his arrival in Durham, was interviewed about the political activities of students. The Manchester *Union* of April 2, 1937, contained the following: "The number of collegiate 'reds,' 'light reds' and 'pinks' about whom so much is written and said these days, is exaggerated in Dr. Engelhardt's opinion . . . . The charge of 'parlor pinks' arises naturally, in his opinion, because young people today are more interested in world and national problems."

World War II brought with it a suspension of dissent. For example, Sidney A. Dimond '43 (a scion of Ezekiel Dimond's family), who had been excused from ROTC as a conscientious objector, served as commander of a landing craft in the Pacific.

A number of the faculty were leaders in the New Hampshire Independent Voters for Roosevelt and Truman in 1944, and in a successive Independent Voters group in 1946. They were suspected of being Communists, and President Stoke found it necessary to conduct an investigation to prevent one of them from being discharged on this ground.

Although the students had gone willingly to war against the Nazis, when they returned to the campus they were not unanimous supporters of the status quo. In the fall of 1946 a campus charter was denied the American Veterans Committee, a liberal group, on the grounds that the university recognized national organizations only if their main purpose was to serve the educational needs of students. (Although denied a charter, members of the group were active on campus. The *New Hampshire* of October 9, 1947, reported that they were holding their first meeting of the year "co-sponsored" by the International Relations Club.) No other national veterans' organization applied for a campus charter.

In September 1947 a new and informally organized group calling itself the Student Committee on Lectures and Concerts arranged for Henry Wallace to speak on campus. Wallace had been Secretary of Agriculture, Vice-President, and then Secretary of Commerce under Franklin D. Roosevelt, but many considered him dangerously

In conference with the Dean of Student Administration, Thompson Hall, 1950.

radical. After discussing the matter at their September meeting, the trustees voted to send a letter to Dean Ruth J. Woodruff, chairman of the Committee on Student Organizations, reading in part:

It was the unanimous opinion of the board that the procedure followed by your committee in giving approval to this unofficial group was most unusual and irregular and under such circumstances does not meet with the approval of the board of trustees . . . . [The board] requests that in the future . . . there be no repetition of the unusual and irregular procedure which was adopted in this instance.

Although displeased, the trustees did nothing to stop Wallace's speech, delivered to an overflow audience of 2,500 in the Field House on October 7, 1947. Wallace was still nominally a Democrat.

In his talk he said that allowing his engagement at the state university was a great credit to New Hampshire tolerance: he had been barred by the University of California.

The Manchester *Union Leader* did not reflect New Hampshire tolerance.° It said: "No cheap Nazi demagogue, no cheap Italian Fascist ranting from a minor balcony in a provincial town in Italy, no Huey Long at his worst, ever harangued audiences and fed them so much plausible poison as did Henry Wallace."

Although disturbed by the Wallace event, the trustees did not close the campus to politicians. In response to a request to use campus facilities, trustee president Frank W. Randall wrote the Young Republican Club: "It will be necessary to avoid conflicts with the regularly scheduled events of various campus organizations. The board suggests that a request be sent to the President's Office for each meeting as far in advance as possible. By securing specific permission for each proposed meeting, it is felt that no misunderstanding can arise." The Young Republicans were one thing; the Progressive Citizens of America (which in 1948 became Wallace's Progressive party) were another. In December the trustees denied a request from G. Harris Daggett, assistant professor of English, to allow that organization to hold meetings on campus. (William Loeb, publisher of the Manchester *Union Leader,* wrote the trustees at this time to tell them that John G. Rideout, professor of English, was state chairman of the PCA and that Daggett was vice-chairman

for the Seacoast Region. The trustees acknowledged the letter but took no other action.)

Although the Wallace speech had been arranged by an *ad hoc* committee, many on that committee were members of the Liberal Club, which had been formed on February 26, 1947. Some of the leaders of the club were suspected of having Communist leanings, if not actual party membership. One Liberal Club member claimed he had been threatened with a beating because of his participation. There were rumors of undercover agents, of spies, of students' papers being surreptitiously ransacked for incriminating evidence.

The Liberal Club petitioned for the privilege of publishing a magazine. This was denied, first because the constitution of the club did not mention such a project, later because the material proposed for publication lacked literary merit. Dean Lauren Seeley, who was serving as executive officer, took the matter to the trustees. They supported the denial.°

The state executive committee of the Progressive Citizens of America elected Professor Daggett a member of the national board. At Henry Wallace's request, Professor Rideout became a member of the national Wallace-for-President committee. A chartered bus took UNH students to a Students-for-Wallace conference in Cambridge, Massachusetts, on February 14, 1948. Early in March the local Students-for-Wallace group met in the Durham Community Church, where they heard Rideout propose a plan for student participation in the campaign. The group di-

---

° The morning *Union* and the afternoon *Leader* were purchased by William Loeb in 1946 and became editions of a single newspaper. To this organization was added the *New Hampshire Sunday News* in 1948. The result was New Hampshire's only seven-day, state-wide newspaper. Loeb owns newspaper properties in other states, but has nowhere else achieved the influence he has enjoyed in New Hampshire. A staunch conservative, he has taken great delight in making life uncomfortable for those of more liberal persuasion. An exasperated John F. Kennedy once complained: "I believe that there is a publisher who has less regard for the truth than William Loeb, but I can't think of his name."

° The *New Hampshire Sunday News* commented on February 8, 1948: "A student publication was killed before birth at our university, killed with some evasive words about the lack of literary quality. Because censorship can live in the cold death of unborn books just as well as in the hot accusing embers of books burned by Hitler, we smell the dank, royal odor of censorship at our state's university . . . . Free speech doesn't have a literary qualification attached to it. The Constitution doesn't say that freedom of speech is guaranteed to those who are able to distinguish a gerund from a participle."

verted its attention from the presidential campaign long enough to stage an outdoor peace rally in April.

Arthur Adams assumed the presidency of the university during the summer of 1948. In conference with the university deans, he worked out a policy on political activity which was adopted by the trustees in September. Basically, it provided that major candidates would be invited to campus to debate each other but that there would be no other campus politicking. The Progressive Party protested the restrictions of the policy.*

The first "civic forum" under the policy was held October 21, 1948, featuring candidates for Congress. The Progressive Party was represented by Professor Rideout, candidate for U.S. senator; Harold H. Horne '49, candidate for the second congressional district; and Alexander Karanikas '38, candidate for the first congressional district. John Pillsbury represented the Republican candidates. No Democrat showed up. The major-party candidates may have been wise to bypass the forum. Of the 221,136 ballots case in the state in November, the Progressives received fewer than 2,000.

Although the political campaign was over, the controversy continued. The legislature met in January 1949. Harold Hart, a representative from Wolfeboro, introduced a resolution calling for an investigation of rumors that "certain persons connected with the University of New Hampshire and other educational institutions in the state

---

* In January 1950 the trustees replaced this policy with a more general and liberal one in order to give freedom of discussion to the extent permitted by the state and federal constitutions. It provided: the right of assembly and speech at the university would be limited only to the extent applied to other citizens advocating the illegal overthrow of the government; there could be reasonable use of the campus for political meetings; political organizations could invite outside speakers in the same way as did other organizations; the university could not accept responsibility unless overthrow of the government were advocated; the political activity of faculty members would be governed by the policy on this matter of the American Association of University Professors.

have been teaching or advocating the overthrow of the government by force if necessary." He also introduced a bill, one section of which would have prohibited the teaching of the doctrines of Communism or overthrow of the government by force. Another section provided for an oath to be taken by all teachers in the state that they would not advocate overthrow of the government by force and that they belonged to no organization which did.

On February 1, a public hearing was held in Concord on the resolution calling for a legislative investigation. A substantial number of students attended, and a few spoke before the joint committee on judiciary and education. They made a generally favorable impression, although one committeewoman did ask: "Are you boys getting credit for coming over here to defend the faculty?"

President Adams and members of the Board of Trustees were invited to appear before an executive session of the joint legislative committee on February 24. Adams read a twenty-one page statement, which was released to the press. In it he detailed rumors about communistic activities on campus. He identified seven such rumors, in each case indicating what he believed had given rise to them and what he had found the facts to be. He listed five conclusions:

First, that there is a student club on campus which had been much interested in explosive questions of social philosophy and that there are members of this club who in their politics might be called left-wing extremists. I am convinced, however, that the membership of the club is not Communistic dominated and, since there is no law making membership in the Communist Party illegal, I see no basis on which we may deny the opportunities of the University to a student on the basis of his political affiliation.

Second, that two faculty members [Rideout and Daggett] have engaged in political activity in the Progressive Party and that all of those in a position to know these individuals are prepared to testify that they do not believe them to be Communists, that they have not been guilty of subversive acts, and that they have conformed to stated University policy . . . .

Third, no evidence has been brought to light by which unethical or subversive activity can be successfully charged against any faculty member.

Fourth, that the University Trustees and administration have been and are continuing to exert every effort to see that the faculty makes completely objective presentations of all the controversial issues of the day, and

Fifth, that the University Trustees and administration have been keenly sensitive all along to the determination of the proper place of political activity on the University campus and have by their acts in individual instances as well as by their establishment of specific policy taken effective measures to safeguard the integrity of the University.

The resolution was amended by the committee to kill the legislative investigation, but to set up an interim commission to study subversive activities in the state without specific reference to the university. The law requiring the disclaimer oath was passed, however. In October Adams reported to the trustees that the oaths "have been executed by all members of the faculty and staff without question, and have been transmitted to the Office of the Attorney General."°

On the campus, meanwhile, a petition for a chapter of Students for Democratic Action was denied. Several requests for campus talks by real

---

° Rideout did not have to sign the disclaimer. Although not threatened with dismissal, he was given to understand that his future at the university was uncertain, and he had resigned at the end of the college year to take a position at Idaho State College. The disclaimer stayed on the books in New Hampshire until 1969. In that year it was amended so that teachers only took the simple oath required of all office holders in the state.

or alleged Communists were turned down, either because they were judged to be in violation of the policy on political meetings or because the speakers were under indictment for such crimes as defiance of state or federal investigative committees. Some meetings barred on campus were held in the Community Church. Herbert Phillips, recently dismissed by the University of Washington, was denied permission to speak on the open triangle in the center of town and ended by having coffee with a group of students in Notch Hall. A group wanting to hold a peace rally was unable to get a recognized campus organization to sponsor it.

In the spring of 1949, G. Harris Daggett was backed for promotion from assistant to associate professor by the English department and by Dean Blewett of liberal arts. The promotion was not approved by the trustees and became a public issue. Student representatives met with individual trustees, and 1,500 students signed petitions supporting the promotion. The trustees reviewed the matter at their May meeting and issued a statement saying that promotions were not automatic, that only four assistant professors had been promoted that year, that failure to win promotion was not evidence of unsatisfactory work, and that in seven years on the faculty Daggett had had four pay increases. In a statement after the meeting, Daggett said he was looking for another position "so that I may gain the professional recognition that is denied here." He did not leave, and a year later received his promotion to associate professor.

22. Return of the Beanie

In December 1948, the trustees had voted to increase tuition. In-state tuition had gone up only ten dollars in twenty years, in spite of rising prices, and was then $160 a year. The new rate was $200, effective in September 1949. The out-of-state rate had been raised to $360 in 1946; it now went to $450. To help ease the impact on the students, the sum set aside for tuition grants was raised from $18,750 to $37,500. Previous tuition grants had paid $75 each and were limited to freshmen. A new policy made some $100 grants available, and all classes except seniors were eligible. Room rents went up by seventeen percent.

Most student jobs paid forty-five cents an hour, with a few at fifty cents. Letters and editorials in the *New Hampshire* complained of this low rate. It was pointed out that a student in Durham had to work ninety-one hours a month to pay for a meal ticket, whereas at Dartmouth a student worked sixty hours a month for his meals. The number of students employed also was down. There was, however, plenty of cash available for student loans.

A trust fund for scholarships, starting with a gift of $500 but later growing to more than a third of a million dollars, was accepted by the trustees in June 1949. The donor was Charles E. Stillings '00. From his graduation until his retirement, Stillings held a modest job as a foreman with the New Haven railroad. In the Benjamin Thompson tradition, Stillings never married, lived with extreme frugality, and invested his savings with skill. He returned to the campus each spring for the alumni reunion, a cadaverous figure clad in black, wearing a wing collar. His host on campus was Treasurer Raymond C. Magrath.

Upon studying the terms of the trust, Adams found that it provided:

No money from this trust shall be used for assistance of any except men of Caucasian race, whose parents are American citizens, and who may prove themselves to be free of any taint of Communism, Nazism, Socialism or any other foreign "ism" or ideology, and any applicant for aid from this trust, about whom there is any doubt of his belief in the American form of government, shall be required to take a non-Communist oath and/or oath of allegiance before receiving any such aid.

Adams questioned accepting such a restrictive gift, and the trustees voted to rescind their acceptance in January 1950. A conference with Stillings resulted in his changing the terms to: "worthy male students, whose parents are American citizens, and who believe in the American form of democracy and the preservation of the American way of life." With this revision, the trustees in February again accepted the gift.

The development of research and graduate study continued to accelerate. Lauren Seeley, dean of technology, doubled as dean of the graduate school during 1948-49; William A. Medesy, associate dean of students, was his administrative assistant. They prepared a report on graduate study in the past and suggestions for its development. A. Fred Daggett '28 was named dean of the graduate school in June 1949.

During the summer of 1949 a sponsored research council was formed. Fred Daggett was named coordinator of research in addition to his position as dean of the graduate school. A committee on radioactive materials had been established to assure compliance with safety practices in this area. Notable horticultural developments included the New Hampshire midget watermelon, the Granite State muskmelon, the Durham raspberry, the Great Bay strawberry, and several new varieties of blueberries, all developed under the leadership of Professor Albert F. Yeager.

In the fall of 1949, the presidents of the six New England state universities met to discuss what specialties each might develop to serve the region. This was the beginning of an interstate compact.

The drive to raise funds for a memorial student union, started during World War II, had faltered when pledges reached $150,000. At a meeting with trustees and alumni directors in June 1948, Adams suggested that a new start be made. The first step was to bring the alumni records up to date: $4,000 of university funds was voted for this purpose. The next step was to bring to campus the directors of student unions at Brown, Bowdoin, and the University of Wisconsin. Porter Butts, director of the Wisconsin union, eventually was retained as a consultant. On his recommendation a Union Planning Committee of sixteen members—representing trustees, alumni, administration, faculty, and students—was set up. Surveys were made of student organization needs, student traffic patterns, and recreational facilities desired by students. On the basis of these data, the site of the present Union and its facilities were determined. Butts recommended that a building costing from $750,000 to $900,000 be planned. By now, almost two years had passed since the decision to get a fresh start on the project.

Student life did not stand still waiting for the erection of the new Memorial Union. There was a reaction from the serious atmosphere that had marked the campus during the peak of the enrollment of veterans following World War II. The new attitude was expressed in an editorial in the January 20, 1949, *New Hampshire* headed "Bring Back the Beanie." It urged: "Bring back those rah-rah customs that made college life something more than a diploma grind . . . . Let's have some of the finer customs of the past which tend to knot student with student, student with class, student with college." Another sign that some lightness was returning to student life was the first "Night of Sin" at Notch Hall in March 1950. Faculty members presided over whirling roulette wheels and rolling dice, with students boldly plunging with phony money.

At the same time, students were showing increasing interest in university government. Edward D. Eddy, then assistant to the president, in October 1950 organized the first annual Conference on Campus Affairs at the Rolling Ridge conference center in Andover, Massachusetts. About seventy-five students and two dozen members of the faculty and administration spent the weekend in serious discussion. This gave impetus to the movement to combine the men's Student Council and the Association of Women Students into a single Student Senate. Students already had been given token representation on the faculty committee on discipline. After the Rolling Ridge conference, student judiciary boards were set up to handle most disciplinary cases.

The trustees denied a request from a group of students to publish a literary magazine of a light and humorous nature to be called *Oyster Stew*. The *New Hampshire* in 1947 was rated "first class—excellent" by the Associated Collegiate Press. Professor Carroll Towle's students continued to lead the nation in winning prizes in the *Atlantic Monthly* contest for college writers. In January 1949 Professor Karl H. Bratton conducted the University Choir in its first coast-to-coast broadcast over the Mutual network. Shirley Hoyle '50 was chosen Queen of New England Coeds in May 1949, the *New Hampshire* memorializing the event by devoting its entire front page to her portrait.

Because of the financial difficulties of fraternities during the Depression, the trustees had voted in 1935 that no new fraternities would be allowed on campus. The Ritrian Club, a non-campus organization, petitioned for the establishment of a chapter of Acacia in the spring of 1949, and this policy was reexamined. A review committee of five—a trustee, an administrator, a faculty-alumnus, a fraternity man, and a non-fraternity man—was appointed to study the matter.

The committee found that the membership of

fraternities and sororities had fallen from 52.5 percent of the student body in 1935-36 to 27.7 percent in 1948-49. The enrollment had more than doubled, but the number of fraternities had not increased. As a group the houses were in satisfactory financial condition. Since World War II, national attention had been directed to the clauses in the constitutions of many fraternities restricting membership on the basis of religion or race; at the university, administrators and some students had been working to eliminate such clauses in the local organizations. That Acacia was associated with the Masonic order introduced a complication on this point, but the group held that Catholics could join if they wished. In October 1949 the trustees approved the establishment of the chapter, the first and only new fraternity on campus since 1929.

With a team made up largely of World War II veterans—a number of them veterans also of the university's undefeated team of 1942—"Biff" Glassford's 1947 Wildcats won all eight of their regular season games. The university was asked if it would be interested in bids to play in the Glass Bowl in Toledo, Ohio, and in the Sun Bowl in El Paso, Texas. After discussion by the athletic council and the trustees, the bid to the Glass Bowl was accepted. In spite of a great second half rally, New Hampshire bowed to the University of Toledo 20-14, December 6, 1947.

Their appetites whetted by success, alumni and students began to campaign for financial support of athletes. Under the Cowell regime, athletes had been aided from Athletic Association funds. For a decade, however, they had benefited only by a slight favoritism in the dispensing of student aid funds, and from a few hundred dollars from individual alumni given the football coaches to dispense. The Glass Bowl team members were virtually all receiving support under the GI Bill.

In the spring after the Glass Bowl game, Glassford told Ernest Christensen '23, F. Samuel Knox '34, and Ralph B. Craig '27—three of the alumni who had been informally helping athletes—that he needed $1,800 to recruit three or four boys he had lined up. The four men met in Knox's office in Dover and organized the 100 Club.°

The club officers dispensed money directly to athletes, by-passing the university financial aid machinery. This was in violation (but not unusual on other campuses) of codes adopted by collegiate athletic conferences. Hearing of the situation, Adams consulted with the officers and secured their agreement to have the funds handled by a special committee, which was appointed by the trustees in September 1948. This group shortly decided that the regular Financial Aid Committee could be trusted with the distribution, the coaching staff making recommendations with respect to athletic prowess, and the committee applying its usual standards of financial need.

Although the 100 Club helped attract athletic talent, the advantage was not sufficient to hold Glassford, who had been unhappy with his salary. After three seasons in Durham, he resigned in January 1949 to become head coach at the University of Nebraska. He was succeeded by Clarence E. "Chief" Boston. Boston had graduated from Harvard as a French and classics major in 1939 and had starred as a quarterback and a wrestler. He came to Durham from a position as backfield coach at West Point. Boston's 1950 team won all its games. Because of the continuing power of the Wildcats, they were having difficulties with their schedule. Several of their traditional rivals were finding the competition discouraging and wanted to drop New Hampshire.

° Another version claims that the 100 Club was formed on the train bringing the Wildcat supporters home from the Glass Bowl game. "Dutch" Knox had been a great football star in the early 1930s. After his final season at New Hampshire, he sought to continue his exploits by enrolling as a freshman at the University of Illinois. His success was so sensational that his press notices got back to New Hampshire, and somebody informed the Illinois officials that their star had already had one college football career. That ended Knox's days at Illinois, so he turned professional, playing tackle for eight years with the Detroit Lions. He later showed equal ability in business, rising to the presidency of the Drackett Products Co. of Cincinnati.

23. Dean Chandler Is Promoted

The spotlight of national attention focused on the University of New Hampshire by Adams's leadership cast reflected light on him. After less than three years in Durham, in May 1950 he was offered the presidency of the American Council on Education, and he accepted.

In his letter of resignation to the trustees, Adams said: "The decision with which I was faced was one of the most difficult, if not the most difficult, of my entire life, and the only reason I decided to accept the presidency of the American Council on Education was because of the broad opportunity that position offers to serve all education."

There was some criticism of Adams in the state press for leaving his post in Durham after so short a time. The *New Hampshire* replied that the rapid turnover in the presidency of the university only proved that the trustees picked outstanding men for the job. Before Adams's departure in November, 1,200 students gathered before his house one evening to give him a surprise rally. It was the biggest demonstration for a president since that given Hetzel in 1923.

A trustee committee was appointed on May 20, 1950, to formulate qualifications for the next president and to make recommendations to the full board. This committee was authorized to designate faculty representatives to serve with them. Selected were professors Thomas G. Phillips of agriculture, Thomas O. Marshall of liberal arts, and Leon W. Hitchcock of technology. "It was made clear," the trustees noted, "that the Board of Trustees in no way would delegate its responsibility and authority in coming to a final decision on the naming of the president, but that the Board sought the counsel, advice and help from the faculty in screening the candidates from its viewpoint."

In September, with the faculty representatives present, the trustees voted unanimously to appoint Robert F. Chandler, dean of the College of Agriculture, as president of the university. As Chandler already was on campus, no interim administration was necessary. He officially took over as head of the institution on November 17, 1950.

At the time of his election, Chandler was forty-three years old. Although born in Columbus, Ohio, he had been reared in New Gloucester, Maine, and had entered the University of Maine in 1925. After a year as state horticulturist in Maine, he spent the next three years at the University of Maryland, where he earned his Ph.D. He did further graduate work at the University of California at Berkeley before going to Cornell in 1935 as an assistant professor. He had advanced to full professor when he left Cornell in 1946 to do research on the corn and wheat crops of Mexico for the Rockefeller Foundation. His appointment as dean of agriculture at New Hampshire followed a year on the Mexican project. As a hobby he bred for exhibition silver-laced Wyandotte poultry at his farm on the outskirts of Dover.

Chandler was inaugurated on April 25, 1951, the first University of New Hampshire president to have been elevated from within its own faculty.

Chandler's early months in office were concerned with budgetary matters. The Interim Commission on Future Policy and Financing of the University, established by the 1949 legislature, presented its report to the 1951 session. Among its recommendations were: (1) that the administration of the university continue to be separate from other educational activities of the state, but that a Council on Teacher Education be established to coordinate this activity in the university and the two teachers' colleges; (2) that the millage formula be continued at one and one-half mills but that it be computed on equalized rather than assessed valuation, thus substantially increasing the base; and (3) that a comprehensive study of higher education in the state be conducted by a professional group.

For university action the commission recommended: (1) that tuition, both in-state and out-of-state, be increased by fifty dollars, with room and board charges also increased; (2) that the allocation of university funds for tuition grants be increased from $37,500 to $50,000; and (3) that a master plan for construction be established and revised annually.

The commission argued that its recommendations would result in adjusting faculty compensation to the level of other New England state universities, and still provide about $225,000 annually for buildings. The trustees endorsed the commission report on February 17, 1951, and voted to take the actions recommended for the university. The legislature did its part by making the change in the millage formula suggested by the commission, but the $1,420,237 yearly appropriated under the new formula clearly was less than needed.* Consequently the legislature appropriated an additional $300,000 annually, provided there was this much surplus money in the state treasury. Fortunately there was.

The main budgetary problem concerned faculty and staff salaries and fringe benefits. The increases in the state appropriation and in tuition made some improvement possible, but the Faculty Welfare Committee pressed for substantially

---

* In 1953, Representative Emile Soucy of Manchester introduced a bill to repeal the millage law and put the university on a line-item budget. The bill was defeated, as were similar bills in later years. In truth, the millage formula has become obsolete as a means of financing the university, especially since Keene and Plymouth State Colleges were joined to the university system in 1963. Its only virtue has been to preserve the principle of a lump-sum appropriation, free from line-by-line prescription by the legislature.

more. A report of the committee to the University Senate in March 1952 indicated that faculty salaries, when adjusted for increases in the cost of living, were below those of 1940. They also were below the salaries at other New England state universities, except for Vermont. (A year later the trustees approved the following minimum salaries: professors, $6,000; associate professors, $5,000; assistant professors, $4,000; instructors $3,200.)

The trustees tentatively decided to seek to have the 1953 legislature raise the millage allotment to two mills. The special committee of trustees, administrators, and faculty prepared for wide distribution a pamphlet, *Information on the Financial Condition of the University of New Hampshire*. The January 1953 *Alumnus* also included material on the financial situation. Chandler and the finance committee of the trustees met with the newly elected governor, Hugh Gregg. He held that the state did not have enough money to increase the millage formula, but offered to add $275,000 (later raised to $280,000) to the university's allotment in each year of the biennium. The trustees agreed, but asked that millage funds which had not been appropriated in the current biennium be added. The governor went along with this request.

Both university and state officials agreed that the 1953 action was a stop-gap arrangement, and in November 1953 Chandler and Treasurer Raymond C. Magrath met with a legislative committee to make proposals for the future Included in the university estimates was $7,500,000 in capital funds within the next fifteen years.

In December 1953 the trustees received the report of an audit of university accounts made by the office of the Legislative Budget Assistant. Although finding that funds had been adequately accounted for, it was critical of the concentration of all controls in the hands of a single individual, the university treasurer. As a result, a national auditing concern was retained in 1954 to recommend changes in the institution's business proce-

*Memorial
Union
Convocation
1953.*

dures and to conduct an independent audit. The report was received in December and resulted in new positions being added in the business office. Treasurer Magrath, who believed that his largely one-man operation had brought efficiency and economy, was unhappy that the trustees raised so few questions about the state audit. He resigned in March 1955 when he was offered the newly created position of comptroller and business manager of Tufts University.

Substantial private gifts came to the university during this period. Harry C. Batchelder '13, a Boston North Shore skating rink impresario, offered a used ice-making machine (valued at $25,000 to $30,000) if the university would adapt it for use in an outdoor skating rink. A study showed that about $60,000 in university funds would be needed to complete the rink; the trustees hesitated to accept the gift but eventually did so. (The rink was dedicated February 12, 1955, at the Colby game, which New Hampshire won 8-0. A northwest wind congealed the spectators during the ceremony. Batchelder Rink was eventually converted into Snively Arena.)

Mrs. Irene Hale, widow of the music critic Philip Hale, left the residue of her estate toward the erection of an arts building. Brandeis University also had a claim on this estate, and after negotiations the University of New Hampshire wound up with cash and securities with a net value of $58,990, plus some personal effects.

The biggest windfall was a gift of $50,000 for scholarships, plus the residue of the estate of Miss Harriet Paul and her sister Isabel. The estate was valued at about half a million dollars. The Paul ladies were the last members of a family which had operated a nineteenth-century foundry in Newfields, New Hampshire.

Building on the foundation laid during the Adams administration, the drive to complete raising funds for the Memorial Union was launched with a three-day convocation on the "Enrichment of Lives on a University Campus," April 23-25, 1953. The speakers ranged from the British ambassador to Olympic skier Andrea Meade Lawrence. This came a decade after the start of the original campaign in February 1943.

A contest had been held in 1951 to select an

architect for the Memorial Union building. Thirteen entries had been received, the judges picking Ronald Gourley of Boston and Dan Kiley of Franconia, New Hampshire, as the winners. Gourley and Kiley were retained, and their design was featured in the campaign. The design was not accepted without spirited debate in the university community: it was contemporary, and many held that no departure should be made from the "Georgian Colonial" style of the rest of the campus. Compromise was reached by substituting a pitched roof for the flat one originally proposed.

Jere Chase '36, who at the time was director of admissions, was picked to head the fund drive for the university. The goal was set at $650,000, which, added to the $150,000 on hand from the original drive, would make $800,000 available for the building. By the end of 1954 the goal had been exceeded by about $25,000.

Meanwhile, a less ambitious drive was conducted for a memorial to Oren V. "Dad" Henderson, who had died in 1951. More than $8,500 was raised in three months. Part of the money was used for the purchase of the Henderson carillon in Thompson Hall, and the balance went to a scholarship fund. The carillon was dedicated April 22, 1952.*

Expansion of academic facilities during the Chandler administration was confined to remodeling the top floor of Pettee Hall for the home economics department, and Hewitt Hall for the department of the arts. A nutrition barn was built by the university crew, utilizing the lumber salvaged from College Woods trees blown down in the 1938 hurricane. Construction of a broiler test plant ran into difficulties when it developed that the cost would exceed the money available, but the situation was eased when faculty, students, and poultry men organized two work bees in October 1952. Grant House on Garrison Avenue was remodeled in 1951 as a headquarters for the Alumni Association.

Sawyer Hall for women and Alexander Hall for men were ready when classes started in September 1951. A rare situation developed the following semester when an appreciable number of spaces in the men's dormitories were vacant. To help keep all beds occupied, a war surplus building on College Road was rented to the Portsmouth Vocational Institute, which transported its students in two old buses used at the end of World War II for bringing university students from Wentworth Acres in Portsmouth. Fairchild Hall, which had always housed men, was refurbished and used for women beginning in 1951-52. Their proportion in the student body was growing as the enrollment of veterans declined.

Stories and editorials in the *New Hampshire* in the fall of 1952 alleging fire hazards in campus buildings, especially East-West halls, resulted in a request to the state fire marshall to investigate. He found the situation not particularly alarming, but a decision was made to start installing automatic sprinkler systems in buildings not of fire resistant construction. Steps also were taken to improve the University-Durham fire department. A seventy-five foot aerial ladder replaced the 1913 hook and ladder truck (which was purchased by the Pi Kappa Alpha fraternity) and additional firemen were provided, so that two would be on duty at all times.

The 1953 legislature was asked to authorize a self-liquidating bond issue for another women's dormitory and for a men's dormitory to replace East-West halls. Authorization was given for borrowing for a women's dormitory (McLaughlin Hall) but not for a men's residence.

Plans to offer the Ph.D. in chemistry, botany, zoology, and horticulture had taken shape in

---

* The electronic instrument has sixty-four bells, with thirty-two notes and three octaves. During its first year of operation, a university official took a visitor to view the console in the Thompson Hall tower and was more than a little surprised to find the room occupied by a cot, cooking utensils, an electric hotplate, and laundry drying on a line. Henry K. Baker '55, a music major who had been engaged as carillonneur, was sharing quarters with the instrument. Dispossession orders were issued promptly.

1950. The next year outside authorities were invited to evaluate the capacity of these departments to offer doctoral degrees. They recommended more staff and equipment. The Graduate Council and the graduate faculty had endorsed the proposals, but in March 1952 the University Senate rejected them by a vote of 47 to 32. Cost was a major issue.

In support of the proposal, the Graduate Council had prepared a seven-page report. It showed that in 1952 there were twenty-seven departments with master degree programs, with 950 candidates (200 of them currently in residence) for that degree. It predicted that Ph.D. programs would not increase the number of graduate students, but would attract more competent graduate assistants, thus reducing the teaching burden on the faculty. It also argued that the proposed programs would increase the number and amount of research grants, then amounting to $120,000.

In June 1953 Herbert Moss, who was then dean of the graduate school, moved that the University Senate approve Ph.D. programs for the four departments seeking them. On a 51 to 20 vote the senate approved the new degree, and the trustees confirmed the action a few days later.

That undergraduate programs had attained a high level was evidenced when the university was granted charters by three outstanding honorary fraternities. On December 9, 1950, a chapter of Tau Beta Pi, honorary engineering society, was installed on campus. A chapter of Phi Beta Kappa was installed on December 16, 1952, with membership limited to students in the general liberal arts programs. In May 1954 was installed a chapter of Sigma Xi honorary scientific research fraternity.

Other recognition came to the university community during this period. A volume of poetry by Professor Babcock, *For Those I Taught*, was published in an enlarged second edition in 1951. A number of Babcock's poems also appeared in the *New Yorker* magazine. Professor Eric Huddle-ston, designer of many campus buildings, was elected a fellow of the American Institute of Architects in 1953. In 1954 the *New Hampshire Alumnus* was picked as the "magazine of the year" in the American Alumni Council contest, and editor L. Franklin Heald '39 was awarded the Sibley medal. An event of only local interest—but one which probably would attract national attention should it occur today—was the awarding in 1954 of the "outstanding citizen" award of the Inter-Fraternity Council to Louis Bourgoin, long-time chief of the campus police.°

Not all of the developments redounded to the academic glory of the university. On January 31, 1954, it was revealed that a high school drop-out named Marvin Hewitt had been teaching physics at the university for a year. New Hampshire was not the only victim of this talented imposter, who in the previous ten years had taught at four different colleges under different names. In Durham he posed as Kenneth P. Yates, Ph.D., a physicist with a good record. He had been hired in 1953 after submitting fake letters of recommendation and a genuine transcript of Dr. Yates's doctoral studies. Although graduate students and colleagues noted inexplicable gaps in his knowledge, the self-taught genius escaped discovery until Wayne N. Overman, a graduate student, became suspicious of him. "Yates" was unfamiliar with the work of a certain German physicist and could not read German—rare for a Ph.D. in physics. Inquiry revealed that the real Yates was innocently pursuing his career in the Midwest.

° Louis Bourgoin retired in June 1955 after thirty-seven years as chief of campus police. Although he had left grammar school at the age of fourteen, Louis was a master in dealing with his better-educated charges. From 1928 to 1955 he jailed only four students. Countless others, picked up by the police of neighboring communities, were released to Louis without being taken to court. Professor William Hennessy said of him: "Louis tempers justice with mercy . . . good judgment, fairness, and humanity." Of himself, Louis said: "If I caught them a second time, it went pretty hard on them." He once stopped, in the space of thirty seconds, a pitched snowball fight between the residents of three dormitories.

24. Johnson's Building Program

Chandler resigned in 1954 to return to the foreign agriculture program of the Rockefeller Foundation, from which he had come to the university seven years previously. His assignment was to establish and direct an International Rice Research Institute. He chose a site in Luzon's Laguna Province, Philippine Islands, where under his leadership new rice strains and methods of culture were developed that revolutionized the production of this basic food in Southeast Asia. The university recognized Chandler's achievements by awarding him in 1972 an honorary Doctor of Science degree for his work as horticulturist, educator, researcher, and foundation officer.

Although not an aggressive president, he supported others in their activities on behalf of the university.* Notable achievements during his administration were the establishment of four Ph.D. programs, the installation of Phi Beta Kappa and other honorary societies, and the successful conclusion of the Memorial Union drive.

Upon Chandler's departure, the trustees named Edward D. Eddy, Jr., as interim executive officer. In February 1955 his title was changed to acting president. It became his task to shepherd the 1955-57 budget through the legislature, which he was able to do with a minimum of controversy. Rather than press for an increase in the millage formula, the university had already agreed to Governor Hugh Gregg's request that it submit a detailed budget—a practice that has been followed since. In addition, the trustees had

voted to raise tuition rates again, effective September 1955. The increases amounted to $50 for in-state students, $100 for out-of-state students.

The appropriation recommended by the new governor, Lane Dwinell, was only slightly modified in the legislature. Bond issues for another women's dormitory (Lord Hall) and for the long-sought new library were also approved. The only battle was over out-of-state students, who now accounted for thirty-one percent of the university's enrollment. Senator Erasley C. Ferguson advocated that their number be reduced by 400. He estimated that $125,000 would be saved by this move; for the university, Eddy pointed out that $240,000 would be lost in tuition income. Although resisting pressure for a sudden cut in out-of-state enrollment, Eddy did say that the university was planning for a gradual reduction, in order to prepare for the jump in New Hampshire applicants expected to start in 1959.

The task of choosing a new president was coming to the trustees so often that a standard operating procedure had been established. The usual committee of three trustees, the president of the board, and three faculty members was appointed. The candidates numbered over sixty by August and over one hundred by October 1954. The four top candidates and their wives visited the campus during the spring. At a special meeting in May, the trustees unanimously elected Eldon L. Johnson president. At the same meeting a new office of vice-president and provost was established, and Eddy was named to it.

Johnson took office on August 1, 1955. He had been born forty-six years before in Indiana, and had received his baccalaureate degree from Indiana State Teachers College. He subsequently earned his Ph.M. and Ph.D. from the University of Wisconsin. He became a high school teacher

---

* Chandler seemed to welcome assignments which took him out of his Thompson Hall office. A regular participant in Professor Babcock's Bible class at the Community Church, Chandler once remarked that he enjoyed the class because it was quiet, and because Babcock was sure of something. Chandler was having domestic difficulties which later culminated in divorce.

Commencement exercises at Lewis Fields, 1957.

of English and history, then moved on to teach political science at the college level. During World War II he was national academic director of the Army Air Force's pre-meteorology program; at the same time, 1940-45, he was director of the graduate school of the United States Department of Agriculture. Following this he went to the University of Oregon as chairman of the political science department, and in 1947 he became dean of both the liberal arts college and the graduate school of that institution, a position he held when called to New Hampshire.

The product of public higher education, Johnson was a strong advocate of it. To the opening faculty meeting in September 1957 he said that a state university cannot devote itself to "education for the elite . . . . It may turn away all youth who do not give promise of successful pursuit of a college education, but it cannot skim off the cream of the intellectual crop and stop there . . . or specialize in class consciousness." He went on that it was important to reach increasing numbers of qualified youth: "insofar as other colleges and universities cannot or will not the state university must." He feared that higher education was neglecting fundamental problems while solving apparent ones. "We make better doctors than men, better lawyers than citizens, better scientists than human beings," he said at a 1956 conference of educators at Crawford Notch, New Hampshire.

Johnson told the trustees that he preferred to have no formal inauguration. In deference to his wishes, the title of president was formally conferred on him during the commencement exercises in June 1956.

One of Johnson's first official acts was the signing of a $974,000 contract for the construction of

The Memorial Union Building (above) and the new library (below) were major additions of the 1950s.

Two views of Spaulding Life Sciences Building, which stands where the B&M tracks once crossed the New Hampshire College campus.

the Memorial Union building. There was a ground breaking ceremony before the football game on Saturday, October 8. Work was halted, however, in February 1956 when the foundation had to be redesigned because of the nature of the subsoil. This delay, plus difficulty in obtaining steel, put off completion for a year. The temporary Notch Hall, after a decade of service, was torn down in May 1957. The new building was dedicated during Homecoming Weekend that October, but it was not opened for use until November 22. To cover the cost of operation and to retire a $100,000 loan made to cover part of the construction cost, a Memorial Union fee of twelve dollars was assessed each student.

Meanwhile, plans for enlarging the library facilities were taking shape. Arthur S. Adams had told the trustees in 1949 that Hamilton Smith Library was too small, with the less-used volumes

being stored in the Service Building. Little was done until the fall of 1953. At that time the decision was made to press for a new building instead of enlarging Hamilton Smith, and a bond issue of $1,400,000 was secured from the 1955 legislature. The library itself was to cost $984,578, with the balance to be used for remodeling Hamilton Smith for other uses. The new library was dedicated on October 5, 1958.°

With enrollment rising steadily—and expected to jump dramatically in the near future—it was obvious that more than a new library would be

° Thelma Brackett, soon to retire as university librarian, was asked how many students the new building would accommodate. Optimistically she replied: "As many as will come." They soon came, and within a very few years classrooms in nearby buildings had to be designated as overflow study areas for library users. In the summer of 1969 an addition was completed, doubling the library's capacity.

needed to house the academic program (see Table 1). The trustees held a special meeting on January 12, 1957, with Governor Dwinell present. They voted to ask the current legislature to approve bond issues for an ambitious building program:

- $1,900,000 for a life sciences building (Spaulding).
- $2,000,000 for a creative arts building (Paul)
- $1,150,000 for a 300-person dormitory (Randall-Hitchcock).

In addition, $200,000 was requested to expand the heating plant. Legislative committees visiting the campus readily agreed that additional academic facilities were needed, but they pressed Johnson to give priority to either the art or the science building. Johnson stoutly maintained that both were vital. As a result, the whole program was approved, including an additional $250,000 for remodeling space vacated by departments

Table 1—Predicted and actual enrollment, 1959-1969

Academic year	Low estimate	High estimate	Actual enrollment
1959-60	3,600	3,700	3,767
1962-63	3,950	4,100	4,400
1965-66	4,250	5,250	5,683
1968-69	5,300	7,200	7,097

moving to the new buildings. Spaulding Life Sciences Building was dedicated May 6, 1960, and Paul Creative Arts Center on October 15, 1960.

Fires plagued the university agricultural establishment during this period. In April 1955 a fire did more than $5,000 damage to the cow barn; in November of the same year another fire destroyed the entire structure. The horse barn burned in September 1961. In both cases farm employees with the help of students rescued all

Paul Creative Arts Center on College Road.

of the stock. The animal metabolism laboratory, located behind Nesmith Hall, was destroyed by fire in October 1956. A replacement was built near the College Woods, and was named for Ernest G. Ritzman whose pioneer work in animal metabolism had brought international notice to the university.

Of the dormitories being built, McLaughlin Hall had been occupied in January 1955. A year and a half later a contract was signed for Lord Hall. The group of women's dormitories on the newly developed circle near Edgewood Road was completed when construction of Jessie Doe Hall was started in the summer of 1962. In the meantime, what was then the largest dormitory on campus was being constructed as the fourth side of the quadrangle of men's dormitories built at the end of World War II. The building was designed to operate as two units, Randall Hall and Hitchcock Hall, each housing about 150 men. When it was completed in 1959, the balance of enrollment was such that it was assigned to women instead. (Even though one or more dormitories was always under construction during Johnson's administration, capacity was not keeping up with demand. In September 1960, 164 men found themselves without a place to sleep. Doubling up in the three original quadrangle dormitories took care of 106 of them, 40 found places in fraternities, and the rest had to commute.)

Married students, a new phenomenon at the end of World War II, had not disappeared as expected when the veterans finished their studies. Some of the temporary student apartment buildings had been razed to make room for new construction, but the large buildings on College Road remained. The quantity—let alone the quality—was far from sufficient, more than one hundred couples being denied accommodations in September 1956. Construction was held up while an answer was sought to the problem of designing apartments with rents low enough for students to afford to pay, but high enough to amortize the costs. (The man primarily concerned with finding

a solution was Norman Myers '50, university treasurer, who himself had lived on College Road as a student veteran.) Finally, in December 1958, the trustees voted to ask the legislature to authorize a $1 million bond issue for new apartments. The bond issue was approved, and a contract was signed in May 1960 for building ninety-eight units, which were ready for occupancy in September 1961. The temporary apartments were then torn down, much to the relief of local fire officials.

Changing times gave the university a bargain in real estate when, in 1958, the Boston & Maine Railroad decided to shut down its passenger and freight operations in Durham. Long gone was the day when students traveled to Dover by train for an evening on the town. The Craig Supply Company of Durham purchased the freight structure; the university bought the passenger depot. The university has put its acquisition to use as a dairy

Horse Barn lost to fire, September 15, 1961.

*Z building, last of the College Road
apartments, dwarfed by Randall-Hitchcock.*

bar and as a practice facility for students in the two-year food preparation curriculum of the Thompson School.

An eight-year effort to establish an educational television station in New Hampshire came to a successful conclusion in the summer of 1959 when WENH-TV went on the air. President Chandler had applied for VHF Channel 11 for a non-commercial station in Durham. The Federal Communications Commission made the reservation in 1952 with a provision that substantial progress must be made within the year. Governor Hugh Gregg therefore appointed a state commission on educational television, and called a three-state conference of educators from New Hampshire, Maine, and Vermont. These efforts led nowhere, but they were sufficient to hold the reservation. In January 1957, former governor Charles M. Dale offered to donate FM transmitter facilities located on Saddleback Mountain in Northwood; the facilities belonged to radio station WHEB in Portsmouth, which Dale owned,

and which had abandoned its FM programming. The Fund for Adult Education then offered $100,000 for the project, provided that the grant be matched on a two-for-one basis.

Jere Chase headed the drive for matching funds, which finally consisted of $50,000 in cash and equipment, $50,000 as the value of the facilities on Saddleback Mountain, and $100,000 as the university's contribution in the form of the basement of the Memorial Union, which was to house the TV studios. Meanwhile the New Hampshire Educational Broadcasting Council had been formed. Consisting of seven colleges and universities, the state Department of Education, the educational officials of the Catholic diocese of Manchester, and a number of private schools, the council was to be the governing body of the proposed station. The license, however, was to be issued to the University of New Hampshire.

With construction funds in hand, a drive was hastily organized for operating money. In two months, $65,000 was contributed in small dona-

Forest Park apartments, a welcome change to student couples and to fire officials.

tions from numerous individuals, and the FCC was finally asked for a construction permit. Channel 11 was to have financial problems in the years ahead, but it was on its way at last.°

At the end of 1960 George W. Collier, owner of a 148-room resort hotel in Franconia, gave the entire property to the university. It was expected that the hotel would serve as a laboratory for students in the hotel administration curriculum, but this plan did not work out. After operating the hotel as a commercial venture for two seasons, the

° It had been expected that the TV station would be used in the instructional program of the university, but only two attempts were made to do so. Under Professor George M. Moore, lectures for the basic freshman course in biology were broadcast starting in 1960-61, with students gathered in a large lecture hall which had been equipped with TV receivers. Professor David Long gave his course in U.S. history over open-circuit TV in 1960-61. Long's lectures appealed to the off-campus audience and were picked up by stations in Boston and Albany. It developed, however, that university students did not like the television classes, preferring live if less colorful teachers, and both experiments were soon abandoned.

university sold it to Franconia College as a campus for that new institution.

While new buildings were going up in Durham, a landmark was coming down. Ballard Hall, which had been built as a rooming house by Albert DeMeritt in 1894, was razed in 1961. After its initial use as a rooming and boarding house, the building had been leased by the bachelor members of the faculty and called the Durham Club. In 1903 it was used as a chapter house by Zeta Epsilon Zeta fraternity. It next was purchased by the university for a women's dormitory, at that time acquiring its name of Ballard. From 1932 to 1934 it housed men students, after which it served as headquarters for student organizations and departmental offices for education and music. Space was found for education in Murkland Hall, the student organizations had moved when the Memorial Union was built, and finally music left when the Paul Creative Arts Center was completed. Stoke Hall now occupies the site.

25. Strengthening the Academic Side.

The biennial budget prepared for the 1957 legislature included pay increases for the faculty—not as much as they wanted, of course, but enough to mark some progress. Otherwise the budget provided little gain for university operations. Lane Dwinell, following the tradition of New Hampshire governors, requested a "hold-the-line" budget. His sentiment toward university appropriations was demonstrated in his January inaugural address. The governor pointed out that the public gave free education to anyone through elementary and high school, adding:

> But in essence we say that two-thirds of our elementary and high school graduates must go to work to earn money, to pay taxes, to provide a heavily subsidized education for the more fortunate of their fellows . . . . We must explore every means through loans, through repayable scholarships, through alumni contributions, to assess more of the cost of higher education on its beneficiaries, and to lessen the burden on the general public.

Of the $1,360,000 biennial increase asked by the university, Dwinell recommended only half, suggesting that the rest be made up by increasing tuition and room and board charges. The legislature proved more generous than the governor, and eventually the budget was passed at a figure only $80,000 below that requested. As noted earlier, all the requests for new construction were approved.

For the next biennium, an appropriation increase of $1,090,000 was asked for fiscal 1960 and $1,170,000 for fiscal 1961. Of this nearly half was intended for salary increases. A little over a quarter of the increase was for debt service resulting from the extensive building program. Wesley Powell '38, a determined and economy-minded young man who became governor on January 1, 1959, followed a policy of recommending virtual-

ly no new money for any state service except highways. The campus reacted vigorously. On February 2 the University Senate passed a resolution viewing with grave concern Powell's failure to recommend any money for salary increases. There were predictions that thirty to forty percent of the faculty would leave for elsewhere. On March 5 New Hampshire Hall was crowded by 1,300 students for a mass meeting at which Johnson presented the budget situation. The *New Hampshire* urged students to contact their legislators.

The legislative session dragged on through the summer. In the end, the university received an appropriation substantially above Powell's proposal. It was October 17 before Johnson was able to present to the trustees the salaries proposed for the fiscal year that had started July 1. Governor Powell (who as an *ex officio* member of the board was present) raised questions about the proposed administrative salaries. They were referred to the personnel committee for review. They finally were approved, with a few dissenting votes, six days before Christmas—at which time a budget was adopted for the year that was already half gone.

For the 1961-63 biennium, the university requested an increase in its appropriation of $1,700,000. Nearly two-thirds of the new money was earmarked for salary increases. Governor Powell's recommendation for operating funds was forty-four percent under the university's request, but the appropriations committee voted to appropriate the sum which the university was entitled under the millage formula. This resulted in an appropriation nearly $300,000 short of the university's request, but the controversy of the previous session was largely avoided. The trustees were able to adopt the 1961-62 budget on July 7, instead of on December 19 as had been the case two years before. (A bill authorizing construction of a $2,500,000 gymnasium was passed by the legislature but vetoed by the the the governor.)

Students as well as the state were called on for help in meeting the rising costs of the university. Room and board rates kept climbing as did charges for such items as extension courses and special fees. Out-of-state tuition went from $600 to $700 in September 1958. For 1960-61, in-state tuition was raised from $300 to $380, and the out-of-state charge went to $800.

As charges were increased, so was the financial assistance to help the less affluent stay in college. The aid program was becoming so large that a half-time position as financial aids officer was established in the fall of 1956. When out-of-state tuition was raised in September 1958, up to $20,000 of the increased income was allocated for out-of-state tuition grants; when in-state tuition was raised in 1960, the upper limit on a tuition grant was increased from $200 to $300. The minimum rate for student labor was moved from sixty to seventy cents an hour in 1959, with the top set at one dollar.

There had been difficulty in collecting some of the student loans made during the Depression. In 1958 some $11,000 in principal and a like amount in interest was written off. At the same time, the loan policy was reviewed and more definite regulations adopted. The maximum loaned to an individual was to be $1,000, on which no interest would accrue until the student left the university, at which time it would be five percent. Graduate students were eligible to borrow. No student operating an automobile was to get a loan unless the vehicle was essential. The federal National Defense Education Act loan program became a reality when $5,948 was allocated to the University in early 1959; the NDEA fund eventually surpassed the university fund by a ratio of five to one.

Private gifts enabled the university to enrich its programs during Johnson's administration. In

1958, the Harriet M. and Huntley N. Spaulding Charitable Trusts gave the university $500,000 to improve the quality of undergraduate education. Gifts from the Spaulding-Potter Trust and the Alumni Fund made it possible to bring distinguished persons to the campus. From the Spaulding-Potter fund came $12,000 to bring distinguished lecturers for a major address and smaller discussions over a two- or three-day period. The series included such speakers as Archibald MacLeish, Lewis Mumford, and Aldous Huxley, who each drew a capacity crowd of one thousand to New Hampshire Hall.

The Alumni Fund contributed $10,000 to support a lecturer-in-residence who was to spend a semester on campus, conducting seminars, meeting discussion groups, and giving an occasional lecture. Edmund W. Sinnott, a noted botanist and dean emeritus of the Yale Graduate School, occupied the post for the semester starting in February 1958. Finding individuals of the desired stature proved to be so difficult that after Sinnott's tenure the format was changed to bring someone for a week or two instead of a semester.

In 1960 the Alumni Fund undertook to support, on a continuing basis, distinguished professors. The first man appointed was Asher Moore in philosophy. His salary was $14,000—very high for the university at the time—and he was given a reduced teaching load and relieved of the obligation to serve on faculty committees. The position was named in honor of Donald C. Babcock.

A four-year experiment in synthesizing the freshman program in liberal arts was initiated under Dean Edward Y. Blewett in September 1956. Supported by a $35,000 grant from the Carnegie Corporation, five faculty members met weekly with groups of about twenty-five freshmen to discuss the relationships of the materials they had studied in their regular courses. The program ended when the grant ran out. An attempt to achieve synthesis at the other end of the liberal arts program had been started in 1951, with Professor John T. Holden managing a course, Senior

Synthesis, enrolling about fifty students a semester. The course, combining lectures and discussion, was passed in 1956 to Professor Carleton P. Menge, who carried it on for a decade.

Technology meanwhile was moving toward a broader curriculum. Acting Dean Edward T. Donovan reported to the University Senate that the technology curriculum committee had agreed on a common freshman year for all programs in the college, and that there would be less emphasis on applications and more on basic science. A requirement of twenty-seven semester hours in social science and the humanities would more than double this segment of the technology curriculum.

Two new graduate degrees for teachers were authorized in December 1958. The Master of Science for Teachers was designed to up-date and deepen the knowledge of high school teachers. The Master of Arts in Teaching was to give professional preparation to liberal arts graduates who planned to become teachers.

As part of a nation-wide project by the Ford Foundation to prepare outstanding students for college teaching, in the summer of 1960 the university received a grant of $136,000. Students were to be identified in the freshman year. Through scholarships, special seminars, and some participation in departmental teaching, they were to complete requirements for the baccalaureate and master's degrees in five years, and to graduate prepared to become college teachers. Few completed the master's degree in the specified time. Instead of entering college teaching when they did, many went on to doctoral study.

In June 1959 the trustees voted $12,500 (later increased to $18,000) from the Spaulding grant for the "purpose of undertaking study of the university curriculum and teaching methods" by a six-member faculty committee. The committee report resulted in revision of the university-wide curriculum requirements, a reorganization of the faculty committee structure, and many changes at the departmental level. A recommendation

that a major change be made in the university calendar provoked much discussion but no action.

Independent of any organized effort on the part of the faculty, a revolution was taking place in the reading habits of the students, thanks to the growing availability of paperback books. In the summer of 1959 Mortar Board circulated to the students a fifteen-page list of paperbacks suggested for summer reading. Dayton M. Henson '36, manager of the University Bookstore, helped things along by building a large stock of the inexpensive volumes and selling four for the price of three. His paperback sales increased four hundred percent from 1958 to 1960.

An expansion in the dramatic activities of the university was made possible by the completion of theater facilities in the Paul Creative Arts Center. Accordingly, the speech and drama section of the English department was set up as a separate department in 1960 under the chairmanship of Joseph D. Batcheller. A full-time director of theater, John C. Edwards, was employed.

To the four original Ph.D. programs (in botany, chemistry, horticulture, and zoology) new programs in microbiology and physics were added in 1960. There was also progress at the service level. A new curriculum in medical technology had been approved in January 1954, consisting of three years on the Durham campus and a fourth year at the Mary Hitchcock hospital in Hanover. New programs were proposed to train nurses and elementary-school teachers, the latter to consist of three years of liberal arts study followed by a senior year devoted entirely to professional study. Both programs were eventually staffed in 1962.

Johnson suggested to the trustees in January 1957 that the department of economics and business administration in the College of Liberal Arts be made a separate school of business administration. The trustees encouraged him to study the matter, and in June 1959 he presented them with a tentative proposal. The trustees voted formal approval in November 1960, and the following

April it was voted to adopt the name of Whittemore School of Business and Economics.°

The institution's faculty had long been in demand for off-campus assignments, and the trend accelerated during Johnson's administration. By 1958, it was necessary to revise university policy in this matter. Henceforth, faculty members were to limit their outside activities to the equivalent of one day a week. Among those who were embarrassed by this policy was the president himself.

In March 1959 Johnson accepted an invitation from the International Cooperation Administration, U.S. Department of State, to serve as its representative on a commision to advise on the founding of a new university in Eastern Nigeria. (In December of the same year, Johnson paid a visit to San Marcos University in Peru, where Professor Albert F. Daggett '28 was directing a three-year project to reorganize the chemistry department. Several other members of the UNH chemistry department also went to Peru from time to time, and San Marcos chemists came to Durham to study and observe.) In July 1959, Dr. Nmamdi Azikiwe, premier of Eastern Nigeria, visited New Hampshire to inspect its facilities and programs. Johnson made two visits to Nigeria in 1960 and another the following year.

Johnson also served in Washington as a member of the Army ROTC advisory panel. In February 1961, he was invited by the International Cooperation Administration to go to the British West Indies as a consultant on the administration problems of the University of the West Indies. Some of the trustees felt that Johnson was spending too much time off campus, but after a discussion in an executive session of the board he was told that the matter was one for him to decide.

Regional cooperation in higher education had been initiated by a meeting of the presidents of

° Laurence F. Whittemore of Pembroke was a trustee for sixteen years and president of the board for five years. Among other positions he had been president of the Boston Federal Reserve Bank; of the New York, New Haven, and Hartford Railroad; and of the Brown Company. He died August 10, 1960.

Assembling the payload for a rocket to be used in scientific space research.

the six New England state universities in 1949. The program was formalized late in 1955. An early project was to arrange for the attendance, at in-state rates, of a student in a curriculum not available in his own state but which was designated as a regional program at another New England state university. Regional programs at New Hampshire, beginning in September 1958, were occupational therapy, hotel administration, and art. Soon added were art education and physical education for women.°

University faculty members obtained access to a digital computer through a cooperative arrangement with Massachusetts Institute of Technology. In the spring of 1956 UNH was one of twenty-

° The list changes from time to time. Not supervised by the New England Board of Higher Education was the pre-existing arrangement between New Hampshire and the University of Vermont, where several New Hampshire residents were enabled to attend the UVM medical school.

four New England institutions allowed to share the use of a $4 million installation at MIT. The university installed its own digital computer in December 1961.

The university rose into the space age when it negotiated a contract in May 1958 for a trailer-housed satellite tracking station, operated by Professor Robert E. Houston, Jr., of the physics department.

This exotic development was not at the expense of research in agriculture. A major project in the feeding of poultry broilers was being carried on, as was research on poultry diseases. The horticulture department gained national recognition with the development of a midget watermelon, sized to fit modern refrigerators. There also was a blue bean which turned green when cooked and a bean for baking which was claimed to be "gasless." A long list of fruits and vegetables was being improved by imaginative experimenters. The same was apparently not true of the local horse population. Letters to the *New Hampshire* in 1957 complained that the university's Morgan horses were being neglected, as indicated by their dependence upon the services of the twenty-three-year-old stallion Melysses to keep the herd going.

At the November 1957 meeting of the University Senate, Johnson reviewed the institution's admission standards. In 1915, graduation from high school had been adopted as a substitute for entrance examinations. In 1926 the catalog added the warning: "applicants with poor records will be advised to withdraw their applications." Three years later *advised* was changed to *required*. In 1931 the policy was modified to require those in the lowest quarter of their high school classes to take entrance examinations; in 1940 this requirement was extended to include those graduating in the lower three-fifths of their high school classes. In the seventeen years the policy had been in effect, Johnson told the senate, the proportion of entering classes admitted by examination had varied from thirteen to twenty-five percent. About two out of three of those so admitted were able to succeed in college work. Although the class standing standard was not changed, in 1960 the University Senate voted to require all applicants to take the Scholastic Aptitude Test of the College Entrance Examination Board.

26. Free Speech: Round Two

The academic-freedom issue continued unabated during the Chandler and Johnson administrations. In 1953 the New Hampshire legislature passed a bill intended to control "subversive activities" within the state. The bill charged the state attorney general, Louis Wyman '39, with conducting an investigation of this perceived threat. It was generally expected in Durham that the attorney general's interest would sooner or later focus on those who had brought left-wing speakers to the university campus.

At the opening faculty meeting in September 1954, Chandler mentioned the expected investigation and suggested that anyone under investigation speak the truth as he knew it. He also announced that a standby committee on freedom of thought and speech had been created by the trustees to act in an advisory capacity if the occasion arose. The committee members were Trustee Austin Hubbard '25; administrators Herbert Moss and Edward Eddy; professors Thomas G. Phillips, John A. Hogan, and Edmond W. Bowler; and students John C. Driscoll and Jean Gilmore, both of the class of 1954.

A number of the students who had been active in the Liberal Club and in the Progressive Party were questioned by the attorney general, but most attention was focused on G. Harris Daggett and Paul M. Sweezy.[*] Sweezy, a resident of Wilton, was a self-styled Marxist economist and author, who before serving in World War II had been an instructor at Harvard for eight years. Sweezy's connection with the university was unof-

ficial. He had spoken to the Liberal Club in 1948, and for three years—1952-54—he gave a single lecture each spring to the humanities class at the invitation of Professor Daggett and other staff members.

Daggett was summoned to Concord to be questioned by the attorney general on December 29, 1953, and again on May 18, 1954. Sweezy was examined on January 8 and June 3, 1954. Both men answered most of the questions asked them, but both refused to answer questions which in their opinion went beyond the attorney general's authority or which violated their constitutional rights. Neither invoked the Fifth Amendment, relating to self-incrimination. Attorney General Wyman petitioned the Superior Court to order that all questions be answered or that the men be held in contempt of court. After three days of legal argument in each case, the judge ruled that Daggett and Sweezy must answer questions relating to their activities in the Progressive Party and about Sweezy's last lecture to the humanities class. They were told they need not answer hypothetical questions or those relating solely to opinions and beliefs.

Rather than risk the uncertainty and expense of an appeal to higher courts, Daggett consented to answer questions about his activities in the Progressive Party. Several months later he turned over to Wyman what he termed the "reconstructed text" of Sweezy's controversial lecture. (Sweezy did appeal. He lost in the New Hampshire Supreme Court but won by a 6-2 decision in the United States Supreme Court, June 17, 1957. The high court in its decision declared that a free society depends upon free universities and that it makes little difference "whether such intervention occurs avowedly or through action that inevitably tends to check the ardor and fearless-

[*] Most of the material on the Daggett-Sweezy case, as well as some of the other material in these free-speech chapters, is from *Academic Freedom at the University of New Hampshire, 1947-1957,* by Professor Robert B. Dishman of the UNH political science department. The paper was written in support of the university's nomination for the Meiklejohn award for academic freedom.

ness of scholars, qualities at once so fragile and so indispensable for fruitful academic labor.")

These developments were closely watched both in Durham and in Manchester. The Manchester *Union Leader* of May 26, 1954, carried a front page story with a five column head: "Professor at UNH Balks in Red Quiz." Chandler was out of town at the time. Edward Eddy, his assistant, told a reporter for the *Union Leader* that Daggett's resignation had not been requested and that no judgment would be made before a decision of the court. A few days before, Daggett had been chosen to speak on "The College Teacher, His Duties and His Privileges" at the university's annual honors banquet. The *New Hampshire* on May 27 put out a special two-page issue devoted entirely to the case. A petition supporting Daggett was signed by seven hundred students.

The university had not heard Sweezy for the last time. On April 24, 1956, a committee of the Student Union requested permission for him to speak at its next regular monthly coffee hour. The matter was referred to Eldon Johnson, who had since become president. After a conference with other administrators, he decided that there should be a request from the Student Union board rather than from one of its committees. The board met on May 4—eleven students and three faculty—and voted against issuing the invitation. Not to be balked, Sweezy's supporters at a meeting in Daggett's house organized what they called the Student Committee on Academic Freedom. On May 7, this group asked for recognition as a student organization and requested that they be allowed to invite Sweezy to lecture on campus on May 17. Both requests were denied. Johnson issued a statement in which he said that "there was about as much need for such a committee at the University of New Hampshire as for the recently organized National Association for the Advancement of White People in the South."

In the meantime, campus leaders had become concerned that the maneuvering had made it seem that the university was screening speakers. As a result, the honorary society Senior Skulls requested permission to bring Sweezy to Durham, along with a recognized conservative to present the other side of the picture. Johnson asked the trustees to hold a special meeting to review the situation. The trustees reaffirmed the existing policy on speakers and political activity, and specifically approved inviting Sweezy and someone to present an opposing point of view. The *Union Leader*, Governor Lane Dwinell, and Attorney General Wyman all criticized the trustees for their decision. The Senior Skulls invited Wesley Powell '38 (who was about to become a candidate for governor) to appear with Sweezy; but he declined in an open letter severely criticizing the university. Dr. Leonard E. Reed, president of the Foundation for Economic Education, agreed to counter Sweezy, who spoke to an overflow audience in Richards (Murkland) Auditorium on May 24.

In April 1958, the American Association of University Professors announced that the first Meiklejohn Award for academic freedom would go to the University of New Hampshire's president and trustees, in recognition of their defense of academic freedom in the face of strong journalistic and political opposition. Laurence F. Whittemore, president of the board of trustees, went to Denver to accept the award. He explained that the opposition would have a harder time pinning the label of "Communist" on him than it would on a college president like Johnson.

The controversy over the Meiklejohn Award rivaled that over the events which had led to it. Both Attorney General Wyman and Governor Dwinell urged Whittemore not to make the trip. Johnson was moved to remark: "UNH should have received the Meiklejohn Award in 1959 for having the courage to accept it in 1958." The excitement died down, however, and there followed a period of relative quiet. This interlude came to an end in the spring of 1961.

Wesley Powell '38 had been elected governor in 1959. On April 28, 1961, he ordered an "Operation Alert" or air raid drill throughout the state. The New Hampshire Civil Defense Code provided that, during such an alert, all persons not involved in conducting the exercise must take cover under penalty of the law. Robert F. Kingsley, a graduate student at the university, decided to flout this requirement. He sent letters to the press announcing that a group of students would march down Main Street during the alert, as a protest against nuclear weapons. The president of the Student Senate, Karl H. Van Ledtje '64, urged the student body to ignore the advertised protest. About seven hundred students naturally headed downtown to see the excitement. According to a story in the *New Hampshire*, there had been little interest in the matter before Van Ledtje's appeal.

Forewarned, state and local police were out in force. When the marchers refused to take cover, eighteen of them were arrested. A comparable number of newsmen on the street to cover the event were not jailed.° Although there was no turmoil, the press reported the event as a "riot." The arrested students appeared a week later before Judge Bradford W. McIntire '25, who fined each of them fifty dollars. Half that amount was suspended, except for one culprit who maintained he would do it again if he had the opportunity.

Between the protest and the court action, Governor Powell wired Johnson, calling for "prompt dismissal" of the students who had participated in the "open disobedience" of civil law. He went on to say: "It is my further opinion that the University administration should have warned these students prior to Friday that such flagrant disobedience of civil law would result in their dismissal. I was convinced that the University

would take prompt action, and I deliberately waited until this hour before expressing my position as Governor and as trustee *ex officio* in this way."

In reply Johnson issued a statement saying: "Violation of the law always brings students under disciplinary review at the University of New Hampshire. A calculated violation occurred last Friday . . . . Therefore all students arrested last Friday have been placed on disciplinary probation. At present, pending the decision of the court, there is no basis for summary dismissals."

In the meantime the Manchester *Union Leader* learned that Willard Uphaus, a minister who had been jailed for a year because he refused to give Attorney General Wyman a list of those who had attended a meeting at his summer camp in New Hampshire, had passed through Durham the night before the demonstration and had stopped to see his friend, Professor Daggett. Robert Kingsley happened to be at Daggett's house at the time. A plot under Daggett's leadership was therefore deduced. Daggett and the student demonstrators both denied that he had been the leader in the April 28 protest, and Daggett issued a statement in which he said: "I am not committing acts of civil disobedience. We live under law, and it is only with law that we can enjoy order and civilization." But he could not resist adding: "It is my observation that the Durham demonstrators made their gesture with conviction and courage."

When Judge McIntire found the students guilty, Johnson took no further action against them. Governor Powell announced that he would attend the trustee meeting on May 20, to urge the board to overrule Johnson. A thousand students showed their support of Johnson by lining the walk from his house to Thompson Hall as he made his way to the meeting.

Daggett came to the trustee meeting and was questioned, mostly by the governor, for two hours. Altogether the meeting lasted eight and one-half hours, with time out for lunch. At one point Governor Powell moved that Kingsley be

---

° Among the journalists was Daniel Ford '54, who later used the episode in his novel, *Now Comes Theodora*. Ford was employed by the university News Bureau at the time, and his book consequently became another political hot potato for the university to handle.

dismissed from the university. Only one other trustee supported his motion. Later Powell moved that the students be informed that participation in similar demonstrations would, in the future, mean summary dismissal. After discussion, the governor's motion was amended to read: "that the student body be informed that we reaffirm our belief in the right of citizens and students to freedom of assembly and demonstration, except that participation in a demonstration during a time designated for taking cover during a civil defense alert shall be cause for suspension or dismissal from the University." The motion passed, eight to three. The negative votes were cast by Frank Randall, Austin Hubbard, and Dean P. Williamson. Johnson abstained because of his involvement in the issue.

There was a sequel to this meeting. On June 2, the trustees met at the Highway Hotel in Concord and prepared a statement that was unanimously approved by the trustees present for the voting. Powell left just before the vote. The statement in its entirety read:

A meeting of the Board of Trustees and the top administrative officers of the University of New Hampshire was held at the Highway Hotel, Concord, New Hampshire, June 2, 1961, at 2:00 P.M. The purpose of the meeting was to discuss University educational policy.

Each of the administrative officers expressed his philosophy regarding the future development of the University of New Hampshire.

The Board expressed its full confidence in President Johnson and the administrative officers and faculty.

At the meeting of the University Senate three days later, Johnson said that the June 2 meeting had clarified the matter of interference with academic freedom. The Senate adopted unanimously a resolution "to express their appreciation to the members of the Board of Trustees for their renewed expression of confidence in the integrity of the President, the Administration, and the Faculty."

There was a further sequel to the civil disobedience affair. On October 21, 1961, the trustees voted an "official reprimand" for Daggett. This action led to repercussions from the American Association of University Professors. At another meeting on April 21, 1962—with an AAUP representative on hand—the board voted to rescind the reprimand. A motion to give Daggett a $500 raise was tabled, however. In the letter informing Daggett of the board's action, there was this revealing sentence:

Although the letter that President Johnson addressed to you on October 25, 1961, was undoubtedly too terse a communication, the intention was and still is to convey unmistakably that the Board of Trustees believes that you, over a period of many years, have displayed a lack of judgment in your combined roles as faculty member and private citizen, the total effect of which has been both unfortunate and deleterious to yourself as a member of the faculty of the University.

In voting the reprimand in the first place, the trustees must have intended that it be tersely worded. If Johnson went a little beyond his instructions, however, his enthusiasm would be understandable. Successive presidents defended Daggett with courage and vigor. They would have been more than human, however, if they were not annoyed by the recurring crises he precipitated. Years before, Harold Stoke had observed that defending academic freedom would not demand so much time and effort if it were not that someone was always trying to discover just where the limits were.

27. Power to the Students

A student protest like that of April 1961 would have been unthinkable ten years earlier. Subtle but important changes had come to student life in the decade of the 1950s.

The honorary societies reached new heights on campus during the Chandler administration. At the same time, the social fraternities were having problems. At the urging of Dean William A. Medesy, in November 1951 a weekend workshop was held to discuss such topics as "hell week" and the perennial drinking problem. The Inter-Fraternity Council went along with Medesy's proposal to substitute a "help week" for the traditional hazing period, with its absurd and sometimes dangerous rides and assignments. While endorsing the idea of help week, the *New Hampshire* sounded the same complaint that had led to the demise of New Hampshire Day: there weren't enough tools to go around.

The University Senate adopted a policy that any fraternity whose members had a composite grade-point average of less than 2.25 would be placed on probation, with subsequent limitations on its social activities. Two or three houses enjoyed this status more or less permanently.

A more serious problem was the matter of racial and religious discrimination by the houses. Discussion went on for months about the issue. A resolution was debated in the Student Senate to bar from campus any fraternity or sorority which did not promptly remove restrictive clauses from its constitution, but those in favor of a campaign for gradual removal won the day, by a 30-9 vote. In May 1955, the Inter-Fraternity Council finally adopted a resolution: "that the fraternities at the University of New Hampshire are opposed to discrimination clauses. Those fraternities who are forced by national clauses to practice discrimination hereby pledge themselves to work at their na-

tional conventions for the removal of these clauses." That satisfied the critics, and the goal of abolishing discriminatory clauses was eventually reached.

Under the leadership of Edward Eddy, assistant to the president, student convocations and gatherings flourished during the Chandler administration. These events included Freshman Camp, the Rolling Ridge Conference on Campus Affairs, and Hi-U Day.

Attendance of 200 freshmen at Camp Carpenter in Manchester in 1951 taxed the facilities. To provide more room the site was transferred to Camp Fatima in Gilmanton. There at the twenty-first annual camp, 270 freshmen and 70 staff members were hit by Hurricane Carol in September 1954. Buildings rocked, electrical and telephone lines were down for several hours, and the twenty-four-hour downpour flooded access roads. (The hurricane caused $18,000 damage on campus.) Soaked and isolated, the students kept their spirits dry by singing and cheering in the creaking assembly hall.

The first Hi-U day on October 31, 1952, attracted about 2,500 high school students from all parts of the state. The purpose was to interest the high schoolers in attending college by having them experience a day on campus. Cynics held that the hoopla characterizing the affair gave a distorted picture of college life.

By 1950 the men's Student Council had expanded and rid itself of faculty participation. The women's organization had become the Association of Women Students (AWS). There was no group which could speak for the students as a whole, however, and sentiment developed for forming a coeducational body which could. This sentiment had been reinforced by the first Rolling Ridge Conference on Campus Affairs in the fall of 1950. Representatives of the Student Council and the AWS drew up a constitution for a joint student government, with a senate as the legislative body. By vote of the students on March 21-22, 1951, the new constitution was approved. Student senators were elected a month later. The Student Senate held an organizational meeting on April 30, and on May 7 elected Robert N. Merchant '52, a twenty-four-year-old navy veteran, as its first president.

A seven-member men's Judiciary Board, with broad authority delegated to it by the Division of Student Personnel, started to operate in the fall of 1950. Richard A. Morse '51, its first chairman, reported that during the year it expelled one student, put ten on probation, warned thirteen, and reprimanded four.

That the students were interested in academic matters as well as campus politics was evidenced when the Student Committee on Educational Policy, College of Liberal Arts, submitted a report suggesting changes in the required freshman courses in English, history, and biology. No changes resulted. Trying again on May 1-2, 1954, the committee sponsored a student-faculty conference on academic problems at the Highland House on Bennett Road. Again the faculty took little notice of student suggestions.

Students were getting a foot into campus government, but no more. In 1955 a joint student-administration committee was formed to set policies for the new skating rink. A similar committee on the examination schedule was getting closer to infringing on the jealously-guarded domain of the faculty. A move initiated by a class in educational psychology resulted in the University Senate's vote to allow smoking in seminar-type classes. The Student Senate was held for downs in the fall of 1956 in an effort to clean up what had become an annoying amount of drunkenness at football games. After student leaders failed to persuade their peers to mend their ways, so that police action would be unnecessary, the Student Senate supported an administrative

edict by voting: "The Student Senate hereby endorses the policy that policemen and ushers prevent intoxicating beverages from being brought into the University stadium."

A 1958 request from the Student Senate that it be allowed to participate in the University Senate was referred to the Faculty Council. The council recommended, and the senate voted, that the student representatives be invited to the University Senate and to committee meetings "when matters involving student activities are to be discussed." (Evidently academic affairs were not yet recognized as being of student interest.) Two students were added to the Committee on Student Organizations, and a liaison committee of three members from each senate was established. Also in 1958, selected students were used to help faculty advisers counsel freshmen during orientation week.

Student government received a set-back in May 1959. President Johnson overturned a student judiciary board penalty of suspension for one man and probation for four others, by dismissing the suspended student and suspending those given probation. The five students had set off a home-made bomb in a dormitory toilet bowl. The explosion not only showered the washroom with water, as the culprits had intended, but with fragments of the bowl as well. Fortunately no one was in the room at the time. The *New Hampshire* commented that it hoped the student board would henceforth, as in the past, "be allowed to make some final decisions free of control or influence."

The important Liberal Arts Policy Committee rejected, by a unanimous vote, a request from students for three of the eleven seats on the committee. An organization of one student from each dormitory was, however, entrusted with bringing under control disorderly conduct that had developed in the freshman dining hall. These students even were allowed to forward complaints about the food.

There had been no publication devoted to stu-

"Whoop" Snively consoles a player.

dent literary efforts since the demise of the *Student Writer* at the beginning of World War II. The *New Hampshire* attempted to fill the gap from time to time. It ran an occasional column, also called the "Student Writer," between 1953 and 1955, and in October 1956 it published a literary supplement. There was a second such supplement in November, but there the venture ended because the volume of contributions was so small. In March 1960, after months of planning, a literary and humor magazine called *Cat Tales* made its appearance. It lacked the proverbial nine lives of its namesake.

Although student literary output was sporadic, it sometimes created controversy because of its earthy content. Outrage over realistic fiction, plus an intemperate letter attacking Attorney General

Louis C. Wyman, caused an investigation into the management of the *New Hampshire*. The investigation was carried out by a committee of editors from the state press. They defended the freedom of the student paper from administrative censorship, but recommended that a board of governors be appointed in an attempt to improve the paper's quality and responsibility. The board would have responsibility for the *New Hampshire's* staffing and budgetary decisions, and would consist of the paper's faculty adviser, an appointee from the administration, and five students. The trustees adopted this recommendation, as well as one to add instruction in journalism to the English department offerings. The first journalism instructor left at the end of a single, controversial year. He was succeeded by Donald M. Murray '48, an established writer and Pulitzer Prize winner in journalism.

The students still had energy for sports, of course. Although not as dominant as it had been two decades before, New Hampshire was still a power in winter sports. Ralph J. Townsend '49 had been a member of the Olympic team in 1948, and at the national intercollegiate ski meet in 1949 was first in the Nordic combined events; his classmate, Si Dunklee '49, was first in the cross country event. By the 1950s, however, New Hampshire's skiing star was an accidental import. Jon B. Riisnaes '56 was one of four Norwegians admitted in a student exchange program in September 1952. Unheralded as an athlete, with the first snow Riisnaes took to the ski jumps. Entering all the big meets in the country, he was undefeated in 1952-53. Fearing his academic work would suffer from his almost weekly participation, for the rest of his time at the university he put his classwork first, losing the fine edge as a jumper that had made him unbeatable.

Under the coaching of "Whoop" Snively, lacrosse attained new status. The 1955 team won the official Class C national championship, with a record of fourteen wins to one loss, four of the wins being over Class B teams. The only loss was to Class B champion Hofstra on a spring training trip. The basketball jinx remained potent. In 1955 Billy Pappas '55 of Manchester and J. Frank Mc-Laughlin, a sophomore from Belmont, Massachusetts, were two of the five named to the all-Yankee Conference team, yet New Hampshire ended the season at the bottom of the standings.

The trustees, concerned with the quality of the marching band, voted in November 1958 that "immediate action be taken to see that the University band becomes a real credit to the University." The result was that the band, under Donald A. Mattran and then Stanley D. Hettinger, changed from a necessary evil to an organization that could hold the spectators for a post-game exhibition.

A new feature was added to the Winter Carnival in 1957, when the event was initiated by the arrival in Durham early Friday evening of a lighted torch. The torch had been lighted from a bonfire atop the Old Man of the Mountain, carried down Cannon Mountain by a skier, then taken to Durham by a relay of twenty-five runners. The runners covered the 134 miles in thirteen and one-half hours.

Baseball claimed the spotlight in 1956 when Henry C. Swasey's team won the New England district playoff and went to the N.C.A.A. championship series in Omaha, Nebraska. Roger W. Magenau '61 won the New England intercollegiate tennis championship in each of the three years he competed on the varsity team. William R. Lochhead '61 was the first golfer to win the New England collegiate title two years in a row. And even the basketball team made history of a sort: on February 9, 1961, it defeated the University of Connecticut, 98-84, its first victory over that team in more than two decades.

New Hampshire students were newly aware of their role in the university community, but they were far from being radicalized. It was as late as February 1960 that Edward Eddy, vice-president and provost, speaking before the Massachusetts Schoolmasters' Club, was able to characterize the student of the day as "deeply conservative . . . interested in maintenance of a very comfortable *status quo* which makes him the sought-after darling of business and industry . . . . He simply lacks passion. He is a member in good standing of a vacuous majority which dictates a stance devoid of enthusiasm, excitement, or involvement."

Eddy was not alone in his analysis. Johnson, speaking before alumni in the summer of 1961, said: "Despite some trumped-up public fears, students at the University of New Hampshire are, like the homes they come from, conservative. Sedition is not one of their normal impulses. I am more disturbed by their quiet than by their daring."

28. McConnell's Years of Ferment

In August 1961, Johnson told the trustees that he was leaving the university to become the first head of the Great Lakes Colleges Association, a consortium of twelve leading private colleges in the Midwest. The trustee resolution accepting his resignation noted that his six-year administration "marks the greatest development in the history of the University, in the growth of its physical plant, in the quality of its educational offerings and in the tone and atmosphere of its campus life." In three legislative sessions, Johnson had succeeded in more than doubling the state's financial support of the university.

When he first arrived in Durham, Johnson had said that he wished to be recognized for his accomplishments rather than for his promise. This wish was realized on November 28, 1961, when more than eight hundred persons crowded New Hampshire Hall for a testimonial banquet. Two days later, 250 students attended a testimonial dinner at the Memorial Union.

To head the university after Johnson's departure on December 1, 1961, Vice-president John F. Reed was designated as acting president. The committee named to recommend the next president consisted of five trustees and three faculty members. A suggestion that the president of the alumni association be added to the committee was tabled. Jere Chase was to be assistant to the acting president during the interim.

No decision had been reached when, in May 1962, Reed announced his resignation in order to accept the presidency of Fort Lewis College in Colorado. The university was accustomed to frequent changes of president, but losing an acting president was a novel situation. The trustees promoted Chase to executive vice-president and made him the chief administrative officer.

The selection committee had decided in April 1962 on John W. McConnell, who refused the offer because he was committed to stay through the fall at Cornell, where he was dean of the School of Industrial and Labor Relations. In September it was decided to renew the offer. This time McConnell agreed to accept as of February 1, 1963.

Born in Philadelphia in 1907, McConnell was granted the B.A. by Dickinson College in 1929 and the Ph.D. by Yale in 1937. In the years between, he had taught at the American University in Cairo, where he became enamored of Harriet Barlow, the daughter of a Rockefeller Foundation medical research scientist. McConnell proposed to her while they were climbing the pyramids. He was an assistant professor of economics and sociology at American University in Washington, D.C., from 1937 to 1939, when he moved to New York University. He went to Cornell as professor of industrial and labor relations in 1946 and was dean of the graduate school for four years before heading the new School of Industrial and Labor Relations. In addition to writing four books, he had had extensive experience as a labor arbitrator and had served as a consultant to the Tennessee Valley Authority, the U.S. Air Force, the Department of Labor, and the Department of Health, Education, and Welfare.

McConnell arrived just in time to be involved in deliberations over the future of higher education in New Hampshire. Chaired by Raimond Bowles '47, an interim commission had been established by the 1961 legislature. The commission proposed that the state teachers colleges at Plymouth and Keene be removed from the jurisdiction of the State Board of Education, placed under new boards of trustees, and upgraded by adding liberal arts programs. Over the boards of these two institutions—and over that of the university as well—it was proposed to establish a co-ordinating board with broad budgetary and planning functions.

Senate Bill 68 was introduced embodying the recommendations of the commission. Governor John W. King had introduced House Bill 450, providing for the appointment by the governor (and advisory to him) of a board of regents with responsibility for all education from kindergarten through the university. Also introduced was House Bill 547 putting all state four-year colleges under a single board. The university's point of view was represented by McConnell, Chase, and Dean P. Williamson, president of the board of trustees. Together with Joseph A. Millimet, the governor's legislative assistant, and representatives of the two colleges and the state board of education, they worked with a legislative sub-committee to amend House Bill 547 until it was acceptable to all concerned. As passed, the bill established a state university system comprising UNH and the state colleges at Plymouth and Keene. To govern this system, the university Board of Trustees was expanded to twenty-four members, adding alumni representatives of the two state colleges and, as *ex officio* members, the presidents of the two colleges and the state commissioner of education.

The business and construction functions of the two state colleges had been centered in the state government at Concord, so it was necessary to integrate these activities promptly with the university offices at Durham. In recognition of his added responsibilities, Norman W. Myers '50 was named Vice-president and Treasurer in August 1963. Arrangements were made to combine the purchasing and cataloging of books for the three institutions, and for facilitating interlibrary loans by means of a trucking service. Academic coordination came more slowly. Until 1971, students transferring from one of the state colleges to UNH were processed in the same way as transfers from any other institution.

A new unit was added to the university system with the establishment in Manchester in September 1967 of the Merrimack Valley Branch. The branch started as an extension center. There were thirty-one credit courses, taught almost entirely by regular faculty members from the main campus, and enrolling 590 students. There also were seven short-term certificate courses enrolling 231. The first branch director, Frederick J. Robinson '49, had a small office in the Manchester Memorial High School and the classes met evenings in the high school. A year later, a house in the neighborhood was rented as an office and library building, while the growing number of classes continued to meet in Memorial High School and in nearby Southside Junior High. The unit got its first recognition as a separate entity when the 1969 legislature voted an appropriation of $60,000 for planning a campus.

In the beginning, the university faculty had been cool toward the Merrimack Valley venture, but in October 1970 the University Senate voted to support its continuing development. In the same meeting, the senate voted approval of a System Planning Committee to include representatives of the university at Durham, Keene and Plymouth state colleges, and when feasible Merrimack Valley. To further the move toward cohesion, in January 1971 the University Senate recommended that all undergraduate credits be transferred freely between the institutions, the receiving institution retaining control only of courses to be counted toward a major. The trustees confirmed this action in March.

The university faculty's growing awareness of the other units of the state system was due in part to a rapid increase in enrollment. Fall enrollment, pushed to a peak of 3,700 in 1949-50 by returning veterans, dropped off to 2,900 in 1953-54. It then increased an average of 133 a year until, in 1960-61 an enrollment of 3,835 exceeded the previous record. There followed three more years of modest increase until the first of the "war babies," sired by returning servicemen in 1946, reached campus. Enrollment went from

First day of the semester: an unchanging ritual.

4,530 in 1963-64 to 6,120 in 1966-67. By the fall of 1969 there were 7,730 full-time students on campus. Students were finding it hard to get into the classes they wanted, and the faculty were under pressure to increase the size of sections.

During the winter and spring of 1970 the University Senate became alarmed by a forecast of 350 more freshmen and 75 more transfer admissions than there had been the previous fall. The Academic Planning Committee favored holding the growth at Durham to four or five percent a year, with an eventual enrollment of between 10,000 and 11,000. The committee recognized that realizing this limitation would depend upon the development of the other units of the state system. It was not until January 1971 that the senate voted to limit enrollment at Durham to 10,500

within five to ten years—subject to review.

The unprecedented surge in enrollment demanded an unprecedented burst of construction. A division of plant development was established in September 1962 with Richard M. Brayton as director. Stillings Dining Hall was completed in September 1963 but could not be operated until the second semester, when steam became available from the expanded power plant. The 1963 legislature approved $3,660,000 for rebuilding the Field House and providing a cover for the skating rink (Snively Arena), $1,645,000 for the first phase of a new chemistry building (Parsons Hall), and $365,000 for alterations and additions to other buildings. Also approved was a $1,560,000 bond issue for the initial phase of the university's first high-rise dormitory (Stoke Hall).

Stillings Dining Hall (above) and Stoke Hall
(below) were major projects of the 1960s.

To avoid frequent major additions to the heating plant, Stoke Hall was heated by electricity, as have been most of the subsequent large buildings. Because of its eight-story height, elevator service was provided. This technical advance led to the two-hour entrapment of three students when the power failed during a blizzard in March 1966.

In January 1965 the trustees authorized McConnell to ask the legislature for $9,156,630 for academic construction, $869,000 for alterations and service facilities, and $7,219,346 in self-liquidating projects. Federal or private funds were available for some of the buildings, so that the costs were higher in some cases than the amounts requested of the legislature. Following is a list of the items sought:

- New wing and alterations to Nesmith Hall: $895,000 (denied).
- Addition and alterations to Putnam Hall: $350,000 (approved; a new building, Barton Hall, was later substituted).
- Addition and alterations to Hamilton Smith Hall: $361,750 (approved).
- Addition and alterations to Kingsbury Hall: $545,000 (approved).
- Social science building: $1,312,500 (approved).
- Phase two of Parsons Hall: $2,152,280 (denied).
- Addition to phase one of Parsons Hall: $556,500 (approved).
- Addition and alterations to the library: $2,130,000 (approved).
- Residence hall: $1,186,660 (approved; Hubbard Hall).
- Residence hall: $1,055,470 (approved; Devine Hall).
- Graduate residence: $1,160,000 (approved; Babcock Hall).
- Addition and alterations to Stoke Hall: $1,542,550 (approved).
- Addition to the Forest Park apartments: $959,418 (approved).
- Addition to Memorial Union: $908,000 (denied).
- Housing unit for New England Center for Continuing Education: $500,000 (approved; Adams Tower).

So much construction was taking place that the booms of construction cranes replaced the power plant stack, the old water tower, and the tower of Thompson Hall as the main features of the campus skyline. Ready, or essentially so, for the opening of college in the fall of 1966 were Parsons Hall phase one, Stoke Hall phase two, Devine Hall, the Kingsbury Hall addition, and the expanded Field House. Also opened was the U.S. Route 4 by-pass, which took the heavy trucks and other through traffic off Main Street. The by-pass did not remove the traffic congestion, however. In the second semester of 1965-66, 3,000 cars were registered on campus, competing for 1,800 parking spaces.

Authorization for three projects denied in 1965—the additions to Nesmith, the Memorial Union, and Parsons—was granted by the legislature in 1967. To relieve the chronically crowded housing and dining facilities, authorization for a new residence hall (Christensen) to cost $3,161,500 and a new dining hall (Philbrook) to cost $1,303,000 was secured in 1967. Christensen was designed as a coeducational hall, with a ten-story tower housing 250 women and two smaller towers housing 190 men. Designed by Franzen Associates of New York City, it won one of ten annual design awards given by the American Institute of Architects in June 1971. It was the only campus residential structure so honored. To avoid the mass-feeding atmosphere of the typical college dining hall, nearby Philbrook has six areas each with a capacity of one hundred diners.

In 1969 the legislature approved the addition to Paul Creative Arts Center for $810,000 (up from the $361,750 requested in 1965). Also authorized in that session was a companion residence hall (Williamson) to Christensen, costing $3,600,000.

Upon arriving in Durham, McConnell had told the trustees: "It is becoming increasingly apparent that in order to do some of the things we want to do, it will be necessary to secure private funds." He was authorized to appoint a full-time director of development, Daniel A. Ferber. Ferber's first project was a drive to raise $3,700,000—later raised to $4,200,000—in connection with the forthcoming centennial observation. Trustee Sinclair Weeks agreed to be chairman of the drive. The funds would go for a building to house the Whittemore School (McConnell Hall) and for a continuing education center.

Knowing that the Kellogg Foundation had financed continuing education centers at other state universities, McConnell wrote to Emery W. Morris, president and director of the foundation, asking for an opportunity to meet with him. The meeting took place in Battle Creek, Michigan, on April 23, 1963. There, McConnell and Jere Chase developed the advantages of Durham as a location for a conference center to serve not only New Hampshire but Vermont, Maine, and Massachusetts as well, and possibly all of New England. McConnell and Chase met with the Kellogg officials again in June. Plans progressed during the summer, and McConnell and Daniel Ferber proceeded to gain the support of the presidents of the other five New England state universities. A meeting was arranged for November 3, 1964, in Durham. Following this meeting, the university presidents drew up an agreement formalizing their cooperation in the venture. Announcement of the plan for the fund drive was released to the press on December 3. In late December, the university made a formal proposal to the Kellogg Foundation for $1,810,000 for construction and program development. At the same time, each of the other state universities requested $60,000 to support its part of the program. A ten-acre tract at the corner of Edgewood Road and Strafford Avenue was set aside for the New England Center.

The Kellogg trustees took favorable action on the requests at their mid-February meeting in 1965. With the construction funds assured, William Pereira, noted architect from Los Angeles, was retained to draw the plan. His problem was to fit the buildings to the site with minimum destruction of the lofty pines and huge granite outcroppings. The solution was to make the living towers eight stories high—about the height of the tallest pines. The exteriors were to be green glazed brick, with exposed columns of steel.

Former President Arthur S. Adams, retired as president of the Salzburg Seminar in 1965, returned to Durham as special assistant to McConnell, devoting most of his time to the New England Center project. Harry P. Day was appointed director of the center in February 1966. It was in October 1969 that the first conference was held in the dramatic new buildings.

Plans for observing the university's centennial year had been initiated when Acting President Reed sought the advice of the trustees at their February 1962 meeting. It was agreed that Philip M. Marston '24, professor of history, would be appointed university historian with the charge of writing a history. A twenty-six member University Centennial Committee was appointed in July 1963, with Laurence E. Webber '34, director of the Engineering Experiment Station, as chairman. In May 1964 the trustees voted to spend up to $10,000—later increased to $28,000—for the affair during the academic year 1965-66. The celebration was divided into three parts: Man in Science, Man in the Arts, and Man in Society. Symposia on the first topic were scheduled for the first semester and for the third topic during the second semester; events and exhibitions related to the arts were spread through the year. The opening convocation on October 7, 1965, was addressed by former president Arthur S. Adams, who spoke on "Science, The Arts, and Society in New England." The final centennial address was given at the 1966 commencement by James B. Conant, former president of Harvard.

Although at the end of its first century there was little resemblance between the modern university and its modest beginning in Hanover, McConnell had one problem that had earlier plagued Ezekiel Dimond. This was securing financial support from the legislature. With the university growing much faster than the income of the state government, the situation was no better at the end of the McConnell administration than at the beginning.

The budget request for the 1963-64 biennium was cut back so that it would be within the estimated yield of the millage formula. When time came to submit the 1965-67 biennial budget, the two state colleges had been added to the university system, making the millage formula useless as a guide. For Durham the operating budget request was $6,197,875 for each year of the biennium—a forty-five percent increase over the preceding biennium. The legislature voted approximately the full amount sought for the first year of the biennium, but it made $750,000 of the second-year appropriation contingent upon a surplus in the state treasury. As fiscal year 1965-66 approached its end, it appeared that there would not be a sufficient surplus. There was a demand for a special session of the legislature. No progress was made until it was discovered in Concord that a one-cent increase in the gasoline tax, voted some sessions previously, was due to expire on June 30, 1966, and that no one had thought to extend it. A special session was called to care for the gasoline tax extension, and at the same time the university system was granted its $750,000 without reference to a treasury surplus.

The battle of the budget was fought along familiar lines in the 1967 and 1969 sessions, and reached a climax of sorts in 1971. Under the twin pressures of inflation and rising enrollment, the university requested for operating expenses $24,537,659 for 1971-73—an increase of fifty-two percent over the preceding biennium. Only $14,141,867 was appropriated. With New Hampshire the only one of the fifty states trying to balance its budget without either a sales tax or a personal income tax the university was unable to mount an effective campaign for more money. President McConnell observed that it was unseemly to ask money for higher education when other state agencies needed the funds to feed or-

phans. To keep the university solvent, in-state tuition—already the highest in the country for a state university—was boosted once again.

In order to permit students of modest means to attend the university, each time tuition was raised part of the added income went to student aid. The income from an anonymous bequest from a member of the class of 1898, amounting to $340,000, was received in 1967 and was designated for scholarships. The same year Mary F. Simpson of Salem, New Hampshire, gave $106,979 for the same purpose. These, added to the Lord and Stillings gifts and dozens of more modest ones, brought the scholarship endowments up to over $1.75 million.

The swelling enrollment had an impact on academic as well as physical aspects of the campus. It stimulated the formation of new instructional units, the addition of new programs, and the modification of academic procedures.

The Whittemore School of Business and Economics was separated from the College of Liberal Arts in the summer of 1962 and was formally dedicated on March 28, 1963. In June 1963, in anticipation of the retirement of Carl Lundholm '21 as director of men's physical education and athletics, outside experts were called in to make recommendations about these activities. The result was a new Division of Physical Education and Athletics, including women's as well as men's activities. James W. Long, who had held a similar position at the University of Toledo, was named as director. The new emphasis on physical education resulted in unhappiness on the part of those primarily interested in intercollegiate athletics. In June 1966, when Long resigned to go to Oregon State University, the administrative responsibilities were divided, and Andrew T. Mooradian '48 was named director of intercollegiate athletics.

In 1966, three years after its graduates began to be awarded the Associate in Applied Science degree instead of a mere certificate of graduation, the Thompson School of Agriculture became the Thompson School of Applied Science. New pro-

Study area in the library.

grams had been added to train technicians in commerce, forestry, soil and water, construction, landscaping, and food preparation.

In 1969, a new School of Health Studies was established, made up of programs which had been offered through the College of Liberal Arts.

Signaling a change in emphasis away from techniques and toward scientific theory, in 1963 the degree awarded graduates of the agricultural departments was changed from a Bachelor of Science in Agriculture to an undesignated Bachelor of Science. Specialized departments in the college were combined into more inclusive units—for example, the departments of animal husbandry, dairy husbandry, and poultry husbandry became a single department of animal science. To indicate more accurately the changing mission of the college, in 1969 its name was changed to College of Life Sciences and Agriculture. Reacting to the widespread interest in ecology three departments merged as an Institute of Natural and Environmental Resources, which in 1970 was authorized to add a major in environmental conservation.

Liberal Arts offerings were substantially increased in most departments. The German department initiated a Junior Year Abroad at Marburg University in 1963, followed two years later by a similar program in French at Dijon University. Students of Spanish could take a year abroad at a university either in Spain or in Latin America. Professional degrees of Bachelor of Music and Bachelor of Fine Arts were authorized.

In the Graduate School, new degrees included the Master of Public Administration, the Master of Business Administration, and the Master of Arts in Teaching. A Certificate of Advanced Graduate Study, based on two years of graduate work, was authorized in student personnel work. The mathematics department won the right to offer the Ph.D. in 1963. The first discipline outside the sciences to offer the Ph.D. was psychology, which was authorized to do so in 1965.*

* As of 1973, the Ph.D. had been authorized in biochemistry, botany, chemistry, economics, engineering, English, genetics, history, mathematics, microbiology, physics, plant science, psychology, sociology, and zoology.

Political science class in Hamilton Smith Hall.

Even more remarkable than the development of the educational programs of the university was the rapid expansion of research activities. An experimental farm had been one of the institution's first acquisitions in Hanover, and on it Jeremiah W. Sanborn began in 1877 to carry on research leading to published results. The first substantial financial support for research was $15,000 received from the federal government in 1887 upon passage of the Hatch Act. Organized research grew steadily. In fiscal year 1958 the treasurer's report showed research expenditures of $408,374, about half of it sponsored. Twelve years later, research expenditures totaled $3,640,243. Of this $2,177,804 was sponsored, largely by the federal government. Agricultural research is still important, but in recent years it has been eclipsed by that in the physical sciences.

Basic changes affecting all the undergraduate programs in the university resulted from the work of two faculty committees. The Committee on Academic Programs and Teaching Methods, appointed in June 1959, recommended university-wide "group requirements," to ensure a

foundation of general education for all undergraduates. The recommendations finally were approved in detail by the University Senate in March 1963.

The increased enrollment, rapid changes in subject matter, and improved preparation of students in the high schools led to the appointment of a faculty Educational Policy Committee in November 1965. Members were Professors Dwight R. Ladd, business administration, chairman; Robert W. Corell, mechanical engineering; Raymond L. Erickson, psychology; Herman Gadon, business administration; Francis H. Hall, soil and water science; Hans Heilbronner, history; Asher Moore, philosophy; Donald M. Murray, English; and Richard C. Strout, animal science. After forty-nine meetings, the committee released its preliminary report as a ten-page supplement to the *New Hampshire* on October 6, 1966. The final report, *Toward Unity through Diversity*, was published in February 1967, leading to a comprehensive reorganization of undergraduate programs effective with the academic year 1969-70. University requirements were stated in terms of "courses" instead of semester-hour credits, the typical course carrying four credits instead of the traditional three. Courses were reorganized; some that had been two semesters long were cut to one. A student was expected to take four courses a semester instead of the traditional five. Provisions for satisfying university-wide requirements were made more flexible. A two-week reading period preceded the final examinations each semester. Intercollege seminars dealing with various contemporary issues and values were introduced.

Adoption of these reforms did not end the educational ferment, nor did all of the changes meet with universal acclaim—the two-week reading period especially was a target for dissent.

Impatient with the pace of academic innovation, a group of faculty and students—copying a pattern initiated on a few other campuses—started a "Free University." This was to offer non-credit, non-fee courses not otherwise available on campus. The courses were to be taught on a voluntary basis by faculty members or qualified students. At its height, during the fall semester of 1967, about 220 registered. Typical enrollment in a course was fourteen to twenty; the largest number, twenty-eight, were attracted to "Introduction to Poetry" taught by Julian H. Smith III, an instructor in the English department.

The most innovative addition to the official university offerings was the Life Studies Program. As outlined by the faculty-student Council on Educational Innovation, this was to enroll in 1970-71 about fifty freshmen and fifty sophomores, all volunteers. The course was organized in workshops, each dealing with a large issue.

A controversy arose in February 1970 when the students wishing to register for political science 401 in sections taught by a part-time instructor, Robert M. Winston, exceeded the capacity. Room was available in other sections of the course, but the students demanded Winston. After heated debate, the University Senate voted to refer the matter to a special committee. When

word was leaked that the committee was deadlocked, more than a hundred protesting students crowded Murkland Hall lobby, in an office off of which the committee was meeting. President McConnell and Academic Vice-president Eugene S. Mills were called on for help, and they got the original committee to agree to the appointment of a new committee of three hitherto uninvolved faculty and three students. After conducting lengthy hearings the next day, a compromise was reached by arranging for Winston to teach an additional section under the auspices of the Continuing Education Division. Four students registered in it.

On the grounds that the creation of these committees took from the Political Science department a decision that rightly belonged to it, all seventeen department chairmen in the College of Liberal Arts submitted resignations of their chairmanships. President McConnell and Vice-president Mills met with the chairmen and discussed scheduling and other prerogatives of academic departments; also, these deliberations brought to the fore the difficulty students were having, because of the rapidly climbing enrollment, in getting the programs they wished. Plans were made for an improved response to department needs and it was agreed that the scheduling of courses continued to be departmental and college responsibilities. Fortunately, the chairmen agreed to continue in their positions.

An Educational Innovation Week was held on campus, March 8-12, 1970, involving local and off-campus speakers, films, and other attractions. Editorializing on the result, the New Hampshire said: "Following recent academic crises on campus, the turnout was expected to be enthusiastic and overwhelming. Student and faculty responses were in fact enthusiastic but could not be termed overwhelming . . . . Attendance was poor." To give more freedom to the student unable to find fulfillment in one of the fifty-eight organized majors, in March 1971 the University Senate voted approval of a "student designed major," subject to acceptance by the several undergraduate schools and colleges.

The restructuring of the curriculum led to the death knell for two traditional requirements—physical education and ROTC. In January 1971 the University Senate voted for immediate elimination of all physical education requirements, but "enthusiastically" endorsed a voluntary program. The requirement that all freshmen and sophomore men take ROTC was abolished in 1964. The Army and Air Force continued their programs, and in the fall of 1969 there were thirty-nine freshmen in the Army program and thirty-two in that of the Air Force. To review the ROTC programs, a Board of Governors with Arthur Adams as chairman was established. The board recommended that elements dealing with international affairs, engineering, management, and the like be covered in the regular courses of the university or in special courses taught by regular faculty. These would carry academic credit. The military "skill" courses would be taught by military personnel with credit for them to count only toward commissioning. The revised program was accepted by the Senate in May 1970, and was approved by the Army and later the Air Force.

Reflecting national interest in improving educational opportunities for blacks, a special program was started in 1969. (The special advising, tutoring, and program adjustments established for them also were open to a few disadvantaged whites.) James T. Johnson, a black recruiter, was added to the admissions staff, and Myrna C. Adams was employed as a coordinator of the program. Twenty-six students were admitted to the program the first year, only three of them from New Hampshire. Six black administrators and faculty members were employed. Difficulties were encountered both in recruitment and in financial support, and the program was eventually reduced in size.

There were social problems as well. It was desired to make the blacks part of the university community but at the same time to encourage racial identity; they were encouraged to room together if they desired, and six rooms in Richards House were assigned as an activity center. There was some friction between blacks and whites which culminated in a confrontation in front of Stoke Hall on February 23, 1971. Two students were arrested, with one held for a court appearance.

Of the disadvantaged whites on campus, six women organized themselves as Disadvantaged Women for Higher Education, Inc. A day care center for their children was established in the Durham Community Church. They had a difficult time financially because no special state or federal funds were available for them.

29. Free Speech: Round Three

When McConnell assumed the presidency in February 1963, he was confronted by a matter relating to G. Harris Daggett. A raise for Daggett had been tabled the previous fall. The trustees took it up again in January but decided to delay discussion until their February meeting, giving McConnell an opportunity to review the matter. The decision was favorable. Daggett wrote the trustees on March 6 to express his appreciation for their action, and commending them for the patience and considered judgment they had shown on his behalf.

Almost immediately, the trustees and McConnell had another opportunity to use patience and considered judgment. On April 21 Daggett spoke at a campus meeting of the Youth Peace Fellowship. His subject was "The Role of the Revolution in Promoting Peace." He said that the United States and the Soviet Union were working toward the same goals, he advocated the admission of mainland China to the United Nations, and he suggested that the U.N. flag should fly above that of the United States. For the time, these opinions were highly inflammatory.

Daggett's audience was small, but it included a reporter from the Manchester *Union Leader*. The newspaper then secured a statement from Louis Wyman, who had recently been elected to the U.S. Congress. Wyman said: "Were I on the Board [of Trustees] I would vote to let Daggett go elsewhere." Congressman Wyman was even more outspoken in an interview for the *New Hampshire*, in which he termed Daggett "a troublemaker, a real troublemaker . . . not dangerous but insidious and undesirable. Free speech need not be paid for by taxes." The American Legion District 4 called for Daggett's dismissal. The trustees held a special meeting on June 6, 1963, and according to the minutes of that meeting:

The Trustees, having discussed the publicity anent the recently quoted remarks of Professor Daggett, have noted the manner in which the university administration has handled the matter and, having complete confidence in President McConnell, have by motion made by Mr. [Sinclair] Weeks and duly seconded by Mr. [Frank W.] Randall, voted that no further action is necessary at this time.

This incident occurred when salaries for the next year were being determined. Wishing to avoid anything that might aggravate the situation, the administration did not recommend Daggett for an increase. The Faculty Welfare Committee learned of this in the fall, took the matter up, and persuaded the trustees to vote Daggett another raise.°

With the freedom of the campus for political speeches well established, Nelson Rockefeller opened the 1964 primary campaign with a campus speech on October 18, 1963. He was followed in the early months of 1964 by Harold Stassen, Margaret Chase Smith, and Barry Goldwater. Although the partisan activities of the major party candidates went smoothly, the same cannot be said for those of a student group calling itself "No Time for Politics." This group invited George Lincoln Rockwell, head of the American Nazi party, and James Jackson, editor of the communist *Worker*. Governor King, who had also agreed to talk to the group, withdrew when he learned of the other invitations.

In the ensuing controversy, the trustees appointed a committee to review and amplify the 1950 speakers' policy. The members were trustees Randall and Bernard I. Snierson '35, Presi-

---

° Daggett was promoted to full professor in July 1966. In the spring of 1969 he was elected the first faculty chairman of the reorganized University Senate. He died—while about to go water skiing—of a heart attack in August 1969.

180

dent McConnell, professors John T. Holden and Richard S. Dewey, and students Allan A. Osgood '64 and William E. Lunt '65. There was a panel discussion on free speech on March 11 and an open hearing on March 17. A new statement resulted from these deliberations, but the faculty felt that to change the speakers' policy at such a moment would be an admission that it had been faulty. By unanimous vote, the trustees reaffirmed—as they had done once before—their 1950 statement on academic freedom.

McConnell told a rally of seven hundred students that the right of faculty and students to invite outside speakers—"even speakers as objectionable and insubstantial as Jackson"—had been reaffirmed. He was cheered by the students. In a confusion of dates and sponsors, however, George Lincoln Rockwell never did get the chance to speak in Durham. (Rockwell and one of his "storm troopers" had earlier met, unannounced, with the leaders of No Time for Politics at the Memorial Union.) James Jackson fared better. Sponsored by the Socratic Society, a philosophy club, Jackson talked before an audience of eight hundred in the Field House on April 24.

Governor King, addressing the annual meeting of the university chapter of the American Association of University Professors in April, had forcefully declared his opposition to "tax-supported platforms" for "subversives." During the fall, the trustees discussed speaker policies at other state universities and considered steps to head off legislation that might limit the university's freedom in the matter. Such legislation seemed a real possibility in the 1965 session of the legislature.

When the legislative session opened in January 1965, Richard C. Plumer, then editor of the *Alumnus*, inquired into the matter.* He was told by Stewart Lamprey, president of the Senate and three-times speaker of the House, that restrictive legislation would probably pass in both houses.

---

* Plumer wrote a 200-page manuscript on the "Feldman Bill" controversy, which is available in the university library, and upon which the following discussion is based.

Lamprey avoided committing himself to vote against such legislation. The leadership in the House took a different stand. Speaker Walter R. Peterson, Jr., and majority leader Alexander Taft both opposed a speaker ban.

Representative Saul Feldman '32 prepared a bill which would add to the state's anti-subversive act the provision that: "No state agency, university, school, or other state institution or agency deriving financial support in whole or in part from the appropriations of moneys collected by state taxation, shall make available to or permit an official, representative or member of a subversive organization or foreign subversive organization to use its facilities or its premises." Those allowing such use were to be fired.

Feldman did not file his bill before the deadline, so he sought to introduce it through the rules committee. Peterson at first opposed this move. When Governor King came out strongly for the bill, however, Peterson decided it would be better to let the bill come in without a fight and to refer it to the education committee (chaired by James E. O'Neil '42) which was known to be favorable to the university. A public hearing on the bill was set for February 24, and the university's administration, faculty, and students joined in organizing opposition to the measure.

When the hearing opened, seven hundred persons crowded into Representatives' Hall, filling the floor, the gallery, and the aisles. Feldman, as sponsor of the bill, spoke first. He held that his goal was "not to restrain academic freedom anywhere in the state but to define the term and to prevent it from becoming a synonym for academic license." The university's case was opened by Forrest M. Eaton '26, chairman of the Board of Trustees. Eaton argued that both law and tradition gave control of university policy to its trustees.

Among those who spoke for the university were former governor Sherman Adams; Placidus Riley, O.S.B., president of St. Anselm's College; John Sloan Dickey, president of Dartmouth; Mrs.

*Protest march of May, 1966; Professor Daggett
is in third line wearing light-colored jacket.*

Mildred McAfee Horton, former president of Wellesley and a UNH trustee; Lawrence Golden '65, president of the Student Senate; Robert B. Dishman, professor of government; McConnell, and trustees Snierson and Maurice Devine. Finally there was Joseph A. Millimet, the governor's legislative counsel, who offered the opinion that King had been "mouse-trapped" into supporting the bill.

Supporting the bill were the governor, one of his staff members reading a statement from him; William Craig, House minority leader; Herbert S. O'Neil, departmental adjutant of the American Legion; and James Glatis, who introduced himself as an undercover agent for the FBI. A number of legislators also spoke for the bill.

The hearing went on for two days. Adjournment on the second day was hastened by reports of a destructive storm in the northern part of the state. Despite the stormy weather, two thousand gathered for a bonfire rally on campus that night, at which a torch was lighted to burn until the defeat of the Feldman Bill.

The university won an easy victory in the education committee, which voted the bill inexpedient to legislate, 19-3. The minority planned to continue the fight on the floor when the matter came to a vote there on March 11. An intensive campaign was launched to have students and their parents contact their legislators. McConnell prepared a two-page letter which was individually typed for every member of the House. All polls indicated that the vote on the floor would be close, the most optimistic predicting defeat of the bill by twenty votes. On the morning of the vote the Manchester *Union Leader* carried on its front page a statement from Congressman Wyman supporting the Feldman Bill.

The debate on the floor of the House went on for nearly six hours, with forty-two members speaking. When the roll was called, the vote against the bill was 205-176.

A year later, on April 21, 1966, a mob of two thousand students tarnished the university's record for upholding free speech on the campus. Two dozen members of the New England Committee for Non-Violent Action were on a march from Exeter to Durham. The demonstrators were unmolested until they reached the Durham town line. There police stopped them because they had no parade permit. Five of the marchers decided to ignore the police order, and were taken off to jail. The others broke formation and walked in a group into town. In front of the Memorial Union, a crowd of students swarmed down on them, blocked the way, and threatened the marchers with physical violence. Some eggs were thrown. The affair had been planned in advance, with posters urging participation put on display in the Quadrangle dormitories.

The *New Hampshire* commented: "It is ironic and it is nauseating that a student body which last year cried out and fought . . . for freedom of speech . . . should so quickly and blatantly not only ignore those freedoms but deny them to others."

The faculty and many students reacted quickly. The AAUP chapter, the Memorial Union Student Organization, and other groups joined in inviting the pacifists back to the campus. Seven hundred signed a resolution condemning the mob action. For the return visit on May 10, a parade permit was secured and 125 faculty and students joined the march. (The parade permit included a proviso that anyone convicted of violating any town ordinance, except one relating to traffic, could not march. Those arrested in the earlier march did join the procession and were promptly arrested. Judge Bradford McIntire dismissed the charges because no law had been violated.)

All previous controversies paled in comparison with the appearance on May 5, 1970, of Abbie

Hoffman, Jerry Rubin, and David Dellinger. The "Chicago Three," as they came to be known, were among those who had been convicted of a conspiracy to riot at the Democratic national convention of 1968.*

The turmoil began on April 17 when the *New Hampshire* reported that Mark Wefers '73, president of the student body, had invited the three men to speak on campus. They were to be paid $4,000 from student activity tax funds. Wefers had not gone through the established routine for clearing such an event through the Student Affairs office.

Next day, at the regular monthly meeting of the trustees, McConnell brought up the matter. He also noted that the university was committed to maintaining a normal academic program in the face of anti-war protests—these soon reached a climax because of the incursion of U.S. and South Vietnamese troops into Cambodia, and because of the death in Ohio of four students at Kent State University.

The trustees, reporting that they had received numerous critical calls and letters, expressed their dismay about the invitation. They supported the administration in its ruling that $3,000 of the speakers' fee, which was to have been transferred from the reserve funds of the *New Hampshire* and the *Granite*, could not be used for such a purpose. McConnell was asked to seek an opinion from the university's counsel, Joseph Millimet, about the sentence in the university speakers' policy that opened the university to any speaker "who does not advocate the overthrow of government by force and violence." The Chicago Three were believed to be advocates of violence.

Millimet's seventeen-page opinion held that, in the light of current court opinions, advocacy of violence was not a sufficient cause to bar a speaker. There must be evidence that the talk itself would lead to violence.

---

* The convictions were reversed by a federal appeals court in 1972.

At a meeting of the executive committee and some other trustees in Durham on April 26, McConnell was asked to find out if violence had resulted from the appearance on other campuses of any of the three. At a special trustee meeting in Concord on the evening of May 1, McConnell reported that his investigation had failed to uncover any evidence that lives or property might be endangered by the proposed meeting. He recommended that no action be taken to prevent it. A long discussion ensued. Vice-president Eugene Mills told the trustees of the concern of the

A vigil for the dead in Vietnam, held at "the notch" in front of the Memorial Union.

university community that the campus be kept open. Governor Walter Peterson said that, since the speakers would undoubtedly come to Durham whether or not a meeting was officially sanctioned, he thought it wise to set a time and place so that plans could be made to avoid violence. A motion to deny the campus to the speakers lost, 12-6. It then was moved to allow the meeting between the hours of 2:00 P.M. to 5:00 P.M., which passed unanimously. Violence was feared not so much from students as from outsiders, but there appeared no practicable way to limit attendance to the university community.

Immediately after the trustees adjourned at midnight, McConnell telephoned Wefers to inform him of the decision. Wefers then issued a call over the campus radio for a mass meeting at 1:30 A.M. to protest the hours limitation. When only a few responded, another mass meeting was called for the daylight hours. Wefers told the several hundred who attended this meeting that, in effect, the university was denying the campus to the speakers. Because of a court appearance in New York on the morning of May 5, the speakers could not be in Durham before 5:00 P.M.

The Chicago Three affair was not on the agenda of the University Senate—nearly half of its members now students—when it met on April 27. The rules were suspended, however, to allow a long discussion of the matter. One faculty member suggested that the senate take over the matter, but McConnell replied that, although he wanted to confer with the senate, the responsibility was his. Following the trustee action in setting afternoon hours for the speakers, a special meeting of the senate was called for Sunday afternoon, May 3. Chairman Paul Bruns had difficulty maintaining decorum. A motion was passed, with one dissenting vote, supporting McConnell's decision that the visit of the Chicago Three was consistent with university policy. It was voted to ask the trustees if the hours set for the speakers could be extended; then a motion by Wefers that no time limit be set was also passed.

On the morning of the visit of the Chicago Three, Wefers appeared before the U.S. District Court in Concord, petitioning that the hours limitation set by the trustees be put aside. Millimet, representing the university, told the court that he had contacted the New York attorneys for the three men, and said it would be possible for the speakers to be in Durham by 3:30 P.M. The court then set 3:30 to 6:30 P.M. for the meeting.

At three-thirty that afternoon, four thousand students and others filled the Lundholm Gymnasium. At 4:00 P.M., Mark Wefers announced that the speakers were in town but refused to abide by time limits. They would speak at 7:30 instead. McConnell conferred with Attorney General Warren Rudman, the United States Attorney, and others. He then announced that, although the state and federal authorities would have supported the university if it refused to allow the meeting, he had decided to let it be held at 7:30.

At the appointed time, the gymnasium was filled once again. Another three thousand persons listened over loudspeakers in the Cowell Stadium. The event was described by L. Franklin Heald in the *Alumnus*:

The three speakers presented the expected tirade against the establishment, law and order, schools and colleges, the war, the treatment of blacks, President Nixon, even the UNH trustees, and practically anyone you could name who stands for the things most Americans stand for.
The theatrics of Rubin and Hoffman—jumping up and down on the stage, allegedly smoking marijuana, repeatedly using the clenched fist strike symbol, and shouting into the microphone—excited the audience who responded with shouts of approval, cheers, and laughter.

When the meeting ended, however, the thousands departed quietly. The next day Mark Wefers was cited for criminal contempt for disregarding the times set by the court. He was convicted by the U.S. District Court in Concord, but on appeal the decision was unanimously reversed by a three-judge panel.

*Freshmen hi-jinks were still in vogue
in the fall of 1963.*

30. The Quiet Revolution

With expanded physical education facilities and a larger student body, new sports were added to the varsity program during McConnell's administration. Serious intercollegiate competition had begun, with the hiring of specialized coaches, in football in 1915, basketball in 1916, baseball in 1921, track in 1924, skiing and hockey in 1925, and lacrosse in 1931. By 1970 varsity sports also included tennis, golf, soccer, gymnastics, swimming, and wrestling. With the provision of an all-weather rink in the Snively Arena—and the fortunate enrollment of a few players from Canada in the mid-1960s—the hockey team moved into the top ranks nationally and consistently attracted sell-out crowds for its home contests.

The persistent problem of financial aid to athletes came under renewed study in 1963. Consideration by the presidents and athletic officials of the six Yankee Conference institutions resulted in the adoption in 1965 of a formula determining what would be allowed, as well as an agreement to submit detailed annual reports.* The formula was a compromise. It allowed more financial aid to athletes than the University of New Hampshire had been giving, but put a ceiling on its more prosperous conference competitors. In July 1966 the trustees voted to authorize granting the full amount of aid allowed by the formula if funds from outside sources were available.

The evening of entertainment and paper-money gambling which had flourished in Notch

* Briefly stated, the formula permitted each institution to award each year, to incoming athletes in all sports, a sum twenty times the average cost of tuition, fees, room, and board. A student could keep his financial aid for four years, but if he dropped out his portion could not be assigned to the others. Reported aid for 1964-65 was Massachusetts $90,000, Connecticut $75-78,000, Vermont $70,000, New Hampshire $34-35,000, and Maine $18,000. Rhode Island did not report.

Hall as the "Night of Sin" had become a less exciting "Casino Night" in the splendid surroundings of the new Memorial Union. Each student, through the activity tax, continued to be charged $4.30 in 1962 for a copy of the annual *Granite* although it continued to fall farther and farther behind in its publication date. The Memorial Union Student Organization started in 1966 a coffee house featuring candlelight, espresso coffee, and entertainment. Known as "In Loco Parentis," it faded because of its respectable surroundings. A more promising location was found in the basement of Schofield House. The upper floors had been converted to university offices, but no official wanted his desk in the basement with its ladder-like stairway and head-bumping pipes. It was October 1969 before alterations to meet fire safety regulations were completed and the project was back in business as "Aquarius."

The Kappa Delta sorority became dormant in 1962 when it was unable to finance continued operation of its house. A $10,000 debt almost forced Kappa Sigma, dating back to Hanover days, to close in 1964, but a $24,000 grant from its national saved its life. In 1964, also, the Pi Kappa Alpha house was destroyed by fire. In 1966, Lambda Chi sold its house to the university as an office building for the New England Center, and for a time the thirty brothers lived together on the top floor of Stoke Hall. Not all chapters were having difficulty, however. In 1966 and 1967, additions to their houses were built by Alpha Tau Omega, Alpha Gamma Rho, Chi Omega, and Pi Kappa Alpha. In contrast with the rapidly expanding enrollment, the total number of students belonging to fraternities and sororities was holding about even.

In the fall of 1962, the student administration officers promulgated a new rule, approved by the trustees, the purpose of which was to dry up the campus. Dean of Students Robert Keesey said: "I believe the most intelligent and most effective method of controlling the use of alcohol on a campus must be based on the student's conscience." The general observation was that the students' consciences were not equal to the burden. The voters of Durham proved uncooperative when, in the biennial referendum in November 1962, they voted 594-471 to allow beer to be sold in town for the first time. Local grocery stores promptly acquired licenses. In December 1963, the University Senate modified its policy by allowing drinking in university houses by males over twenty-one, and the trustees acquiesced. (The coeds had asked that they not be given equal rights.) An editorial in the *New Hampshire*, commenting on the changes, summed them up: "Wet again, dry again, and now damp."

At a student-faculty conference at the Pembroke Conference Center in November 1966, a resolution was adopted urging abolition of curfew hours for women. The next month the students informally voted ten to one to abolish curfews for sophomore, junior, and senior women, but to keep a curfew for first-semester freshmen women. A committee appointed by McConnell to study the matter also recommended abolishing curfews except for freshmen. In April 1967 the Student Senate, and in June the University Senate, moved to adopt the recommendation in steps: seniors to be liberated the following year, juniors the next, then sophomores, and finally second-semester freshmen. The trustees, with three dissenting, in November 1970 approved ending the curfew for all students.

A portent of what was to follow was the daring 1962 topic for the intramural debate tournament: "Resolved, Housing units should be coeducational." Stoke became the first "coeducational" dormitory in September 1969. Women were assigned to one wing; doors between it and the men's portion were kept locked except during visiting hours. ("Visiting," which until that spring

had been limited to the public parlors, had since been extended to the students' rooms.) The *New Hampshire* reported that the women liked the joint tenancy, and supervisory personnel testified that the change had brought more order to Stoke Hall.

In April 1970 the University Senate voted to allow each dormitory to set its own visiting hours, up to twenty-four hours a day. In May the trustees overruled the senate, but in February 1971 they changed their minds. The new rules would allow each hall to set its own hours by a two-thirds vote of the total residents, within the limits of 7:00 A.M. to 1:00 A.M. Sunday through Thursday, 7:00 A.M. to 2:00 A.M. on Friday and Saturday. Each hall was allowed to decide if it would have a twenty-four hour policy for the public lounge areas.

Students at the university have been reasonably willing to follow national patterns of campus behavior. Should there be a rash of "panty raids" on other campuses, the officials knew what to expect on the next balmy evening of spring. It was not astonishing, then, that Durham fell victim to an acute case of student unrest at the end of the first semester of 1964-65.

The unrest was prompted by an announcement by Registrar Owen B. Durgin, who revealed that student schedules for the second semester would be made up by computer. Student representatives met with McConnell and other administrators to decry this "dehumanization" of the educational process. There was talk of a Thompson Hall sit-in. A specific complaint was that the student would have no choice of section, that boring instructors and eight o'clock classes were to be distributed by an electronic circuit. Section choice had been eliminated because of the limitations of the university computer. When arrangements were made to use an out-of-town computer which could handle section preferences, mutterings about dehumanization persisted but talk of a siege of Thompson Hall by students died.

The incident revealed a weakness in communication. Accordingly, an informal group of a dozen—equally representing students, administrators, and faculty—was established. It met for luncheon fortnightly to discuss potential problems. Students were given added voice when, in December 1965, the University Senate voted to have student members on several more of its committees.*

The desire for greater student participation in university affairs continued to grow. A committee—consisting of Professor R: Stephen Jenks as chairman, McConnell, Dean Richard F. Stevens, Professor Richard W. Schreiber, and students Robert A. Sawyer and David Jesson—was appointed in June 1968 to review the governmental structure of the university. Another committee of five faculty and four students, chaired by Professor Allan B. Prince, was at work on student rights and rules; its report to the University Senate in March 1969 became the basis for a booklet, *Student Rights and Responsibilities*, to replace the *Student Rules Book*.

It was apparent by the end of 1968 that the Jenks committee on governmental structure would recommend student membership on the University Senate. Fifteen students were therefore given voting membership in the old senate for the second semester of 1968-69, as an interim arrangement. The senate as finally reorganized consisted of thirty teaching faculty, twelve administrators, thirty undergraduates, and five graduate students. All members from McConnell to the youngest student had equal status; the chairman, instead of being the president of the university as before, was elected by the membership. The University By-laws specified: "The University Senate shall be the legislative body of the entire University at Durham. Subject always to the approval of the Board of Trustees, the University Senate shall have legislative jurisdiction in all

* The gap between students and administrators was further bridged when McConnell began to teach a course entitled "Public Policy in Social and Labor Legislation"—the first president since Murkland to go into the classroom regularly.

matters of student government, faculty government, and educational policy." Subsidiary to the senate there was an executive council; faculty, undergraduate, and graduate caucuses; and student and faculty forums.

Professor G. Harris Daggett, the first chairman of the new senate, died suddenly in August. In September Professor Paul E. Bruns was chosen to succeed him. The vice-chairman was Susan Poppema, probably the first student in the country to preside over a meeting of the governing body of a major university, which she did on May 22, 1970. Coming on the scene in the most turbulent year ever experienced on the campuses of the country, the new senate faced not only procedural uncertainties but a staggering agenda. There were twelve meetings between September and April. The regular meeting of May 4 was continued to May 11, then to afternoon and evening sessions on May 18, and finally to May 22, at which time it was voted to commend Bruns for his "admirable patience." In addition there were special meetings on May 3, 7, and 12 in connection with the appearance on campus of the "Chicago Three." A proposal was made, but not adopted, to give student senators academic credit for their services in recognition of the time required.

The reorganized senate brought national attention to the university. It was one of four institutions studied by a national commission on university government, headed by President R. W. Flemming of the University of Michigan. Philip W. Semas spent several days on campus gathering material for a story that appeared on the front page of the July 6, 1970, issue of the *Chronicle of Higher Education*.

Nettled when the Board of Trustees did not accept all of its actions on visiting hours in dormitories, the senate sought a means of improving communication between the two bodies. It was suggested that the most effective means of coordinating the work of the senate and the board would be for their equivalent committees to get

together. The trustees made this official in March 1971 by approving faculty and students as "participating members" of the standing committees of the board, with particular reference to the committees on student affairs, educational policy, and personnel. It also was voted to have three official "participant-observers" from the Durham campus, Keene, and Plymouth at the board meetings.*

The most demanding issue faced by the University Senate during its initial year was unrest caused by the Vietnam war. The first such demonstration had been promoted by the Students for a Democratic Society in April 1967.

* The 1971 legislature revised the membership of the Board of Trustees to provide full voting membership for a student from one of the three campuses. The first appointee was David Gagne from Keene State College.

Left: Ben Thompson would have been startled neither by the bowler hat nor the hair beneath it.
Below left: Transcendental meditation on Thompson Hall lawn.
Below: Suntans and studying at Christensen Hall.

They proposed that the faculty turn their classes into war workshops, and that the students walk out on those refusing. Rallies and leaflets were substituted for this proposal. The *New Hampshire* termed the event one of the most disorganized of the year. Much more widely supported was Vietnam Day on October 15, 1969. The University Senate passed a motion encouraging participation in the activities, but refrained from stating an official position on the conflict other than to recognize the concern of the campus. The resolution made no call for dismissing classes, as some advocated. McConnell issued a statement saying: "In accordance with long-standing policy, each faculty member will decide whether or not to hold classes [on Vietnam Day]." The Young Americans for Freedom, a conservative group, urged all professors to hold classes, and let the individual student make his choice. Under a headline "Panel on Impact of War Draws Little Student Interest," the *New Hampshire* reported that the faculty did all of the talking and that most students stayed in bed. It was estimated that perhaps five hundred students left campus to participate in activities elsewhere.

When forty-five students chartered a bus to take them to a peace rally in Washington on November 15, 1969, about sixty-five Young Americans for Freedom marched to the departure point to dissuade them. The bus peacefully left.

On many campuses, recruitment by corporations engaged in military work and by the military services was meeting with physical interference. The university policy was that such recruiters would be invited to defend the activities of their organizations at a forum, but whether or not they chose to do so they would be allowed to recruit. A room adjoining the recruiting site would be provided, where up to three objectors would be permitted to present their arguments to would-be interviewees. Demonstrating was allowed if it did not involve physical interference. This policy was violated on December 9, 1969, when the General Electric company had scheduled interviews for the third floor of Huddleston Hall. The opposition to General Electric was based less on its munitions making than on its failure to reach an agreement with striking workers. Students for a Democratic Society, together with a few non-students, overflowed the room that had been assigned them and blocked access to the entire third floor. The interviews were conducted on the second floor of Huddleston.

The demonstrators refused to leave the building and were still inside when Dean Richard Stevens ordered it locked at 6:00 P.M. (Security guards had entered the building two hours earlier to stand guard over the files of the Placement Service.) The executive council of the University Senate met in emergency session at 7:00 P.M. After two hours of discussion, the council went to Huddleston in an ineffectual effort to get the demonstrators to leave. It was then decided to have McConnell give written notice that a court injunction would be sought. It took until 3:00 P.M. the next day to get the injunction, which was served on nine students and one non-student. They left at 4:15 P.M., having done no damage to the building. Meanwhile, General Electric had concluded its interviews in the Field House.

Christmas vacation being about to start, it was January before thirteen students were brought before the Judiciary Board. Twelve were suspended for a semester. They appealed to the advisory committee on discipline, then to McConnell, who turned the matter over to a committee of three vice-presidents. The sentence was upheld, but the culprits had been allowed to stay in classes pending the appeal and by this time the semester of suspension had ended.

Anti-war action peaked in the spring of 1970, after the invasion of Cambodia and the killing of four students by National Guard troops during a protest at Kent State University. A strike committee was organized, with the objective of closing down the university, and a demand was made that the senate cancel classes for the balance of the year. The *New Hampshire* advocated striking but urged that all classes continue so that each individual could make his own decision.

Much debate and confusion ensued. The senate decided that the faculty must continue their regular academic duties for the balance of the semester. A student not wishing to finish out the year, after conferring with each of his instructors, would be allowed (1) to get a final grade on the basis of his work to May 7; (2) to get a grade of "credit" for a course; or (3) to get an incomplete in a course with the understanding that the work would need to be made up later. Students who disappeared from a course without consulting the instructor were to "be treated in the normal manner"—presumably failed.

To settle disputes, the senate established a committee on adjudication, consisting of the academic vice-president or his associate, three faculty, and three students. The committee had little to do since most questions were handled at the departmental level. Some departments finished the year in a more or less normal fashion; others devoted most of their energies to hastily-organized workshops and study groups on the war and other problems. It was difficult to estimate the disruption of regular academic activities because classes were already ending, to be followed by a two-week reading period and final examinations. As a "strike" it was obviously less effective than that of 1912, caused by the suspension of William Brackett for ringing a false fire alarm. University officials held that, in view of the nation-wide campus disruptions, the unrest had been well contained: not a waste basket had been burned nor a window pane shattered in Durham.

Epilogue

McConnell retired at the end of June 1971. He had announced his plans on March 26, 1970, less than a month before the tumultuous events of April and May. His administration had been one of the longest and one of the most eventful in the history of the institution.

The university he left was far different from the one he had come to guide in February 1963. Instead of a single campus in Durham, it was a statewide system including the established state colleges at Keene and Plymouth and the fledgling Merrimack Valley branch. The outward signs of progress were more than a score of new buildings or major additions. This construction program doubled the physical plant. The enrollment too had doubled, from 4,150 full-time students to 8,275. The addition of nine Ph.D. programs to the six previously existing was a measure of the growth of graduate study and research activity. A School of Health Studies was started, and a School of Social Work gained legislative approval though no money with which to operate. The undergraduate offerings not only were expanded, but the curriculum underwent its most fundamental revision since the first years in Durham. The reorganized University Senate was a pioneer project to bring students into full partnership in governance.

The late 1960s was a period of unprecedented turmoil on college campuses, but the university adjusted to the pressures without harmful disruption. In large part this was McConnell's doing. Reviewing the McConnell administration in the *UNH Magazine*, Richard C. Plumer wrote:

John McConnell has remained available to articulate faculty determined to move the University in diametrically opposed directions. He has listened quietly to the strident eloquence of some irrational but insistent students . . . . He has kept antagonists speaking to one another and the avenues of communication open when minds were on the verge of becoming closed and intellectual as well as emotional barricades were being constructed.

On July 1, 1971, Thomas N. Bonner assumed the presidency of the University of New Hampshire. A veteran of World War II, he served with the Army Signal Intelligence Corps in Europe before returning to the University of Rochester to earn his Bachelor of Arts and Master of Arts degrees. In 1952 he received his Doctor of Philosophy degree from Northwestern. He was an administrator and teacher at William Woods College, the University of Nebraska, and the University of Cincinnati, becoming the academic provost at Cincinnati in 1967 and its vice-president in 1969. In addition, Bonner had been a Fulbright lecturer at the University of Mainz, a lecturer at the Salzburg Seminar, a Guggenheim fellow, legislative assistant to Senator George McGovern, and candidate for the U.S. Congress from Nebraska's second district. He was the author of seven books and some thirty articles in the fields of history and education.

This is not the place to attempt a study of the just-ended Bonner administration. It would be a lively chapter. When his selection was announced, the Manchester *Union Leader* began a series of background articles and editorials with the intent of persuading Bonner to resign before he arrived in New Hampshire. (His friend and former employer, Senator McGovern, was then campaigning for the Democratic nomination for President.) Senator Norris Cotton criticized the appointment on the floor of the U.S. Senate. Undeterred, Bonner came to New Hampshire and began a campaign to rally support for the university throughout the state. He reorganized the administration of the Durham campus, promoting Eugene S. Mills from academic vice-president to provost in charge of the campus. This freed Bonner to devote more time to molding Durham, Keene, and Plymouth into a more cohesive system, and to press successfully for increased state appropriations. Bonner's goal was to make the university a truly public institution. He was able to reduce the high in-state tuition rates; he advocated less stringent admission standards; he organized a university-wide School of Continuing Studies to make educational opportunities more available to adults throughout the state.*

So the University of New Hampshire continues

to evolve. From a student body of ten and a faculty of one—without a campus they could call their own—the present institution has emerged in little more than a century. Imagine the incredulity of Ezekiel Dimond if he could be here to see it. For the sake of sentiment, let us reincarnate him in the library building that bears his name, and where his disbelief would be exceeded only by his joy at the collection of 620,000 books, 5,000 periodicals, and 5,500 tapes and records.

While we are at the business of reincarnation, let us also bring back Benjamin Thompson. As he stands in the tower of Thompson Hall and gazes at his farm, his amazement would at least match that of Ezekiel. (Unlike so many of us, however, he would not be dismayed by the flowing locks adorning a sizeable proportion of the male students. His own hair was shoulder-length.) Off to the west he would see the university's barns, greenhouses, fields, and orchards, and they no doubt would please him. But let us not burden his soul with the details of the main campus—ten thousand students, six hundred faculty members, thirty-five buildings devoted to instruction, research, and administration, and twenty-one residence halls—nor with the contents of the university catalog. Ben Thompson desired a college devoted solely to agriculture. He built better than he wanted.

---

* Amid all the developments, talented teachers have continued to make their classroom impact on students. In a poll of "best-remembered" teachers conducted in connection with the Golden Jubilee fund drive in 1972-73, William Yale, history, took top honors, ranking first with classes graduating over two decades, 1930-39 and 1940-49. Other firsts were Ernest R. Groves, sociology, before 1919; Donald C. Babcock, history and philosophy, and Leon W. Hitchcock, electrical engineering, tied in 1920-29; G. Harris Daggett, English, 1950-59; David F. Long, history, 1960-69. William G. Hennessy, English, impressed students over three decades tieing for second in 1940-49 and receiving honorable mention in 1920-29 and 1930-39. At a disadvantage in the polling because of their more limited exposure to students, teachers in the agricultural and technical departments who ranked high included Frederick W. Taylor, agriculture, before 1919; Charles James, chemistry, before 1919 and 1920-29; Harold A. Iddles, chemistry, 1930-39 and 1940-49; and Edmond W. Bowler, civil engineering, 1930-39.

Appendices

APPENDIX 1: EXECUTIVE OFFICERS

If other than president of the institution, the individual's title follows his name.
In those cases where the trustees specified a title to be used by an interim officer,
that title follows in parentheses.

1866-1877	ASA D. SMITH
1877-1878	GEORGE W. NESMITH, president of the board of trustees
1878-1891	SAMUEL C. BARTLETT, president of the faculty
1891-1893	LYMAN D. STEVENS, president of the board of trustees
1893-1903	CHARLES S. MURKLAND
1903-1912	WILLIAM D. GIBBS
1912	CHARLES H. PETTEE, dean (acting president)
1912-1916	EDWARD T. FAIRCHILD
1917	CHARLES H. PETTEE, dean (acting president)
1917-1927	RALPH D. HETZEL
1927	ADRIAN O. MORSE, executive secretary
1927-1936	EDWARD M. LEWIS
1936-1937	ROY D. HUNTER, president of the board of trustees (executive officer)
1937-1944	FRED ENGELHARDT
1944	ROY D. HUNTER, president of the board of trustees (chief executive officer)
1944-1947	HAROLD W. STOKE
1947	FRANK W. RANDALL, president of the board of trustees (acting president)
1947-1948	LAUREN E. SEELEY, dean of the college of technology (executive director)
1948-1950	ARTHUR S. ADAMS
1950-1954	ROBERT F. CHANDLER
1954-1955	EDWARD D. EDDY, JR., assistant to the president (administrative officer, then acting president)
1955-1961	ELDON L. JOHNSON
1961-1962	JOHN F. REED, vice-president (acting president)
1962	JERE CHASE, executive vice-president
1963-1971	JOHN W. McCONNELL
1971-1974	THOMAS N. BONNER

APPENDIX 2:   **THE UNIVERSITY'S PRESIDENTS**

Asa D. Smith

Charles S. Murkland

William D. Gibbs

Edward T. Fairchild

Ralph D. Hetzel

Edward M. Lewis

Fred Engelhardt

Harold W. Stoke

Arthur S. Adams

Robert F. Chandler

Eldon L. Johnson

John W. McConnell

Thomas N. Bonner

APPENDIX 3: DECENNIAL ENROLLMENT STATISTICS

Decennial Enrollment Statistics

	Full-Time Bachelor Degree Candidates							2-Yr.	Grad.	Other	Grand Total
Year	Ag	L.A.	Tech	Bus.	Men	Women	Total				
1868-9	—	—	—	—	10	—	10	—	—	—	10
1878-9	—	—	—	—	14	—	14	—	—	—	14
1888-9	—	—	—	—	33	—	33	—	—	—	33
1893-4	—	—	—	—	54	10	64	—	—	—	64
1898-9	—	—	—	—	68	13	81	5	1	8	95
1908-9	—	—	—	—	182	15	197	25	1	8	231
1918-9	84	335	170	—	424	165	589	14	0	0	603
1928-9	97	1032	340	—	1046	423	1469	21	61	376	1927
1938-9	208	1267	368	—	1230	613	1843	52	118	437	2450
1948-9	355	2305	768	—	2569	859	3428	115	241	2021	5805
1958-9	264	2388	810	—	2306	1156	3426	77	250	1729	5518
1968-9	478	4380	715	561	3328	2806	6134	245	718	3056	10153

Comment: This table has been derived principally from enrollment statistics contained in the annual catalogs of the institution. There have been changes from time to time in methods of accounting for students. For example, during the Hanover years the few short course and correspondence students were included with the baccalaureate students. As women were not reported separately until 1916, their number before that date has been estimated on the basis of given names. Before the Whittemore School was established, business, hotel, and economics majors were included in liberal arts.

The "other" category includes principally extension, short course, and summer school students. Due to the multiplicity and irregularity of these courses, some error in their enrollment figures is probable. As some students in summer school will already have been counted as regular or extension students, the grand total is likely to be about ten percent above the annual net enrollment.

Taking ten-year intervals eliminates some figures of interest. For example, there were a total of seven graduate students from 1880 through 1886; the first women, six, were enrolled in 1892. Although it does not come at a ten-year interval, the first year in Durham, 1893-94, has been included. This table does not meet the highest standards of statistical accuracy, but it does give a meaningful picture of the growth of the institution.

APPENDIX 4: THE UNIVERSITY AND THE STATE

As the relationship between the university and the state officials in Concord is mentioned from place to place in the text, this skeletal guide is presented as an aid to the person unfamiliar with the governmental organization of New Hampshire.

The Governor is the chief administrative officer of the state and is the only official elected on a state-wide basis. In the New England pattern, there is an executive council of five elected members whose approval the governor must secure for important matters such as appointments and approval of contracts, and for most trivial ones, such as permitting two or more officials of a state agency to travel together out of state. The governor's administrative authority does not extend to the university system, but he is an *ex officio* member of the board of trustees and, with the consent of the council, appoints twelve of the twenty-four members of the board. The university system is a semi-autonomous state agency governed by the board of trustees.

The legislature, or General Court of New Hampshire as it is officially known, consists of a senate of twenty-four and a house of from three hundred seventy-five to four hundred, by far the largest of any state. The university usually receives favorable treatment from the education committees, but any measure involving money goes from those committees to the appropriation or finance committees. Here the hearings are sympathetic until someone asks the inevitable question, "Where is the money coming from?" As New Hampshire is the only state with no broad-based tax, the general fund depends largely on: the tobacco tax, a share of pari-mutuel betting at race tracks, profit from the state liquor stores, a business profits tax, and a room and meals tax. The result is that state appropriations are determined not so much by need as by the income from sources of limited flexibility.

Although there are legislators who would like to put the university on a line-item budget, state appropriations for it are made on a lump-sum basis, with occasional exceptions. The trustees determine the tuition and fees, except that since 1969 the legislature has directed that out-of-state tuition be set to cover the full instructional cost per student. Major university construction is financed by state bonds voted by the legislature for specific projects. The university must meet the interest and amortization costs of these bonds; the money for the bonds related to academic construction comes from the university's general funds and that for dormitory and dining facilities from the income from those activities.

Bibliography

The material on which this history is based has come largely from printed reports and catalogs issued by the institution, from student publications, and from the minutes of the board of trustees. Limited use has been made of the *History of the University of New Hampshire*, published by the university in 1941 in connection with its seventy-fifth anniversary. That volume contains no information on sources, except mention in the preface that a 292-page manuscript by Professor Emeritus Clarence W. Scott had been useful. Efforts to find the manuscript have been unavailing.

The present volume was started by Professor Philip M. Marston, who had completed at the time of his death a draft covering the years 1866 to 1944. Unfortunately neither the draft nor the other papers left by Marston give useful information about his sources, other than indications that they were principally university publications and minutes of the board of trustees. In his papers was a 55-page summary of 2,006 letters to Dean Charles Pettee during the years 1890 to 1893, but the letters themselves cannot be found.

The University Library has what appears to be a complete collection of institutional and student publications, beginning with the first report of the trustees to the legislature in 1867. The early trustee reports were comprehensive, including the college catalog and reports of the agricultural experiment station. The library also has a bound copy of Marston's draft history and a copy of Oren V. Henderson's "Notebook."

The trustee minutes are in a vault in Thompson Hall, to which they were moved in the spring of 1970 when student occupations of administrative offices on other campuses had resulted in the destruction of valuable records. With the trustee minutes is a "Record Book" started in 1891 but soon abandoned. Also in a Thompson Hall vault are minutes of Faculty and University Senate meetings. The minutes for the academic year 1969-70 are especially valuable, because they are supplemented by numerous memoranda and committee reports considered by the senate.

Joseph B. Walker, in 1866 one of the original trustees of the college, presented a memorial sketch of Professor Ezekiel Dimond at the professor's funeral; and at the dedication of the new campus in Durham in 1893 he spoke on the history of the institution while at Hanover.

Lengthy interviews were granted by Adrian O. Morse, who from 1923 to 1927 was assistant to the president and then executive secretary of the university; Donald C. Babcock, member of the university faculty from 1918 until his retirement in 1956; Edward Y. Blewett, an undergraduate from 1922 to 1926 and then, until his resignation in 1958, alumni secretary, executive secretary, and dean of the College of Liberal Arts; Mrs. Marion Engelhardt Fehrs, widow of former President Fred Engelhardt; and the late C. Floyd Jackson, professor and later dean of liberal arts from 1908 until his retirement in 1952. Part of the interview with Babcock and all of that with Blewett are on tape in the University Library.

Two histories of Dartmouth College, the first by Chase and Lord and the second by Richardson, furnished valuable information on the relationship of Dartmouth and New Hampshire College during the years when the latter was in Hanover.

Deposited in the University Library are three versions of the manuscript of this book: 1) the carbon of the original draft on the margins of which is a complete record of the sources of all material, including reference to the pages of Marston's manuscript; 2) a second, somewhat expanded version of the original draft, which Ford edited for the final draft and on the margins of which are indicated the pages to which the material was transferred in making a topical version; 3) the topical version, which includes comprehensive references to sources including germane acts of the New Hampshire legislature. Also deposited in the library are about two thousand five hundred five-by-eight cards used in compiling information.

Annett, Albert. *History of Jaffrey, New Hampshire.* Town of Jaffrey, 1937.

Babcock, Donald C., et al. *History of the University of New Hampshire, 1866-1941.* Durham: University of New Hampshire, 1941.

Blewett, Edward Y. "Tenure Plan Completes Unified Faculty Personnel Policy at N.H." *School and Society,* 24 December 1938, pp. 829-30.

Bowles, Raimond, et al. *Report of the Interim Commission on Education.* Np, nd.

Burns, Charles H. *The Leach Bill.* Concord, N.H.: np, 1895.

Cary, Harold W. *The University of Massachusetts, a History of 100 Years.* Amherst: University of Massachusetts, 1962.

Chase, Frederick; Lord, John K. *A History of Dartmouth College and the Town of Hanover.* Vol. 1. Cambridge, Mass.: John Wilson & Son University Press, 1891. Vol. 2. Concord, N.H.: Rumford Press, 1913.

Chittenden, Russell H. *History of the Sheffield Scientific School of Yale University.* New Haven: Yale University Press, 1928.

Conant, John. *Memorial of John Conant to the Legislature in Relation to the N.H. College of Agriculture and the Mechanic Arts.* Concord, N.H.: np, 1872.

Dishman, Robert B. "Academic Freedom at the University of New Hampshire, 1947-1957." Unpublished, University of New Hampshire Library, Durham.

Eddy, Edward D., Jr. *Colleges for Our Land and Time.* New York: Harper & Brothers, 1956.

Eschenbacher, Herman F. *The University of Rhode Island, a History of Land Grant Education in Rhode Island.* New York City: Appleton-Century-Crofts, 1967.

Fernald, M.C. *History of the Maine State College and The University of Maine.* Orono: University of Maine, 1916.

Heald, L. Franklin. "The Chicago Three." *UNH Magazine,* June 1970.

Henderson, Oren V. "Notebook." Unpublished, University of New Hampshire Library, Durham.

Kelly, Robert L. *American Colleges and the Social Order.* New York: Macmillan, 1940.

Lindsay, Julian I. *Tradition Looks Forward: The University of Vermont, a History, 1791-1904.* Burlington: University of Vermont and State Agricultural College, 1954.

Marston, Philip M. "History of the University of New Hampshire." Unpublished, University of New Hampshire Library, Durham.

New Hampshire General Court. *Report of Committee on Subject of an Agricultural College, with the Proposition of the Hon. David Culver.* Concord, N.H.: np, 1864.

Plumer, Richard C. "Campaign from the Campus." Unpublished, University of New Hampshire Library, Durham.

———— "A Fine University with Its Integrity Intact." *UNH Magazine,* June 1971.

Porter, Noah. *The American Colleges and the American Public.* 1870. Reprint. New York City: Arno Press and *New York Times,* 1969.

Rand, Frank P. *Yesterdays at Massachusetts State College, 1863-1933.* Amherst: Associated Alumni, Massachusetts State College, 1933.

Richardson, Leon B. *History of Dartmouth College.* Hanover: Dartmouth College Publications, 1932.

Ross, Earle D. *Democracy's College, the Land Grant Movement in the Formative State.* 1942. Reprint. New York City: Arno Press and *New York Times,* 1969.

Rudolph, Frederick. *Mark Hopkins and the Log, Williams College, 1836-72.* New Haven: Yale University Press, 1956.

Scudder, Harold H. *Benjamin Thompson.* Durham: np, 1941.

Stackpole, Everett S., and Thompson, Lucien. *History of the Town of Durham.* Town of Durham, 1913.

Stemmons, Walter. *Connecticut Agricultural College, a History.* Storrs, Conn.: np, 1931.

Storr, Richard J. *The Beginnings of Graduate Education in America.* 1953. Reprint. New York City: Arno Press and *New York Times,* 1969.

Tewksbury, Donald G. *The Founding of American Colleges and Universities before the Civil War.* 1932. Reprint. New York City: Arno Press and *New York Times,* 1969.

True, Alfred C. *A History of Agricultural Education in the United States (USDA Miscellaneous Publication No. 36).* Washington: U.S. Government Printing Office, 1929.

University of New Hampshire. "Alumni Register Number, 1866-1935." *Bulletin of the University of New Hampshire,* November 1935.

———— *Toward Unity through Diversity (Report of the Educational Policies Committee).* Durham: University of New Hampshire, 1967.

———— *The University of New Hampshire in the Service of the State.* Durham: University of New Hampshire, 1946.

Veysey, Laurence R. *The Emergence of the American University.* Chicago: University of Chicago Press, 1965.

Walker, Joseph B. *Memorial Sketch of the Life and Character of Ezekiel Webster Dimond.* Np, nd.

Wayland, Francis. *Thoughts on the Present Collegiate System in the U.S.* 1842. Reprint. New York City: Arno Press and *New York Times,* 1969.

Index